MUSLIM WOMEN

EDITED BY
FREDA HUSSAIN

ST MARTIN'S PRESS
New York

Printed in Great Britain
First published in the United States of America in 1984

Library of Congress Cataloging in Publication Data
Main entry under title:

Muslim women.

    Contents: Muslim women / Freda Hussain—The status
of women in early Islam / Barbara Stowasser—Muslim
women : the revolutionary ideal / Zainab Rezai and
Suroosh Irfani — [etc.]
    1. Women, Muslim—Addresses, essays, lectures.
I. Hussain, Freda.
HQ1170.M847 1984   305.4'862971   83-11189
ISBN 0-312-55586-5

CONTENTS

PART THREE: CONTEXTUAL REALITIES

PREFACE

Scholarly books are written for a variety of reasons. Some are written because of the author's particular interest in the subject matter; others because the subject may be a 'hot' issue at that time; and yet others may be written because of pressures of 'publish or perish' that are often found in the academic world. Whatever the reasons, the subject matter is treated within the constraints imposed by the author's orientation in a particular discipline but the end product is considered to be objective. For me, this was not entirely possible because as a Muslim woman, I was writing about Muslim women. I am a part of that contextual reality, the subject matter of which has received considerable attention in recent decades. In compiling this book I have therefore attempted to combine the subjective and objective roles.

In the objective role, I tried to detach myself while examining the situational contexts and the direction of Muslim women in various parts of the Muslim world. One way of presenting my findings would have been to write about them myself through a study of secondary sources. The other way was to call upon those persons who had spent years in the field and had first hand knowledge of the stark realities faced by Muslim women in the context in which they lived. I chose the latter method and would first of all like to acknowledge my debt of gratitude to all the contributors to this book who have given generously of their valuable time and effort in the preparation of their excellent studies and sharing their knowledge and experiences.

In the selection of such a team of contributors, I kept two main considerations in mind. Firstly, I wanted to cover as wide a geographic area as possible to represent a sample of women in the Muslim world. This volume includes contributions on Muslim women in Africa (Sudan), North Africa (Tunisia), the Middle East (Egypt), Southwest Asia (Turkey and Iran), South Asia (Pakistan) and Southeast Asia (Malaysia). Many other countries could have been included but the limitations of space in one volume did not permit it. Secondly, I wanted to explore the subject in the context through a multidisciplinary approach. The contributions therefore reflect the methodology and observations of historians, sociologists, educationalists, political scientists, social anthropologists and an expert in French

Preface

Maghrebian literature, each with a special interest in Islam and Muslim countries.

My second role, as stated earlier, was a subjective one. What I was writing about and thinking of was a part of my life, regardless of the context I was living in. The Introduction and the paper by myself and my co-author give expression to our observations drawn from life experiences, a deep concern about the role of Muslim women and work among Muslim women. It was enriched by observations made last year during my field work in Pakistan on women in urban and rural areas. I would like to thank Miss Mavis Jones for making it possible for me to take a year's leave of absence from school. Much of the work on this book was done during that year.

A book on a sensitive subject such as this is bound to raise some controversy. This book, perhaps, raised more questions than it has attempted to answer. My goal was to awaken the consciousness of the general reader and to draw attention to the direction of research and active struggle needed in the future. Muslim women have to feel socially responsible for each other in order to achieve such a goal.

Any such effort however, could have remained unknown because thinking of a course of action is one thing, executing it successfully is another. For the latter, I am grateful to Mr. David Croom, my publisher, for his encouragement and help in the completion of a task I had undertaken. Three other persons deserve a special mention for their help in the production of this book. Kathy Hollingworth for typing the manuscript with patience and care. Christine Leverton for preparing a camera ready copy for the publisher. Finally, my husband Asaf Hussain, for his advice, unerring support, overall supervision and above all his faith in my ability to complete this book when at times it did not seem possible. The final responsibility, is however, mine alone.

Leicester

Freda Hussain
December 1983

Dedicated with love

to

Shalra, Lubna, Fiza,
Fauzia, Farah, Sophia,
Fatima and Mariam.

INTRODUCTION:
The Ideal and the Contextual Realities of Muslim Women

Freda Hussain

One of the most important issues debated in Muslim societies relates to the role of women in the various spheres of social life. The sensitivity which surrounds this issue borders on irrationality and it is therefore not surprising to find that women have often been treated as if their presence constituted a social problem in their own societies.

The problem starts at the birth of a female child, which is still frowned upon in many Muslim societies and escalates as the girl approaches the age of puberty. Social problems relating to the role of a female in a Muslim society vary at different stages of her life. There are those who feel strongly that she must wear the veil, receive limited education, remain segregated from the opposite sex and in general be prepared for her role as a wife and mother. Others want to oppose such restrictions and feel that she deserves the freedom to choose a career and contribute to national development. Such controversies rage over almost all aspects of the lives of Muslim women and involve wide ranging issues such as marriage, divorce, education, polygamy, virginity and sexual chastity.

Such a sensitive subject could not fail to attract the attention of Western academics as well as Muslim women themselves. Some books in the area of Muslim women studies were written from the modernisation theory or the Marxist point of view. They emphasised some aspects at the cost of others and were thus inadequate in assessing the contextual realities relevant to the situation of Muslim women. Many of these studies used the Western ideal of womanhood as a yardstick for studying Muslim women. They sympathised with the plight of Muslim women and considered that once they became modernised or Westernised, their lives would be free from problems. Their viewpoints were based on an ethnocentric assumption that Muslim women wanted to become Westernised and hence had to gain their freedom from all retrogressive forces in Muslim societies, including Islam. Such a thesis was further reinforced by data which focussed mainly on Westernised Muslim women from the upper strata of Muslim societies. A major fact which was ignored was that this sample was not representative of Muslim women, as these women formed an insignificant minority in all Muslim societies. Westernised Muslim women did not represent aspirations of the majority of Muslim

1

feudalism over done

Islam vs muslim

? normative vs historical Islam

Introduction

women. On the contrary, they were often alienated from their own societies.

On the other hand, a number of studies and viewpoints emanating from Muslim societies and religious authorities posited an Islamic role for Muslim women in those societies. These were, however, representative of feudalistic and not Islamic thinking for they consistently sought to place women under the control of men. They were powerful and effective in their influence on the role of women because they reflected the feudalistic state in which all contemporary Muslim societies find themselves. As there are no Islamic societies to be found in the world today, various distorted interpretations of Islam have manifested themselves in Muslim societies. Such interpretations have been imposed on women and over the centuries have resulted in the institutionalisation of a pseudo-Islam.

The above mentioned factors have been the cause of considerable concern for me. The idea of this study was therefore conceived in an attempt to bridge the gap between the Islamic ideal and the contextual realities to be found in the world today. The ideal had to be uncovered from its historical wrappings while empirical research was necessary to bring out the contextual realities within which Muslim women existed. It was rather an ambitious plan, particularly as it had to be circumscribed to project its message through one volume. Bearing in mind the vastness of the subject, I decided to focus mainly on the roles, role conflicts and adjustments of Muslim women.

ROLE PERSPECTIVES

Sociologists consider role behaviour to be a structural component of every human society as the norms of every society prescribe behavioural sanctions for interaction between the sexes. Such a construction is based on two assumptions which role theorists share. First, that roles are learned. No one knows his or her role from birth unless one is trained in it or learns it through social communication, education and training, social interaction, etc. Secondly, when people see themselves and others interacting with each other as incumbents of particular roles, guidelines are drawn for behavioural modifications. If this were not so, then a child would not know how to behave with his parents, or a woman with a man, etc.

From such sociological studies, the study of role behaviour has developed along two main traditions. One is the structural tradition[1] and the other is the social-psychological tradition.[2] In the former, 'status is simply a collection of rights and duties' while 'role represents the dynamic aspect of status'.[3] The structural position is embedded in the permanency of human behaviour. For example, if being a housewife is a status, then every incumbent would be expected to enact the roles related to this status. The social-psychological tradition, on the other hand, takes into consideration the interactional aspects of role behaviour. Role behaviour may vary according to different situations or may remain the same irrespective of the context. The interactional component is essential and one person may

2

have many different types of interaction. In other words, each person has many roles to perform: for example a woman has to play the role of a daughter to her parents, wife to her husband, mother to her children, etc. Each is interconnected with the other and one may influence the way in which she may behave in regard to the other (role performance). Role expectations give the role incumbent an idea of role performance. They are derived from the role norms which may be prescribed in secular or religious codes. They have an anticipatory quality, that is, in any particular status, certain behaviour is expected. Further, role norms effect role performance but there is an essential link between them in that the role incumbents see their own roles through interpretations (personal role definitions) of the prescribed norms.

Role expectations within a Muslim family are derived from the norms prescribed by Islam. But, in order to have eternal validity they must be applicable in any context and at any time period. Unfortunately this has not happened, because Muslim civilisations have been corrupted and corroded through time and history and women have been one of the greatest casualties of this process.

What then is the reality prevailing in Muslim societies today? We find that female behaviour has to conform to male role expectations. Religious functionaries or patriarchs have never allowed women personal role definitions through the prescribed norms. They have usurped this essential link between role norms and role performance.

Different religious functionaries have given their own interpretations in different societies. This has correctly led to observations that the term Islam has been replaced by 'Islams' emphasising the multiplicity of its expressions in different historical and cultural contexts.[4] Whether they are all equally valid is open to question, but the one thing that is clear is that interpretations of Islam by men have certainly suited their own interests.

It is not surprising to find that male interpretations of role norms vary from one Muslim society to another. Often there may be disagreements between the interpretations of different male authority structures but each one has used Islam to legitimate its views. However one factor that is common to all interpretations is their aim to keep Muslim women subordinated to male role expectations.

THE IDEAL AND CONTEXTUAL REALITIES

In order to study Muslim women the framework of role perspective is very useful. Muslim women could be anchored on a continuum, one end of which is labelled the ideal and the other end, the contextual realities. Any confusion between the two will lead to contradictions in depicting the reality of Muslim women.

The ideal is structured by the Islamic role norms from which are derived the Islamic role expectations for female role performance in Muslim societies. On the other hand, contextual realities relate to the role performance of females as determined by the culture and structure of various Muslim societies. History and tradition in

3

particular, have influenced the role assigned to women. Any deviation from such roles is dealt with through various means of social control.

The female role expectations of the men had emanated from the feudal structures that existed in pre-Islamic societies. Islam was subsequently used to legitimise and reinforce these expectations of female role performance. Religious functionaries stunted the growth and development of Muslim societies by using pseudo-Islamic norms to resolve problems relating to woman and other issues. They failed to transcend time and history by trying to make early interpretations of Islamic laws applicable to later contexts and times. The feudal structures manifested themselves in many ways in different contexts and were closely related to the culture and customs of various Muslim societies. Patriarchy was common and by using biological rational-isations or chauvanistic ideologies of the feudal and capitalist systems, women have come to be treated as a private property under the control of men.[5]

The focus of this study is limited to the implications of Patriarchy in Muslim societies. These cannot be dismissed for 'the major feature of the patriarchal order was the development of a new tribal power structure totally based on patrilineage. Within the family unit, the father became the uncontested and absolute ruler. The wives and daughters were referred to interchangeably as slaves .... He could sell his wives or children, kill them or incarcerate them .... Since the tribe was the highest political economic, military and legal authority, without which the individual had no significance whatso-ever, it followed that the paternal bond became the supreme bond .... it became the core and essence of that patriarchal system .... However, the major contribution of Islam towards the ultimate defeat of Patriarchy .... lies in the fact that Islam replaced the paternal bond of Jahiliyyah totally by the religious bond within which everyone - male or female, black or white, young or old, rich or poor - is equal. By doing that Islam struck at the heart of the patriarchal system. Tribal allegiances were weakened, with brother fighting brother for the faith. New allegiances appeared based on moral and religious principles instead of patrilineage'.[6] Until the feudal structure is dismantled the patriarchal order will persist and will continue to use Islam to exploit women.

Patriarchy has victimised them in every manner, particularly in the area of sexual morality. Fear of a woman's sexuality getting out of hand has led to the cruel practices such as cliterodectomy or female circumcision in some Muslim societies. The childbirth customs as discussed by Heather Strange in her paper on Malaysian women have no Islamic sanction - yet they are followed within the context and form part of that reality.

Role conflicts therefore create contradictions between the ideal and contextual realities and should be taken into consideration when studying women in Muslim societies. The most important question which arises at this point is: how does one distinguish the ideal from the contextual realities? The first point is not to confuse the two, for all that occurs within the context is not Islamic. This is due to various reasons as discussed earlier. Secondly, a knowledge of Islamic norms is necessary for any research on Muslim women. The ideal must be known as it affects the role expectations and role performance of Muslim women in every society. But here an important distinction should be kept in mind. The knowledge about the ideal should be acquired through the study of Islamic and not Muslim history.

Islamic history refers to the period of Quranic revelation and the lifetime of Prophet Muhammad. Muslim women of the Prophet's time have often served as reference groups for role behaviour in their societies. The roles of women such as Fatima (daughter of the Prophet and wife of the fourth caliph), Khadija (first wife of the Prophet who was a business woman) or A'ishah (the last wife of the Prophet), provide important role models in the ideal sense. Their struggle, chivalry and the.r relations with their husbands and other members of the community point out the multi-faceted role of Muslim women which was a far cry from the role of women as chattels that is found in Muslim history. The ideal, during the lifetime of the Prophet was translated into reality, for he was always there to rectify misinterpretations. But after his death all sorts of distortions were incorporated into interpretations of Islam through personal or vested interests and ultimately through the decadence which set in and eventually led to the demolition of Muslim empires.

The 'ideal type' which emerged was the work of religious functionaries who worked closely with the ruling elite throughout Muslim history. They were patronised by the Muslim rulers in every period of Muslim history and in fact ended up legitimising the dictates of the rulers through Islam. The Ulema's vested interest lay in maintaining its class and this could only be done through alliance with the ruling class. The Islam which the Ulema propagated allowed Muslim rulers to keep large harems. Throughout Muslim history, women's rights were infringed and their voices were drowned within the four walls of the harems guarded by castrated slaves. Islam, however, does not sanction the development of a priestly class because it does not separate the political from the religious sphere. Anybody who believes in Islam can interpret the Qur'an. While women read the Qur'an, they have never dared to interpret it for fear of opposing the Ulema. The ideal type created by the Ulema suited the feudal rulers and remained intact for centuries in a male dominated society. It was in this sense that the institutionalisation of pseudo-Islam took place and role sanctions were enacted for the role behaviour of Muslim women.

The interpretation of Islam by women has yet to emerge in the Muslim world. But where it has been done, it has lead to role conflicts because the personal role definitions by women are incompatible with the role expectations of Muslim males. Such role conflicts have often arisen as a reaction to the retrogressive Islamic forces and have led to women adopting alien ideologies such as feminism. Other Muslim women have reacted to Western modernisation and have adopted Marxist ideologies. Both these options chosen by Muslim women have failed to become grounded in the context due to the fact that they are reactionary manifestations. Undoubtedly, such courses of action have been chosen in desperation by Muslim women but they have not resulted in solving the problems of Muslim women. Changes in the role performance must evolve from within the Islamic role structure through personal role definitions evolved by Muslim women. In other words, social change in the role of Muslim women must be brought about, by the elimination of feudal Islam through Islam.

Such a process must start by rejecting all interpretations and re-examining the Qur'an and the Hadith for oneself. Although a cut and dried solution may not be readily available because of the opposition from the retrogressive forces in Muslim societies, but in it lies the salvation for Muslim women. It may take some time, but questioning the traditional and feudal authority structures of Islam will lead to role conflicts and adjustments that will eventually weaken it. The Quranic text must be related to the present context and used to liberate women from male domination.

The papers presented in this volume have been arranged with this framework in mind. The papers contributed by Barbara Stowasser and myself and Kamelia in PART ONE, have merely initiated the direction which the new awakening of Muslim women should take. The discussions focus on the sources which sanction the role performance of Muslim women as derived from the Qur'an and the Hadith and by reference groups of women related to Prophet Muhammad.

Stowasser deals with the ideal of early Islam and the confusion that has arisen from it. She shows why reality did not conform to the ideal because of the intervention of various factors. On the other hand, my paper with Kamelia Radwan discusses the revolutionary role of women in Iran as a case study to depict pseudo-Islamic and Islamic prescription and encourage women to develop.

As pointed out, role conflict took place due to the incongruence between the role expectations of Islam and the role expectations of Muslim males. How do such role changes take place? These are given in PART TWO in which three scholars have contributed papers focussing on different factors. Debbie Gerner has focussed on role transitions among the Arab women and how various factors have affected them. Anne-Marie Nisbet's analysis examines the images of women as portrayed in the French literature. The media often reflects multiple realities of how women are or should be. They are reflections of the context and can in turn exert changes in roles through role models of heroines. Leila Ahmad's paper provides an excellent discussion on feminist ideologies in the context of Turkey and Egypt.

The last section deals with the contextual realities and outlines some important aspects. The legal, educational and economic aspects are closely related to enhancement of the role of Muslim women. Only through legal protection can her rights be safeguarded; education, on the other hand, is a necessity to raise their social awareness and to development personal role definitions for partici-pation in national development of their countries. Both the above factors will help to encourage women to take up careers and fight their own battles against patriarchy. But these problems cannot be solved in a day and therefore it is necessary to probe various aspects of them. Norma Salem has focussed on the legal status of women in

Tunisia; Hind Khattab has dealt with the issue of education in Egypt, while my paper has focussed on the struggle of women in the National development in Pakistan. The last paper by Carolyn Fluehr-Lobban will be helpful to researchers and will also serve to warn them of the male opposition that one encounters during field work and how it can be overcome.

REFERENCES

1.   See R. Linton, The Study of Man. New York: D. Appleton Century, 1964.
2.   See G.H. Mead, Mind, Self and Society.   Chicago: University of Chicago Press, 1934.
3.   R. Linton, op. cit., pp. 113-14.
4.   Dale F. Eickleman, The Study of Islam in Local Contexts. Contributions to Asian Studies, Vol. XVII, 1982, p. 1.
5.   See Roberta Hamilton, The Liberation of Women: a study of patriarchy and capitalism. London: George Allen & Unwin, 1978.
6.   Azizah al-Hibri, A Study of Islamic History: or how did we manage to get into this mess? Women's Studies International Forum, Vol. 5, No. 2, 1982, pp. 212-213.

Part One:

THE IDEAL

Chapter 1

THE STATUS OF WOMEN IN EARLY ISLAM

Barbara Freyer Stowasser

An important aspect of the contemporary Islamic revival, the widespread and still spreading regeneration of the Islamic ethos, is the renewed and visible emphasis that is being placed by Muslims on the 'Islamic way of life'.

As a comprehensive system of beliefs and values, Islam evolved principles that touched upon most aspects of social existence. Few, if any, of these therefore remain unaffected by the Islamic 'regeneration' (*tajdid*). The impact is further intensified by the scale on which this regeneration unfolds. Even societies which seemed securely on the road to secularist modernisation are now drawn into and give evidence of widespread, intensified emulation of Islamic lifestyles. Centrally affected by these developments are the societal patterns of men's and women's status and the interrelationship of the sexes. The question of women's status in Islamic society, the issue of separation of female world from male world by means of secluding and barring women from public affairs, is hotly debated as the forces of tradition cross arms with the forces of modernity in today's open, swiftly changing Islamic world of internal and external pressures and crises. The apologists of the traditional Islamic order who are in the forefront of the battle not only to retain, but to restrengthen 'the Islamic way of life' propagate a distinctive social order which has been described in terms of the *institutionalisation* (1) of the difference in ranking of men and women and (2) of the 'cushioning-off' of the female world (the home) from the male world (public affairs).[1] This order they sanction in religious terms by ascribing it directly to the Koran or to 'the original order of Islam'. By describing the order in religious terms in this fashion, they contribute, or intend to contribute, to the compulsive impact of the institutions concerned.

It is thus a worthwhile undertaking to investigate exactly and in some detail what the Koran and the early Islamic Traditions (*Hadith*) contain of information regarding men's and women's status, inter-relationships, rights, duties, etc. It will also be relevant to inquire how this information was used (or even changed) by later generations of Muslims.

This is, however, a vast area of concern, and only a small beginning can be made here in this presentation. I will attempt simply

11

to indicate and characterise some of the available source materials, map out a course of action for research, and offer some preliminary findings.

The study of the early Islamic sources is enhanced as well as made difficult by their status as well as by the role which they have played in the development of the Islamic order as a whole. Not only the Koran itself, but also the early Islamic Traditions represent infallible, since divinely inspired, sources of the *shari'a*, the Holy Law of Islam, through which their principles and prescriptions are applied to all (or almost all) aspects of social and political existence. The Islamic doctrine that Muhammad as an individual and his Companions as a group acted under tacit divine inspiration, elevated even their daily behaviour patterns to the level of legally binding precedent or model behaviour (*Sunna*) which all believers were expected to follow. This doctrine was developed early on. Already at the end of the first century of Islam, the principle that 'the *Sunna* is the judge of the Koran, and not vice versa' was formed by the pious scholars in their endeavour to raise the *Sunna* to a position of equality with the Holy Book in establishing the law.[2]

A study of the legislative detail of the Koran as well as the *Sunna* of the early believers as depicted in the Traditions, therefore, brings us face to face with the 'blueprint' of the just Islamic order. Even when and where this model order was incompletely realised, it remained the code of ultimate normative value that the individual believer knew – and knows – as a vital part of his faith and against which he measured – and measures – his own, usually imperfect, reality.

This sanctity of the sources certainly endows them with the greatest importance, but also makes for great sensitivity in any attempt at critical investigation. Since even the order described in the Traditions has become part and parcel of the religion of Islam, to use the *Hadith* material critically as one would any other historical source is liable to be taken by ultra-conservative believers as an attack on the religion as a whole.

I   THE SOURCES, NATURE AND FLEXIBILITY

Before presenting at least some limited detail on women's position in the early Islamic society as depicted in the early Islamic sources, it may be of benefit (1) to briefly describe the sources and (2) to indicate how they were used by the early believers themselves to accommodate the staggering rate of political, economic, and social change that occurred during the first centuries of Islamic history.

The Koran, being the sum total of God's revelations to the Prophet and utterly sacred in content as well as in form according to Muslim belief, had legislated deep-going changes in all areas of life. With the Prophet's death in 632, the Koran became a closed book. As the Arabs embarked upon the wars of conquest soon thereafter and as the realm of Islam expanded dramatically within the span of just a few generations, the original message and way of life of Islam had to be made workable in the conquered areas for a multitude of peoples of varied ethnic, linguistic, political and cultural backgrounds many (or most) of whom converted the the new faith. One manner in which innovation and change could be accommodated and legitimised, and even foreign patterns could be assimilated, is constituted by the discipline of Koran exegesis (*tafsir*). Koran commentators set out to legitimise actual usage of their own day by interpreting it in great detail into the Holy Book. The process of change of women's status in Islamic society, e.g. can be traced through a comparative study of Koran interpretations such as those of Tabari (d. 923), Zamakhshari (d. 1144), Baydawi (d. 1286), the *Tafsir Jalalayn*, begun by Jalal al-Din al-Suyuti (d. 1505) and completed by his son of the same name, and many others.

The Traditions (*Hadith*) which provide detail to the doctrines and laws of the Koran constitute source materials of quite a different nature while playing a similar role as the Koran interpretations in the process of accommodating and legitimising changes in the community. The Traditions embody the venerable precedent or *Sunna* of the Prophet and his Companions consisting of what he or they said, did, or tolerated. The *Sunna* was recorded and transmitted in the form of *hadiths*, short narratives or traditions, each of which consisted of a text – containing an element of doctrine, ethics, law or social custom and etiquette – and a chain of transmitters, i.e. a chain of the names of all those men and women who had handled that particular text and had passed it on one to the other. The deep-going changes that engulfed the ever-expanding Islamic community during the formative years of the Islamic Empire were in turn absorbed and legitimised through the *Sunna* as codified in the *Hadith* through the technique of forgery of *hadiths*. Political, sectarian, social and other innovations were legitimised by providing for them a fake 'chain of transmitters' and hence by presenting them as the usage of the Prophet and his Companions. This was an effective way of dealing with changes in the established order since a *hadith* (even if forged) was more convincing than rational argument.[3] In this fashion, the *Sunna* was adjusted by the addition of normative detail to fit the needs of each new generation.

The challenge of uncontrolled proliferation of *hadiths* found its response in the emerging science of *Hadith* criticism with its weighty tones of biographic dictionaries (such as the *Tabaqat* of Ibn Sa'd, d. 844) that established both biographical data and credibility of the individual traditionists, together with a listing of the 'sound' material that they had transmitted. As a result, expurgated editions of *Hadith* material that – so their authors claimed – were free of forgeries were compiled from the mid-9th century onward (i.e. about 250 years after Muhammad's death). Most notable among them are the six canonical collections of al-Bukhari (d. 870), Muslim ibn Hajjaj (d. 875), Abu Da'ud al-Sijistani (d. 889), Abu 'Isa Muhammad al-Tirmidhi (d. 892), al-Nasa'i (d. 915), and Ibn Maja (d. 896).

A detailed study of these collections shows that they reflect and represent[4] (1) the actual way of life of the first generations of Muslims, (2) a nostalgic reinterpretation and idealisation of the early beginnings by later generations, and (3) the growth and change that occurred during later periods. It should be understood, however, that all of the material – no matter what its age or authenticity – is most valuable for our understanding of Islam because of the fact that it reflects actual social reality, even if not necessarily the social reality of the first generations of Muslims.

While it is as yet impossible in most cases to determine the exact age of the information conveyed within a single collection, comparative study of several *Hadith* collections can be enlightening insofar as it helps to establish – with the death date of each compiler serving as the *terminus ante quem* for all material within his compilation – patterns and directions of development within Islamic doctrines and practice through the centuries.

II   WOMEN IN THE KORAN

While the *Hadith* is a source that reflects both early and later usage, and hence tends to be ambiguous as to the age and authenticity of the information it contains, the Koran, on the other hand, is free of ambiguities of this kind. Thus, we find in it in some detail women's rights and duties as put into place during the Prophet's lifetime.

For perspective the Koranic material should be studied against the background of the Jahiliyya. Furthermore, for the reasons mentioned above, the Koran should best be let to speak for itself, without the benefit of Koran commentaries.

Islam is a religion of the city. Far from being a mere 'projection of the Bedouin mind',[5] the new faith with its mutually integrated religious, social, political and economic institutions was born in and shaped by a city environment. Furthermore, Islam arose within the context of a situation of change – change brought about by commercial development that had already profoundly altered the political, social and spiritual structures in Western Arabia.[6] The pre-Islamic trend toward urbanisation was crystallised and enhanced by the Islamic order which in its earliest form combined the patriarchal society of the pastoral nomad with urban life.[7] Desert and urban societies are, of course, structurally different. For one thing, the economic situation of desert life creates a balanced division of labour between the sexes, and permits a high degree of freedom for women. Urban living, on the other hand, disrupts this balance and forces women into the background. This situation of increasing urbanisation generating social change – combined with a deplorable lack of pertinent sources – may be the reason for our uncertainty concerning the status of women in pre-Islamic Arab urban society.

On the other hand, we hear of publicly visible, independently wealthy women who are active in their own rights. The best-known example here is, of course, Khadija, Muhammad's first wife. Much has been speculated about the existence of a matriarchal social order in pre-Islamic Arabia. As I have suggested elsewhere,[8] some details of Khadija's marriage to Muhammad are reminiscent of what Wellhausen[9] has suggested about matriarchal marriages in pre-Islamic Arabia. The whole issue of the Arabian matriarchate is, however, an old controversy[10] and need not be discussed again. What is of interest to us here, rather, is that aside from such rare figures of public visibility, involvement and independence as Khadija, the majority of pre-Islamic urban women appear to have lived in a male-dominated society in which their status was low and their rights were negligible. Most women were subjugated to male domination, either that of a male relative, or that of the husband. The men's rights over their women were as their rights over any other property. This seems to have been so not only in marriages by capture, where the captured woman was completely under the authority of her captor,[11] but also in marriages by purchase or contract. Here, the suitor paid a sum of money (the *mahr*) to the guardian of the bride-to-be (and possibly another sum, the *sadaq*, to the woman herself), thereby purchasing her and making her his exclusive property. The marriage contract, in other words, was a contract between husband and guardian, with the bride the sales object.[12] Furthermore, neither conventions nor laws seem to have existed to put a limit to the number of wives that a man could have simultaneously, so that the only restrictive considerations were economic ones.[13] As to divorce in the Jahiliyya, it was a matter entirely up to the will of the husband who, 'having purchased his wife, could discharge his total obligation to her by payment of any portion of the *mahr* that might remain due to her father or guardian, and be rid of her by pronouncement of the formula of dismissal'.[14] This formula, pronounced three times, was effective instantly. Finally, there is some indication that women in pre-Islamic Arabia were not allowed the holding, or in any case the uncontrolled disposal, of their possessions.[15]

A.   When studied against the background of the Jahiliyya, both the social status and the legal rights of Muslim women were improved through Koranic legislation. Among the laws effecting such improvement were the following:

1.   The Koranic laws putting an end to the pre-Islamic custom of burying baby girls alive.[16]   For example,

> Surah 16 (*The Bee*) verses 58 and 59: When if one of them receiveth tidings of the birth of a female, his face remaineth darkened, and he is wroth inwardly. He hideth himself from the folk because of the evil of that whereof he hath had tidings, (asking himself): Shall he keep it in contempt, or bury it beneath the dust. Verily, evil is their judgement.

> Surah 81 (*The Overthrowing*) verses 8 and 9: And when the girl child that was buried alive is asked for what sin she was slain .... (cf. Surah 6 (*Cattle*) verses 138 and 141, and Surah 17 (*The Children of Israel*), verse 31).

2.   The Koran sanctions marriage as a meritorious institution and invests it with importance and dignity. While marriage in Islam is not a sacramental, indissoluble (or monogamous) union of man and woman,[16] but a contract concluded between man and woman, it is one of the Signs of God, and is meritorious.

Surah 30 (*The Romans*) verse 21:   And of His signs is this: He created for you helpmates from yourselves that ye might find rest in them, and He ordained between you love and mercy. Lo, herein indeed are portents for folk who reflect.

Women are like fields to be cultivated and made fertile.

Surah 2 (*The Cow*) verse 223:   Your women who are tilth for you (to cultivate) so go to your tilth as ye will, and send (good deeds) before you for your souls, and fear Allah, and know that ye will (one day) meet Him . . . .

Men and woman are important as well as comforting to one another.

Surah 2 (*The Cow*) verse 187: . . . . they are raiment for you and you are raiment for them . . . .

Wives should be treated well in marriage.

Surah 33 (*The Clans*) verse 51:   . . . . that they may be comfortable and not grieve, and may all be pleased with what thou givest them . . . .

Furthermore, the laws of the Koran restrict the number of wives a man can have simultaneously to four[17] with the clear recognition that even this number may be so large as to make it difficult to treat all of them with impartiality.

Surah 4 (*Women*) verse 3:   . . . . marry of the women, who seem good to you, two or three or four; and if ye fear that ye cannot do justice (to so many) then one (only) or (the captives) that your right hands possess.   Thus it is more likely that ye will not do injustice. *id.*, verse 129: Ye will not be able to deal equally between (your) wives, however much ye wish (to do so). But turn not altogether (from one), leaving her as in suspense. If ye do good and keep from evil, lo! Allah is ever Forgiving, Merciful.

3.   The Koranic laws guaranteeing women the right to inherit and bequeath property. For example,

Surah 4 (*Women*) verse 7:   Unto the men (of a family) belongeth a share of that which parents and near kindred leave, and unto the women a share of that which parents and near kindred leave, whether it be little or much – a legal share.
id., verse 11: Allah chargeth you concerning (the provision for) your children: to the male the equivalent of the portion of two females, and if there be women more than two, then theirs is two–thirds of the inheritance, and if there by one

(only), then the half. And to his parents, a sixth in the inheritance, if he have a son, and if he have no son, and his parents are his heirs, then to his mother appertaineth the sixth, after any legacy he may have bequeathed, or debt (hath been paid). Your parents or your children: Ye know not which of them is nearer unto you in usefulness. It is an injunction from Allah. Lo! Allah is Knower, Wise.

id., verse 12: And unto you belongeth a half of that which your wives leave, if they have no child; but if they have a child then unto you the fourth of that which they leave, after any legacy they may have bequeathed, or debt (they may have contracted, hath been paid). And if a man or a woman have a distant heir (having left neither parent nor child), and he (or she) have a brother or sister (only on the mother's side) then to each of them twain (the brother and the sister) the sixth, and if they be more than two, then they shall be sharers in the third, after any legacy that may have been bequeathed or debt (contracted) not injuring (the heirs by willing away more than a third of the heritage) hath been paid. A commandment from Allah. Allah is Knower, Indulgent.

4. The Koranic laws guaranteeing women the right to have full possession and control of their wealth, including the dower, while married and after divorce. As it is the women who receives the dower in Islam, and no longer her guardian, the terms *mahr* and *sadaq* have become synonymous. For example,

> Surah 4 (*Women*) verse 4: And give unto the women (whom ye marry) free gift of their marriage portions; but if they of their own accord remit unto you a part thereof, then ye are welcome to absorb it (in your wealth).
> *id.,* verse 24: .... seek them with your wealth in honest wedlock, not debauchery. And those of whom ye seek content (by marrying them), give unto them their portions as a duty. And there is no sin for what you do by mutual agreement after the duty (hath been done). Lo! Allah is ever Knower, Wise.
> *id.,* verses 20 and 21: And if ye wish to exchange one wife for another and you have given one of them a sum of money (however great), take nothing from it. Would you take it by the way of calumny and open wrong? How can ye take it (back) after one of you hath gone unto the other, and they have taken a strong pledge from you? (cf. Surah 4: 127).

> Surah 2 (*The Cow*) verse 229: Divorce must be pronounced twice and then (a woman) must be retained in honour or released in kindness. And it is not lawful for you that ye take from women aught of that which ye have given them; except (in the case) when both fear that they may not be able to keep the limits of Allah. And if ye fear that they

may not be able to keep the limits of Allah, in that case it is no sin for either of them if the woman ransom herself. These are the limits (imposed by) Allah. Transgress them not. For whoso transgresses Allah's limits: such are wrongdoers.

5.   The right of the wife to be properly fed and clothed at the husband's expense. For example,

> Surah 4 (*Women*) verse 34: Men are in charge of women, because Allah hath made the one of them to excel the other, and because they spend of their property (for the support of women) . . . .

6.   The Koranic divorce laws which stipulate the obligatory *'idda* (a waiting period of some three months after the final pronouncement of the divorce formula) also have to be mentioned here, as they entail a slight amelioration of women's position at divorce. While pre-Islamic wives could be repudiated and turned out by their husbands immediately, the Koran legislates:

> Surah 2 (*The Cow*) verse 228: Women who are divorced shall wait, keeping themselves apart, three (monthly) courses. And it is not lawful for them that they should conceal that which Allah hath created in their wombs if they are believers in Allah and the Last Day. And their husbands would do better to take them back in that case if they desire reconciliation. And they (women) have rights similar to those (of men) over them in kindness, and men are a degree above women. Allah is Mighty, Wise.
> *id.*, verse 229: Divorce must be pronounced twice and then (a woman) must be retained in honour or released in kindness. And it is not lawful for you that ye take from women aught of that which ye have given them; except (in the case) when both fear that they may not be able to keep within the limits (imposed by) Allah . . . . etc.

cf. Surah 65 (*The Divorce*) verses 1-7.

The Koranic legislation, in other words, secures adequate time for reflection, and legislates fair treatment of the woman if the man ultimately resolves upon divorce. Resumption of the marriage in the period of "suspended divorce" is both possible without further ceremony, and recommended. Otherwise, a "release in kindness" is enjoined (cf., e.g., Surah 2 (*The Cow*), verses 228, 229, 231, 232). Special rights are also given to the nursing mother (*id.*, verses 233), etc.

B.   The Koranic laws, while improving women's status, do not establish political, social or economic equality of the sexes, as "Men are a degree above women" (Surah 2 (*The Cow*) verse 228).

1. For example, the testimony of a woman is worth half that of a man.

> e.g. Surah 2 (*The Cow*) verse 282: .... And call to witness from among you men, two witnesses. And if two men be not (at hand) then a man and two women, of such as ye approve as witnesses, so that if the one erreth (through forgetfulness), the other will remember.

2. In most cases, women inherit half of what men inherit.

> Surah 4 (*Women*) verse 11: .... to the male the equivalent of the portion of two females ....

3. The marriage laws enjoin women not only to strict monogamy, but to marriage with Muslims only. For example,

> Surah 2 (*The Cow*) verse 221: .... and give not your daughters in marriage to idolators till they believe, for lo! a believing slave is better than an idolator though he please you.[18]

> Muslim men, on the other hand, are free to marry

> the virtuous women of the believers and the virtuous women of those who received the Scripture before you, when you give them their marriage portions and live with them in honour, not in fornication, nor taking them as secret concubines. (Surah 5 (*The Table Spread*) verse 5).

According to this law, then, marriage of a Muslim man to Jewish, Christian and Sabian women is lawful,[19] although marriage to an idolatress is not.[20]

4. Within the context of marriage, the wife is in charge of her husband who has full authority over her, including the authority to admonish and beat her if she is rebellious. For example,

> Surah 4 (*Women*) verse 34: Men are in charge of women, because Allah hath made the one of them excel the other, and because they spend of their property (for the support of their women). So good women are the obedient, guarding in secret that which Allah hath guarded. As for those from whom ye fear rebellion, admonish them and banish them to beds apart, and scourge them. Then, if they obey you, seek not a way against them. Lo! Allah is ever High, Exalted, Great.

5. The Koran does not give the same rights in the matter of divorce to women that it gives to men. Rather, the decision to divorce is left to the men exclusively:

> Surah 2 (*The Cow*) verse 227: .... And if they (the men) decide upon divorce ....

The women may seek arbitration:

> Surah 4 (*Women*) verse 35: And if ye fear a breach between them twain (the man and wife), appoint an arbiter from his folk and an arbiter from her folk. If they desire amendment, Allah will make them of one mind, Lo! Allah is ever Knower, Aware.

She may 'ransom herself from her husband', for a sum agreed upon by both of them, after he has twice pronounced divorce against her, etc. For example,

> Surah 2 (*The Cow*) verse 229: Divorce must be pronounced twice and the (a woman) must be retained in honour or released in kindness. And it is not lawful for you that ye take from women aught of that which ye have given them; except (in the case) when both fear that they may not be able to keep within the limits (imposed by) Allah. And if ye fear that they may not be able to keep the limits of Allah, in that case it is no sin for either of them if the woman ransom herself. These are the limits (imposed by) Allah. Transgress them not. For whoso transgresseth Allah's limits: such are wrongdoers.

This piece of Koranic legislation represents a restriction of a pre-Islamic practice which had made it possible for a woman to buy her freedom from her husband by resigning her dower to him[21] - a practice that seems to have led to considerable abuse. Therefore, Islam sanctions it only if the parties 'fear that they may not be able to keep within the limits (imposed by) Allah'.

The woman desiring divorce has the right of negotiation, however, and the man is enjoined to goodness. He should refrain from any action induced by 'greed', i.e. by reluctance to lose her possessions.

> Surah 4 (*Women*) verse 128: If a woman feareth ill-treatment from her husband, or desertion, it is no sin for them twain if they make terms of peace between themselves. Peace is better. But greed hath been made present in the minds (of men). If ye do good and keep from evil, lo! Allah is ever Informed of what ye do.

Ultimately, however, the inequality of men and women remains in full force as the husband can repudiate his wife, but she cannot repudiate him.

C. Finally, the Koran teaches that as members of the community of the faith, with respect to the spiritual and moral obligations imposed upon them, in their relationship with their Creator, and the Compensations prepared for them in the Hereafter, men and women have full equality.

> Surah 33 (*The Clans*) verse 35: Lo! Men who surrender unto Allah, and women who surrender, and men who believe and women who believe, and men who obey and women who obey, and men who speak the truth and women who speak the truth, and men who persevere (in righteousness) and women who persevere, and men who are humble and women who are humble, and men who give alms and women who give alms, and men who fast and women who fast, and men who guard (their modesty) and women who guard (their modesty), and men who remember Allah much and women who remember - Allah hath prepared for them forgiveness and a vast reward.

> Surah 9 (*Repentance*) verse 71: And the believers, men and women, are protecting friends one of the other; they enjoin the right and forbid the wrong, and they establish worship and they pay the poor-due, and they obey Allah and His messenger. As for these, Allah will have mercy on them. Lo! Allah is Mighty, Wise.

> Surah 40 (*The Believer*) verse 40: Whoso doeth an ill-deed, he will be repaid the like thereof, while whoso doeth right, whether male or female, and is a believer, (all) such will enter the Garden, where they will be nourished without stint.

> Surah 9 (*Repentance*) verse 72: Allah promises to the believers, men and women, Gardens underneath which rivers flow wherein they will abide - blessed dwellings in Gardens of Eden. And - greater (far)! - acceptance from Allah. That is the supreme triumph.

> (cf. also Surah 48 (*Victory*) verse 5; Surah 56 (*The Event*) verses 1-56; Surah 57 (*Iron*) verse 12; Surah 3 (*The Family of Imran*) verse 195, and others.

Both men and women have their full humanity and bear the burden of equal moral responsibility.

The Koran legislates, for example, the same punishment for thieving men as for thieving women.

> Surah 5 (*The Table Spread*) verse 38: As for the thief, both male and female, cut off their hands. It is the reward of their own deeds, an exemplary punishment from Allah. Allah is Mighty, Wise.

Both male and female adulterers will suffer the same punishment, according to Surah 24 (*Light*) verse 2:[22]

The adulterer and the adulteress, scourge ye each one of them (with) a hundred stripes. And let not pity for the twain withhold you from obedience to Allah, if ye believe in Allah and the Last Day. And let a party of believers witness their punishment.[23]

Furthermore, according to Surah 24 (*Light*) verses 6-9, a woman's oath by which she defends herself against her husband's accusation of adultery 'shall avert the punishment from her', i.e. her oath shall weigh heavier than his.

As for those who accuse their wives but have no witnesses except themselves; let the testimony of one of them be four testimonies, (swearing) by Allah that he is of those who speak the truth; And yet a fifth, invoking the curse of Allah on him if he is of those who lie. And it shall avert the punishment from her if she bear witness before Allah four times that the thing he saith is indeed false. And a fifth (time) that the wrath of Allah be upon her if he speaketh truth.

One may even argue that women's essential equality with man is more complete in Islam that it is in Judaism and Christianity. Both in the Old and in the New Testament, Eve is responsible for the Fall and the expulsion from Paradise. She transgressed, and as punishment for her transgression, God cursed Eve (before He cursed Adam) by saying

I will greatly multiply thy sorrow and thy conception; in sorrow thou shalt bring forth children; and thy desire shall be to thy husband, and he shall rule over thee. (Genesis 3:16) (King James Version).

This inequality with man was then extended to other areas, e.g. by Paul in the First Epistle to Timothy, chapter 2 (King James Version):

Let the woman learn in silence with all subjection. But I suffer not a woman to teach, nor to usurp authority over the man, but to be in silence. For Adam was first formed, then Eve. And Adam was not deceived, but the woman being deceived was in the transgression. Nothwithstanding, she shall be saved in childbearing, if they continue in faith and charity and holiness with sobriety.

In the Koran, on the other hand, Adam and Eve are jointly responsible for the transgression and consequent expulsion from Paradise.

Surah 7 (*The Heights*) verses 18-26: He (God) said (to Iblis): Go forth from hence, degraded banished. As for such of them as follow thee, surely I will fill hell with all of you.

And (unto man): O Adam! Dwell thou and thy wife in the
Garden and eat from whence ye will, but come out nigh this
tree least ye become wrongdoers. Then Satan whispered to
them that he might manifest unto them that which was
hidden from them of their shame, and he said: Your Lord
forbade you from this tree only lest ye should become angels
or become of the immortals. And he swore to them (saying):
Lo! I am a sincere advisor unto you. Thus did he lead them
on with guile. And when they tasted of the tree, their
shame was manifest to them and they began to hide (by
heaping) on themselves some of the leaves of the Garden.
And their Lord called them (saying): Did I not forbid you
from that tree and tell you: Lo! Satan is an open enemy to
you? They said: Our Lord! We have wronged ourselves. If
Thou forgive us not and have not mercy on us, surely we are
of the lost! He said: Go down (from hence), one of you a
foe to the other. He said: There shall ye live, and there
shall ye die, and thence shall ye be brought forth.   O
Children of Adam! We have revealed unto you raiment to
conceal your shame, and splendid vesture, but the raiment
of restraint from evil, that is best.   This is of the
revelations of Allah, that they may remember.

It would lead us away from our topic were we here to engage in a
discussion of the concept of original sin and its presence or absence in
Koranic teaching.

Suffice it to say that all the Koranic doctrines cited so far
clearly converge to establish the absence of the doctrine of woman's
spiritual inferiority in Koranic Teaching.

D.   Seclusion and Veiling of Women in the Koran

On these, possibly the most sensitive of all issues, the Koran makes a
clear distinction between the Prophet's wives on the one hand and
believing women in general on the other.

1.   The legislation specific to Muhammad's wives is to be found,
for example, in Surah 33 (*The Clans*) verses 33 and 34. These verses
are preceded by some that indicate clearly that the wives of the
Prophet are not like other women, and are followed by a verse
legislating the proper behaviour for all believing visitors who come to
the Prophet's house.   The context, thus, makes it clear that the
legislation applies to the Prophet's household specifically and not to
the believers in general.

Surah 33 (*The Clans*) verse 28:   O Prophet!   Say unto thy
wives: If ye desire the world's life and its adornment, come!
I will content you and will release you with a fair release.
(29) But if ye desire Allah and His messenger and the abode
of the Hereafter, the lo; Allah hath prepared for the good
among you an immense reward.
(30)   O ye wives of the Prophet!   Whosoever of you

committeth manifest lewdness, the punishment for her will be doubled, and that is easy for Allah.

(31) And whosoever of you is submissive unto Allah and His messenger and doeth right, We shall give her reward twice over, and We have prepared for her a rich provision.

(32) O ye wives of the Prophet! Ye are not like any other women. If ye keep your duty (to Allah), then be not soft of speech, lest he in whose heart is a disease aspire (to you), but utter customary speech.

(33) And stay in your houses.[24] Bedizen not yourselves with the bedizenment of the Time of Ignorance. Be regular in prayer, and pay the poor-due, and obey Allah and His messenger. Allah's wish is but to remove uncleanness far from you, O Folk of the Household, and cleanse you with a thorough cleansing.

(34) And bear in mind that which is recited in your houses of the relevations of Allah and wisdom. Lo! Allah is Subtle, Aware.

(53) O ye who believe! Enter not the dwellings of the Prophet for a meal without waiting for the proper time, unless permission be granted you. But if ye are invited, enter, and when your meal is ended, then disperse. Linger not for conversation. Lo! that would cause annoyance to the Prophet, and he would be shy of (asking) you (to go); but Allah is not shy of the truth. And when ye ask of them (the wives of the Prophet) anything, ask it of them from behind a curtain. That is purer for your hearts and for their hearts. And it is not for you to cause annoyance to the messenger of Allah, nor that ye should ever marry his wives after him, Lo! that in Allah's sight would be an enormity.

(55) It is no sin for them (thy wives) (to converse freely) with their fathers, or their sons, or their brothers, or their brothers' sons, or the sons of their sisters or of their own women, or their slaves. O women! Keep your duty to Allah. Lo! Allah is Witness over all things.

2.   The Koranic legislation that applies to the women of the believers in general is found in Surah 33 (*The Clans*) verse 59

O Prophet! Tell thy wives and thy daughters and the women of the believers to draw their cloaks round them (when they go abroad). That will be better, that so they may be recognized and not annoyed. Allah is ever Forgiving, Merciful.

and in Surah 24 (*Light*) verses 30 and 31, where general rules of chaste and modest conduct are laid down for both male and female believers:

(30) Tell the believing men to lower their gaze and be modest. That is purer for them. Lo! Allah is Aware of what they do.

(31) And tell the believing women to lower their gaze and be modest, and display of their adornment only that which is apparent, and to draw their veils over their bosoms, and not to reveal their adornment save to their husbands or fathers or husbands' fathers, or their sons or their husbands' sons, or their brothers or their brothers' sons or sisters' sons, or their women, or their slaves, or male attendants who lack vigour, or children who know naught of women's nakedness. And let them not stamp their feet so as to reveal what they hide of their adornment. And turn unto Allah together, O believers, in order that ye may succeed.

III ADJUSTMENT AND DEVELOPMENT OF SOME ASPECTS OF WOMEN'S STATUS THROUGH KORAN INTERPRETATIONS

As Islamic society changed rapidly during the course of its early history, the dictates of the Koran were made the basis of interpretation and hence accommodation, adaptation, and adjustment to later reality. While it would certainly be of the greatest benefit here to analyse in bulk in a comparative way the main interpretations of at least the most important Koran verses dealing with women's status, a few samples will have to suffice. As illustrative examples, two verses – and their interpretations – have been selected here. The first deals with the status of women, the other with the veil.

As pointed out above, the Koran is free of any clear or specific legislative detail directed at Muslim women to keep in seclusion to their houses or to veil their faces. Seclusion and veiling, however, – both presumably of Persian and possibly Byzantine origin – were legitimized by exegetes who interpreted the vague and general Koranic provisions to sanction them.

The efforts of the Koran interpreters may also in part have been caused by their desire to ensure maximum application of the Koranic provisions. For, 'in the same way as the Rabbinical Commentators of the Pentateuch placed 'a fence about the Law' by requiring a precautionary margin in order to ensure the entire fulfilment of its dictates, so the interpreters of the Koran demanded more than their original'.[25]

In Surah 4 (*Women*) verse 34, we read that

Men are in charge of women, because Allah hath made the one of them to excel the other, and because they spend of their property (for the support of women). So good women are the obedient, guarding in secret that which Allah hath guarded . . . . etc.

Abu Ja'far Muhammad ibn Jarir al-Tabari (d. 923) comments on this Koran verse in the following way:

Men are in charge of their women with respect to disciplining (or chastising) them, and to providing them with restrictive guidance concerning their duties toward God and themselves (i.e. the men); *by virtue of that by which God has given excellence (or preference) to the men over their wives:* i.e. the payment of their dowers to them, spending of their wealth on them, and providing for them in full. This is how God has given excellence to (the men) over (the women), and hence (the men) have come to be in charge of (the women) and hold authority over them in those of their matters with which God has entrusted them.

Tabari here interprets the Koran verse literally and specifically as endowing the men (a) with authority over their women in the family setting, and (b) with the obligation to provide for their women by way of material support.

Some 350 years later, Nasir al-Din Abu l-Khayr ' Abd Allah ibn 'Umar al-Baydawi (d. 1286) gives an interpretation of the same verse that provides generally applicable restrictive detail and sanctions the view of women as creatures incapable of and unfit for public duties – a view that was fully developed by his time.

Men are in charge of women, i.e. men are in charge of women as rulers are in charge of their subjects . . . . *God has preferred the one (sex) over the other,* i.e. because God has preferred men over women in the completeness of mental ability, good counsel, complete power in the performance of duties and the carrying out of (divine) commands. Hence to men have been confined prophecy, religious leadership (*'imama*), saintship (*wilaya*),[26] the performance of religious rites, the giving of evidence in law courts, the duties of the Holy War, and worship (in the mosque) on Friday, etc., the privilege of electing chiefs, the larger share of inheritance, and discretion in the matter of divorce, *by virtue of that which they spend of their wealth,* in marrying (the women), such as their dowers and cost of their maintenance.

Later Koran commentators not only accepted Baydawi's interpretation, but further categorised and hardened the restrictive detail provided by his exegesis. Ahmad ibn Muhammad al-Khafaji (d. 1659), goes on to specify the various aspects of the restrictions which Baydawi had put forth categorically, for example:

religious leadership (*'imama*) (which is inaccessible to women) is understood to include both the *'imama kubra* and the *'imama sughra. wilaya* he understands not as 'saintship' but as 'assuming of responsibility (*tawallin*) for the woman in marriage matters, which means the power to make decisions' (which by this time, of course, was no longer theirs.

The religious rites (*sha'a'ir*) from which women are barred according to Baydawi, are exemplified and specified as: the call to prayer (*'adhan*), the second call to prayer (*'iqama*), the Friday sermon, Friday worship (in the mosque), and the *takbirat al-tashriq* (certain rites during the Pilgrimage).

Not only the process of ever-increasing exclusion of women from all public concerns, but also the development of the law of the veil is traceable through comparative study of the Koran commentaries. On the basis of vague and general Koranic rules, e.g. those imposing modest behaviour for women, the exegetes prescribe the veil in increasingly absolute and categorical fashion.

> Surah 24 (*Light*) verse 30: And tell the believing women to lower their gaze and be modest, and display of their ornament only that which is apparent, and to draw their veils over their bosoms, and not to reveal their adornment save to their own husbands or fathers or husbands' fathers . . . . (etc.)

Tabari (d. 923) interprets this as an order to believing women to

> *lower their gaze* so as not to look at what God has forbidden them to look at, and to *preserve their private parts* from the glances of him who has no right to glance at them, by veiling them with some garment or other . . . . As for the *apparent ornament* (which may be displayed), it is the face and the hands (up to the middle of the forearm), including eye-make up (*kuhl*), rings, bracelets, and dyes.

Tabari's argument for the lawful *un*covering of the face and the extremities runs as follows:

> Since man has to cover his genitals when praying, and woman has to uncover her face and hands during prayer, but has to cover all else – except that it is transmitted from the Prophet that he forbade her to display more than half her forearm – it follows therefrom that she has the right to display of her body that which is not pudendal, just as the man has the right to do so. Because, what is not pudendal, may lawfully be shown. If she has the right (to show these parts), it is understood that they are of those that God has exempted when He said: 'except that which is apparent', because this much may be seen of her.

As for the prescription *to draw their veils over their bosoms*, i.e. the order to draw their veils over their breast pockets (*juyub*), it implies, according to Tabari, the injunction to veil their hair, neck and ears. The interpretation of the same verse in Baydawi (d. 1285) reads as follows:

> *Let them lower their gaze* before the men at whom it is not lawful for them to look, and *let them guard their private parts* by veiling them, or by bewaring of (or: guarding against) fornication. The lowering of the glances is presented because the glance is the messenger of fornication. *And let them not display of their adornment* such as jewellery, dress and make-up – let alone the parts where they are worn or applied – to those to whom (such display) is not lawful . . . . what is meant by *adornment* is the place where adornment is put (or worn) . . . .

As to the opinion that the prohibition to display does not include the face and hands, because they are not pudendal, Baydawi argues that clearly

> this applies to prayer only, not appearance, because the whole body of the free woman is pudendal, and it is illicit for anyone (except the husband or the *dhawu mahram*) to look at any part of her except by necessity such as (medical) treatment, or the bearing of witness.

As for later commentaries such as al-Khafaji's (d. 1659) *Hashiya* on al-Baydawi, this restrictive interpretation is further heightened and emphasised. Women have now completely disappeared behind the veil. al-Khafaji teaches on the authority of al-Shafi'i that

> the whole body of the women is pudendal, even face and hand, without exception (absolutely).

He also cites the opinion that

> face and hand are pudendal *except* during prayer and that a woman's prayer *does not become invalid* if she uncovers these parts of her body.

Since this interpretation, however, leaves no part of the woman visible, the Koranic exemption *except that which is apparent* has to be given a new meaning. al-Khafaji and others deal with this difficulty by interpreting the verse as

> a command of exception from *the established rule*, which applies to such exceptional circumstances as the giving of evidence in law courts and medical treatment only.

The process of progressive exclusion and increasing restrictions imposed on women is thus clearly visible through comparison of the original Koranic legislation with the series of commentaries which later ages produced. The evidence is furnished both by commentaries that were written as interpretations of the Koran directly, and by the supercommentaries (*hawashi*) that adapted and developed the teachings of earlier commentaries rather than just those of the Holy Book.

IV   THE *HADITH*

The *Hadith* material by virtue of its provenance and role in the shaping of the Islamic order is both a record of the way of life of the early community, and an indicator of later changes and development. Furthermore, in view of the fact that the *Hadith* reflects the formation of the Islamic *Sunna* against the background of Jahiliyya moral laxity and in the face of the indifference of vast numbers of individuals converted, but not yet deeply committed, to the new religion, it is not surprising to find also in the *Hadith* - descriptions of the early Islamic elite the traits of the inspirational example rather than just that of the realistic portrait. Given, therefore, the inevitable gap between the actual and the idealized, between the genuine and later ascriptions, it is only to be expected that the *Hadith* entails much varied and often contradictory information on the society it describes.[27] Because of the limited scope of this paper, only a few aspects of the status and roles of women in the *Hadith* literature can be presented.

A. The Images of Women in the Hadith

The nature of women as reflected in the *Hadith* spans the whole spectrum from the saintly to the evil and unclean.

1. The saintly women

The most extraordinary women who are especially favoured by God and therefore blessed with unusual powers and extraordinary experiences are, of course, Muhammad's wives whose close association with the Prophet lifts them above the realm and ranks of ordinary womankind. Most of them, e.g. had extraordinary dreams or visions prior to their marriage to the Prophet, such as Sawda[28] and 'Umm Habiba.[29]   'A'isha's picture, on the other hand, was shown by the Archangel Gabriel to the Prophet prior to his proposal of marriage to her father;[30]   or, according to another account, she was shown to Muhammad as his future bride and a substitute for Khadija by Gabriel while still in the cradle. This was a favour from God to take away the Prophet's grief over Khadija's death.[31]

Muhammad received revelations while he was in 'A'isha's company[32] and, according to some 'A'isha could even see the Angel and exchanged greetings with him,[33] while, according to others, they sent greetings through the Prophet to each other, although she could not see him.[34] The Prophet took his wife Hafsa back after he had divorced her, because the Angel Gabriel commanded him to do so, as she was a righteous woman and would be his wife in Heaven.[35]   All of the Prophet's terrestrial wives will be his wives in Heaven, e.g. Zaynab bint Jahsh,[36] Hafsa,[37] etc. 'A'isha's image in Heaven is even shown to Muhammad to make his own death easier on him.[38]

The special status of Muhammad's wives as legislated in the Koran imposed specific rights and privileges as well as duties and limitations upon them. Their title, *'ummahat al-mu'minin,* is used through the *Hadith* as a technical term that applies exclusively to them as a finite group. It is noteworthy that the *Hadith* emphasizes the fact that the title endows its bearers with authority over the male believers. We hear, e.g. of a woman who said to 'A'isha: 'Oh Mother!' and received the answer: 'I am not your mother, but the mother of your menfolk'.[39]

It is not surprising, then, to find this group of women presented with all the qualities of piety and religious rightmindedness, such as fasting continuously,[40] overly generous in the giving of free-will alms offerings at the expense of their own food supply,[41] and living in voluntary poverty including possession and wearing of threadbare clothes that they mend themselves.[42] At the same time, they are most knowledgeable about the matters of religion[43] and truthful in their transmitting of information concerning the Prophet of Islam.[44]

In the treatment of the sanctified Mothers of the Believers, however, very human 'female' traits such as jealousy and possessiveness are emphasized by the pious transmitters as well. In the Prophet's household, new arrivals evoked great jealousy on the part of the already established wives, as well as fear of being replaced in the Prophet's favour by a rival.[45] The Prophet, however, was absolutely scrupulous in treating all of his wives equally and visited each of them once a day when he made his daily rounds to their houses, even on the day of a wedding to a new wife.[46] Each wife had her fixed day to spend with him, a prerogative which she most zealously guarded[47] but which she could give to a rival – to please the Prophet – if she so chose.[48] On the occasion of travels, lots were cast to decide which of his wives were to accompany the Prophet and which stayed at home.[49] Some wives attempted to detain the Prophet on his daily visit through the use of some trick or other, such as Hafsa who, knowing of Muhammad's love for sweets, detained him by offering him a honey drink, until this ruse was discovered and terminated by a counter-ruse of 'A'isha, Sawda and Safiyya.[50] Backbiting and bragging matches among the women are also recorded,[51] as are some incidents of unwillingness to help a rival out in a case of need.[52]

The lives of the wives of the Prophet, therefore, are written on several levels: the anecdotal level that reflects their squabbles and therewith the 'foibles of their sex', the normative level where they appear as paragons of virtue and as models for all women to follow, and the level of pious legend with its tales of divine grace and the workings of miracles on their behalf.

2. Ordinary women as spiritual and sexual equals of men

The general attitude toward women reflected in the *Hadith* is a positive one. This fact is intimately linked with the original teachings of Islam, and the lifestyle of its founder. The *Hadith* elaborates on the Koranic teachings regarding the spiritual equality of women and men, and provides detailed information on women who perform all the religious duties enjoined by Islamic doctrine, thereby proving their full membership in the faith, such as prayer,[53] almsgiving,[54] the freeing of a slave,[55] ritual slaughtering of sacrificial animals,[56] and fasting (although the latter, according to some, should be done with the husband's permission except during Ramadan when the husband's consent is not necessary[57]). As for the holy war, its equivalent for women is the blameless pilgrimage.[58] Regarding martyrdom, the woman who dies in childbirth is a martyr.[59] Women also build mosques[60] and can even act as prayer leaders.[61]

Women's spiritual equality with men is matched by – and, indeed, flows from – their human equality of full personhood, including their sexuality. The lack of a tradition of asceticism – or, rather, in all probability, the refusal on the part of the community to permit such a tradition to grow strong enough to drastically alter the substance of Islam - is reflected in those *hadiths* that admonish the believer not to overdo prayer by night and fasting by day. For, as they claim, the self - the body - and the family have their rights which necessitate that one refrain from exhausting oneself through the observance of religious duties.[62] Indeed, the wife is important enough that fasting should be broken on her - as on a guest's - behalf.[63]

The sexual instinct in both man and woman, far from being sinful, is part of God's creation, and hence the pleasures that the sexes bring to each other are rightful, provided they be enjoyed in the context of lawful marriage (or concubinage). Marriage is meritorious and strongly recommended, partly because it preserves modesty better. Indeed, says Ibn 'Abbas, 'the best of His people is he who has the most wives' (i.e. of course, the Prophet himself).[64]

The Prophet advocated marriage both in his words and by his personal example. He was married often and happily. The *Hadith* records expressions of great affection for his wives, such as his words to 'A'isha that he loved her 'more than butter with dates',[65] and that 'her excellence over all other women was like the excellence of bread-soup (his favourite dish) over other dishes'.[66] Furthermore, the *Hadith* tells about his virility as it does about his piety, strength of character, and powers of persuasion. 'Women, pleasant odours, and prayer were the three things which he found most precious in this world'. 'The Prophet loved women, perfumes, and horses'.

A wife should be given her full share of sexual pleasures by her husband who is enjoined to devote himself for 8 days (or 3 days) when marrying a woman who has been married before, for 7 days when marrying a virgin.[67] The woman, on the other hand, may not shun her husband's bed, and if she denies herself to her husband and he is angry at her because of it, the angels curse her until dawn.[68] She is the fully equal sexual partner of her husband. Her consent, e.g. is required before the husband can engage in 'azl (*coitus interruptus*).[69]

The favourable attitude toward sex presented in the *Hadith* is not, however, reflective of a 'deeper awareness of human sexuality',[70] but remains, in James Bellamy's words, 'rather naive and simplistic, even innocent'.[71] The language used to describe sexual acts is unspecific and chaste as well as serious. Only very rarely are particular sexual acts mentioned. A successful wedding night, e.g. is described as one where the groom (the Prophet) 'was pleased by the bride' (Safiyya) and 'did not sleep that night and did not cease to converse with her'.[72] The *Hadith* emphasizes the Prophet's virility as much as his prudishness. Ultimately, the prudishness that pervades the *Hadith* as a whole may indeed stem from the reluctance of the pious transmitters to investigate too closely the most private details of the Prophet's or his household's personal lives.[73]

Women should be cared for well and treated with kindness by their husbands[74] as well as given the right to do their own idiosyncracies, since 'woman is like a rib which will snap if one tries to straighten her natural crookedness'. 'The morsel that a man puts into his wife's mouth will be rewarded by God'. Wives are not slaves and should not be treated as such.[75]

3.   Women as inferior beings

Under the impact of a growing asceticism in the Islamic community, and in the framework of a changed social order which secluded women from public life, the nature of women came to be perceived in a different way. Naturally, the *Hadith* reflects these changes.

Women are naturally, morally and religiously defective.[76] Women, houses and horses are ominous.[77]   Prayer is interrupted if dogs, donkeys (unbelievers) and women pass too closely by the place of prayer.[78] Women are unclean over and above menstruation. There is, e.g. a difference in the degree to which the urine of baby boys and baby girls defiles clothes, the latter being greater.[79] Women are evil temptresses, the greatest *fitna* for men.[80] It is one of the signs of the Hour that there will be only one man for every fifty women.[81] And women make up the larger part of the inhabitants of Hell, because of their unfaithfullness and ingratitude toward their husbands.[82]

Women's inferiority, however, does not only stem from their impurity and moral deficiency, but also from their weaker intellectual powers. Therefore, among many other deficiencies, women do not have the qualities that would render them fit to rule. A people that entrusts a woman with rulership will not prosper and thrive, and her government will not render her people happy.[83] At the same time, it is sinful for women to leave the confines of their sex. The Prophet pronounced a great curse against women who behave and act like men.[84]

B.   **Seclusion and Veiling of Women in the Hadith**

1.   The women of the Prophet

The *Hadith* gives unquestionable evidence that the *hijab* – which implies not merely the face-veil, but the sum-total of practices connected with the seclusion of women[85] – was legislated and hence made obligatory for the wives of the Prophet. The only contradictions evident in the *Hadith* material regarding the *hijab* have to do with the occasion for the revelation of the *hijab*, not with which group of women the *hijab* was imposed upon. Among the several explanations, we find mention of Zaynab bint Jahsh's wedding to the Prophet who became disturbed either because some male guests lingered and would not leave the bridal meal on the wedding night,[86] or because he saw some men loitering in the vicinity of Zaynab's house on the morning after the wedding night.[87] In any case, great emphasis is placed on the use of the *hijab* by the Mothers of Believers. 'A'isha, again evidencing model righteous behaviour, secluded herself behind the *hijab* even from Hasan and Husayn, Muhammad's grandchildren (in super-erogatory seclusion).[88] On travels, Muhammad's wives were secluded in litters so undistinguishable and unrevealing that even the Prophet mistook one for the litter of the other.[89] In 'A'isha's case, her litter was even moved on although she was not in it (*hadith al-'ifk*).[90]

As seclusion in the house and veiling abroad were the prerogatives of Muhammad's wives, great emphasis is laid on their use in the cases of Juwayriyya, Rayhana and Safiyya, all three prisoners of war, as proof that they were in fact Muhammad's wives. That this is indeed the reason for these story materials, and that they do not intend to imply veiling of free women in general, is, for example proven by the following, otherwise incomprehensible account:

> Safiyya sat behind Muhammad on his mount wrapped like a bundle in his cloak that covered her face and back and was fastened under her feet.[91] As the mount stumbled and she and the Prophet were thrown off, Abu Talha covered his face with his own garment before helping her to get up,[92] so as not to look at her. (Because she was now one of the 'Mothers of the Believers').

'A'isha, of course, is again the model of veil-wearing. She was veiled even as a little girl before she reached puberty, after Muhammad's proposal of marriage had been made to her father,[93] and wore a face-veil even during the *tawaf*. For less pious reasons, she sometimes veiled herself when she did not want to be recognised, for example once when Muhammad unveiled his new bride Safiyya in public, 'A'isha mingled with the spectators to have a look at her new rival.[95]

Thus, as the norms of proper 'Islamic dress' were established, detailed instructions were often put into 'A'isha's mouth, e.g. when we hear of Hafsa, 'A'isha's niece, entering 'A'isha's house in a thin veil that revealed her bosom and of 'A'isha ripping it off while saying: 'Don't you know what God has revealed in the *Surah of the Light*?' (Surah 33, see above). She then covered her chest with a thick veil. (IS 8, 49-50). Even in this story, then, where she is the arbiter of correct appearance, the veil she dispenses is meant to cover the chest and not the face of a woman who is not one of Muhammad's wives and therefore is not expected to use the *hijab*.

It is equally clear that some of the sources indicate confinement and immobility for Muhammad's wives after the Prophet's death, which he himself is supposed to have imposed on the Farewell Pilgrimage and which, e.g. Sawda and Zaynab observed, saying that 'no mount would move (them) about after the death of the Messenger of God'.[96] 'A'isha, on the other hand, certainly did not adhere to this regulation. She engaged in numerous manoeuvers in the public sector, among them her battle against 'Ali that centered and surged around her camel.[97] The *Hadith* reports other pieces of evidence on such mobility as well.

As the segregation issue became a prominent feature of Islam, it was extended from life into death. The rule that only those males were permitted to descend into a woman's grave at burial who had been *dhawu mahram* to her applied at first to Muhammad's wives only. The same woman, Zaynab bint Jahsh, at whose wedding to the Prophet the *hijab* was revealed, was put into her grave by her relatives only and the Mothers of the Believers prevented the Caliph 'Umar from descending into her tomb, 'as only he may descend to whom it was lawful to look at her while she was alive'.[98]

2.   Veiling and seclusion of ordinary women?

On the issues of veiling and seclusion, the *Hadith* material is quite contradictory.   Three main characteristics are discernible without difficulty.   Firstly, 'permissive' and 'restrictive' material is found side by side, often anchored in the same early authority (such as Ibn 'Abbas).   Secondly, the relevant material often exists in the form of clusters of related traditions.   In this context, it is noteworthy that the longer and more detailed variants more often than not include restrictive detail which is absent in the shorter versions.   What comes across as an addition, in other words, is often restrictive.   Finally, the restrictive material is therefore generally more abundant in the later, as opposed to the earlier, *Hadith* collections as a whole.

On the basis of these general observations which will have to suffice here, one may argue that the traditions depicting *women's visibility and full participation in society* are of the greatest importance and should be studied with the greatest care.   For there is good reason to believe that they more of less faithfully reflect aspects of early Islamic society which were left behind by later generations. For this reason, it will be beneficial to present some of the available material for illustrative purposes.

In pre-Islamic times, the veil was probably not unknown among women in the Hijaz, since it may have been used as a mark of distinction by the urban high-born as against the slave women.[99]   In any case, however, its wearing apparently did not constitute an essential part of the early Islamic way of life.   In the initial pledge of allegiance (*bay'a*) that the women as a group made to the Prophet, the veil is not mentioned.   Rather, the women pledged that 'they would not take partners unto God, steal, commit adultery, kill their children, lyingly invent slander, or disobey the Prophet in a lawful matter',[100] which 'lawful matter' is then explained as 'that they would not scratch their faces or tear their breasts or undo their hair, and wail';[101]   nor would they 'use obscene language'[102] or 'act dishonestly toward their husbands (by favouring others or giving them of the husbands' wealth)',[103] or 'sit with men in isolated places'[104] 'except with those closely related',[105] 'as the Koran says'.[106]   The veil, thus, is not one of the conditions imposed upon the women, and as a matter of fact only one single *hadith* among the extremely large number of *hadiths* reporting on the women's *bay'a* in Ibn Sa'd's *Tabaqat* mentions that the women were 'wrapped in their cloaks' when they went to see the Prophet.[107]   But even this 'wrapped in their cloaks' certainly does not signify a complete veiling.

(a)   It was a matter of course for women in early Islamic society to accompany their men into battle[108] and even to participate actively in battle, either by trying to instil the courage to fight in their men who had been defeated or whose spirits were lagging,[109] or by nursing the wounded, fetching water, and recovering the dead.[110]   Women could also grant protection in war and asylum to a fugitive.[111]

(b)   In the early years of Islam, many women accepted the new religion and joined the community of believers on their own without the consent of their husbands, even making the *hijra* on their own.[112]

Muhammad's paternal aunt 'Arwa may serve here as a representative voice speaking for the soul-searching that must have preceded such a drastic step:[113]

> To the son of her first marriage who has become a Muslim, 'Arwa laments the fact that women can't do what men can do: 'By God, if we could do what men can do, we would follow and defend him (Muhammad)'. And her son inquires what prevents her from doing the same, she answers that she has to find out first what the other women are doing. He then implores her to convert and pledge allegiance to Muhammad, and she does.

These women who joined the believers in Medina on their own, without their husbands, were submitted to an examination to establish 'that love of God and His Prophet only, not love of a man or flight from a husband' were responsible for this decision.[114]

(c)   Women were travelling widely in the early years of Islam. While Muhammad's wives - at least according to some authorities - were secluded even on their travels with the Prophet to the point where the Prophet himself mistook the litter of one of his wives for the litter of another,[115] other women appear to have been much freer of movement. Notably, we find a discussion in the *Hadith* on how long (24 hours, 3 days) a woman may travel by herself without a husband or male relative accompanying her.[116] By the time of Ahmad ibn Hanbal, however, we find a *hadith* indicating that she may not travel without her husband or *dhu mahram*.[117]

(d)   As to women's participation in the prayers at the mosque, there is overwhelming evidence in the *Hadith* that women prayed in the mosques together with the men.[118] They even visited the mosques at night.[119] The sheer number and variety of traditions indicating that women had the right to and should not be prevented from visiting the mosque,[120] or that they should be admonished to visit the *musalla* on the days of festival,[121] or that they must leave the mosque before the men,[122] that one gate of the mosque is reserved for women,[123] and, finally, that women are advised to perform the prayers in the houses,[124] in all probability reflect the various stages of the debates on this point that were raging in the early Islamic community. These debates eventually ended with women's disappearance from public prayer, 'as the harsh disapproval of the learned succeeded in driving them out of the mosque'.[125] Even the question as to whether or not menstruating women must avoid the mosque is part of this debate; here we find, e.g. the imposition that the prayers of menstruating women are only accepted *if they wear a veil*.[126] The debate was later extended to include women's access to the bathhouse[127] and, not surprisingly, the bathhouse is prohibited to women.[128]

(e)   Men and women often met in the streets and greeted each other.[129] Even in the homes, however, there was ample social contact between the sexes, so that men and women knew each other personally, even if they were not closely related. Some traditions report that men visited their wives' houses and saw and talked to the female guests present,[130] just as they visited sick women to talk to them.[131]   We also find reports on women acting as hostesses to the husband's guests.[132]   One of the many available and well-documented categories of situations which may be used as evidence for the considerable amount of social contact between men and women in early Islam is that wherein a man proposes directly to a woman (in all cases the women described are widows or divorcees), without benefit of a male intermediary. These proposals often occur in the house of the woman which the man is visiting. We hear e.g. of a woman who tells a suitor of a previous proposal by another man. The (second) suitor proposes right then and there and gets the bride.[133]   Similar evidence may be found in the Prophet's proposal to Zaynab bint Jahsh whose house he entered after her divorce from Zayd, but prior to his marriage to her, without even having asked for her permission to enter.[134]   We also hear about Umm Salama to whose house the Prophet came to pay his condolences during a lengthy visit after her husband's death. After her waiting period he then proposed to her personally, and, after some negotiations, she accepted him.[135]   It is not surprising that in this story, as in many others, additional *hadiths* exist which indicate *either* that a curtain existed between her and him on this occasion, *or* that the groom sent an emissary to express the proposal, *or* that he proposed 'to the son of her brother or to her son, or her guardian'. Through emendations/additions such as these, the story was brought into agreement with later expectations.

3.   The *Hadith* as the record of the changing status
       of women in Islam

In his recent work *Zwischen Hadit and Theologie*, Josef van Ess has blazed new trails in the field of *Hadith* research. By concentrating on a particular cluster of related traditions on the predestination issue and by engaging in a criticism of the text (*matn*) and the chain (*sanad*) simultaneously, he succeeded in establishing a system of relationships between the different versions of the material which enabled him to draw up a preliminary time frame for each. Until techniques along these lines are perfected, much has to be left to the reader's intuition in fitting the material into a system of chronological stratification. Side-by-side enumeration of contradictory detail, of course, usually indicates editorial activity on the part of some traditionalists. In many cases, the structure of a *hadith* can throw some light on the intention of the transmitter, and help to prove forgery. For instance, information is usually more reliable if it is merely illustrative detail than if it is the central 'message' of the *hadith*, unless the illustrative detail constitutes a recognisable interpolation into a transmission also transmitted without it. Anachronisms, of course, are clues that give the whole tradition away.

       Unfortunately, all extant *Hadith* collections are younger than the late eight century of the Christian calendar; i.e. they were compiled more than five generations after Muhammad's death. But even so, development of the material is discernible within the compilations as a group. A study of whole collections on a comparative basis, e.g. with the help of *Hadith* Concordances such as Wensinck's, proves that the later the source, the more abundant, detailed, and normative-restrictive the information on women which it contains. The later traditionists who included such material in their collections presumably justified their activities by arguing that as it was meritorious for men to follow the *Sunna* of the Prophet in all matters, so women should adhere to the *Sunna* of his wives,[136] particularly as regarded veiling and seclusion in the home.

While it would be most desirable to study all relevant materials in all of the *Hadith* collections in depth on a comparative basis, particularly with the inclusion of much later collections such as the *Kanz al-'ummal fi sunan al-'ahwal* by Muttaqi al-Hindi (d. 1567) and others, such an ambitious undertaking will have to remain the object of a future investigation.

CONCLUSION

Contemporary conservative authorities who argue for the preservation of 'the traditional order of Islam' with its segregation of the sexes - such as the former Mufti of Egypt, Shaykh Muhammad Hasanayn Makhluf who in his famous and controversial fatwa of 1952 denied women the right to vote or be elected to parliament 'on the grounds of their inherently unsuitable nature' and 'as a protective measure'[137] - speak 'on the authority of Islamic law' and sanction their opinions and decisions by referring to Koran interpretations as well as Traditions that reflect their points of view.

The fact that such sanction, as shown in this paper, rests on shaky grounds has not been lost on those progressive thinkers who have striven to modernise the Islamic social order from within. They argue that the fault for unjust laws and practices such as women's inequality, lies not with God's revelation but with the *'ulama's* interpretation of it, as well as with contrived or inauthentic traditions of later provenance which 'either do not reflect what the Prophet said' or represent fallible 'variations of his *Hadith*'.[138] A representative example of this school of thought may be found in Nazira Zayn al-Din, author of *Unveiling and Veiling: Lectures and Points of View*. She, like many other contemporary Muslim thinkers, laments that the Koran interpreters, 'in disregard and neglect of God's word, put forth undue allegations and assumptions as well as sheer subjective preferences, and obstinately adhered to their individual opinions'.[139] She points out that 'the drastically changed conditions of our modern age with enormous progress and discoveries realised in all fields of knowledge demand that we disregard the efforts of the medieval scholars whose erudition - never complete in the first place - has become totally inadequate, and that we interpret the Koran and the authentic *Sunna* in a new light'.[140] Nazira Zayn al-Din laments the fact that the jurists' interpretations have become more important than the Holy Book itself,[141] and calls for the formation of a committee of contemporary authorities in all fields, 'jurisprudence, sociology, ethics, etc.', who shall work together in *ijtihad*, i.e. independent, fresh, and immediate interpretations of the sources themselves.[142] Only in this way, concludes Nazira Zayn al-Din, will there arise 'great good for the

37

world and the community', and only thus 'will the arrow of criticism against Islam be broken'.

The Koran, as we have shown, provides women with a set number of specific property and personal rights while placing them, within the marriage situation, under the care as well as the authority of their husbands. On the issues of seclusion in the houses and veiling abroad, the Koran, on the other hand, contains only some very general and vague guidelines which mainly serve to establish chastity and modest deportment of women in general. While the revelations concerning the wives of the Prophet are more specific and restrictive, they (the wives of the Prophet) 'are not like any other women'.

The Hadith likewise contains much evidence of women's visibility as well as full participation in communal matters in the early Islamic period. Later generations of pious scholars changed these patterns considerably, or rather, they sanctioned such changes as had occurred within Islam under the influence of foreign (probably mainly Persian and Byzantine) modes of life. Through the centuries, both the Koran commentators and the traditionalists emphasized restrictive norms with the distinct purpose of legitimizing the newly restricted status of women in Islam. The result was that restrictions increased with the progression of time.

By disregarding the secondary material of Koran exegesis and returning to a fresh and immediate interpretation of the Holy Book, and by taking a new and critical look at the *Hadith* - in other words, by engaging in creative *ijtihad* - modern Islamic authorities could very well reform and renew the position of Islam on the issue of the status of women and so work to build a juster order for future generations, within the venerable system of the religion itself.

NOTES

Research for this article was in part made possible by a 1981 Faculty Summer Reserach Grant from Georgetown University

REFERENCES

1. C.A.O. Van Nieuwenhuijze, *Sociology of the Middle East*, pp. 651-53.
2. I. Goldziher, *Muslim Studies*, II, p. 31.
3. G.E. Von Grunebaum, *Medieval Islam*, pp. 110 ff.
4. B. Freyer, 'Formen des geselligen Umgangs . . . .', *Der Islam*, 38, 1, pp. 51-63.
5. P.W. Harrison, *The Arabs at Home*, p. 42.
6. E.R. Wolf, 'The Social Organization of Mecca . . . .', *Southwestern Journal of Anthropology*, 7, pp. 329-30.
7. R. Levy, *An Introduction to the Sociology of Islam*, I, p. 278.
8. B. Stowasser-Freyer, 'Formen des geselligne Umbangs . . . .', *Der Islam*, 42, 1, p. 49.
9. J. Wellhausen, 'Die Ehe bei den Arabern', *Gottinger gelehrte Anzeigen*, 1893, p. 466.

10.   R.F. Spender, 'The Arabian Matriarchate . . . .', *Southwestern Journal of Anthropology*, 8, pp. 478-502.

11.   R. Levy, *The Social Structure of Islam*, pp. 92-93.

12.   id., p. 95.

13.   id., p. 100.

14.   id., p. 121.

15.   id., pp. 95-96.

16.   The Koran is cited in the translation by M.M. Pickthall.

17.   With the exception of the Prophet who is exempt from this limitation. See e.g. Surah 33 (*The Clans*) verses 50, 51.

18.   This revelation reinforces an earlier revelation forbidding Muslims to send back believing women who have escaped from unbelieving husbands, Surah 60 (*She That is to be Examined*) verse 10.

19.   cf. Surah 5 (*The Table Spread*) verse 72.

20.   cf. Surah 2 (*The Cow*) verse 221.

21.   R. Levy, *The Social Structure of Islam*, p. 122.

22.   Surah 4 (*Women*) verse 15, on the other hand, mentions only adulteresses.

23.   This law shows clearly the change in women's status in Islam as compared to the Jahiliyya.   Under the pre-Islamic system of proprietary marriage, a woman was the chattel of her husband, his *muhsana* ('woman to be guarded'). If he failed to guard her, and she engaged in an alliance with another man, no moral stigma was attached to her, since she was merely a possession of his. (R. Levy, *The Social Structure of Islam*, pp. 94-95).

24.   There is good reason to agree with those who reject the translation 'stay in your houses' or 'stay quietly in your houses' for grammatical reasons (in spite of the lengthy explanations on the part of those Koran exegetes who favour it).   Nazira Zayn al-Din, e.g. points out that the verb in this verse cannot be *qarra yaqirru* ('stay') or *waqara yaqiru* ('stay, remain') but must be *qara yaqaru* ('walk noiselessly on the sides of the feet, (so as to avoid the jingle of anklets which incites men's lust)') (Zayn al-Din, Nazira, *al-Sufur wal-Hijab*, pp. 180 ff).

25.   R. Levy, *The Social Structure of Islam*, p. 126.

26.   id., p. 99.

27.   B. Freyer, 'Formen des geselligen Umgangs . . . .', *Der Islam*, 38, 1, pp. 55 ff.

28.   IS8, 38-39.

29.   IS8, 68.

30.   IS8, 44.

31.   IS8, 54.

32.   IS8, 43-44.

33.   IS8, 46.

34.   IS8, 55.

35.   IS8, 58.

36.   IS8, 76.

37.   IS8, 58.

38.   IS8, 45.

39.   IS8, 44 and 46.

40.   e.g. 'A'isha, IS8, 51.

41. e.g. 'A'isha, IS8, 46.
42. e.g. 'A'isha, IS8, 50.
43. IS8, 45.
44. IS8, 47. Ibn al-Zubayr said, when he transmitted from 'A'isha: 'By God, she never tells lies about the Prophet of God' (!).
45. IS8, 66.
46. IS8, 74–75.
47. e.g. IS8, 67.
48. e.g. IS8, 36.
49. IS8, 72.
50. IS8, 59.
51. e.g. IS8, 55–56.
52. e.g. Zaynab's unwillingness to lend one of her camels to Safiyya (IS8, 90–91).
53. see below.
54. Bu 13: 7, 8, 16, 18, 19; 24: 44; 67: 124; 77: 56, 57, 59.
55. IS8, 53.
56. Bu 72: 19.
57. Bu 67: 84, 86.
58. Bu 25: 4; 28: 26; 56: 1, 62; IS8, 50.
59. AbH IC, 200; V, 409.
60. e.g. IS8, 19.
61. AbH VI, 405.
62. Bu 67: 1, 89; 78: 84.
63. Bu 30: 54, 57.
64. Bu 67: 1–4, 8.
65. IS8, 55.
66. IS8, 55.
67. IS8, 64ff; Bu 67: 100, 101.
68. e.g. Bu 67: 85.
69. AbH I, 31.
70. J. Bellamy, 'Sex and Society in Islamic Popular Literature' in *Society and the Sexes in Medieval Islam*, p. 28.
71. id., p. 27.
72. IS8, 87.
73. J. Bellamy, 'Sex and Society in Islamic Popular Literature' in *Society and the Sexes in Medieval Islam*, p. 29–30.
74. Bu 60: 1 ff.
75. Bu 67: 79, 80; 78: 43; IS8, 147 ff.
76. Bu 2: 21; 6: 6; 16: 9; 24: 44; 67: 88, and many others.
77. Bu 56: 47; 67: 17; 76: 43, 54.
78. AbH I, 247; cf. 347; cf. II, 203 ff; II, 299, 425; IV, 64, 86; V, 57, 149, 151, 155 ff; 160, 161; cf. 164; 216, 376 ff; VI, 84 ff, 126, 134, 154.
79. e.g. Bu 4: 59.
80. Bu 67: 17; AbH III, 22; V, 200, 210.
81. e.g. Bu 67: 110; 74: 1; 86: 20.
82. Bu 2: 21; 6: 6; 16: 9; 24: 44; 59: 8; 67: 87; 81: 16, 51.
83. Bu 92: 18.

84. Bu 77: 61; 86: 33.
85. cf. A.F.L. Beeston, *Samples of Arabic Prose*, p. 5.
86. IS8, 74.
87. id.
88. IS8, 50.
89. IS8, 67.
90. Bu 52: 15.
91. IS8, 86.
92. IS8, 88–89. Cf. pp. 84 and 91.
93. IS8, 40 and 54.
94. IS8, 49.
95. IS8, 90.
96. IS8, 37.
97. The Battle of the Camel, 656 A.D.
98. IS8, 79 et al.
99. R. Levy, *The Social Structure of Islam*, p. 124.
100. IS8, 1.
101. IS8, 3.
102. IS8, 4.
103. IS8, 4.
104. IS8, 4.
105. IS8, 5.
106. IS8, 5.
107. IS8, 6.
108. IS8, 90.
109. IS8, 28.
110. Bu 13: 20; 25: 81; 56: 65–68; 63: 18, 22; 76: 2; IS8, 214, 301 ff, 334, 335; AbH III, 108ff, 112, 198, 279, 286, etc.
111. IS8, 21–22.
112. IS8, 20 ff, 27.
113. IS8, 28.
114. IS8, 7, in accordance with Koran 60: 10.
115. IS8, 67.
116. e.g. Bu 18: 4; 20: 6.
117. AbH I, 222; III, 66.
118. e.g. IS8, 37, 49; Bu 8: 13, 14, 15; 10: 93, 164; 77: 19, and many others.
119. Bu 10: 162, 163, 165; 11: 13.
120. Bu 10: 116; 67: 116.
121. Bu 13: 15, 20.
122. AD 2: 196.
123. AD 2: 17, 53.
124. AbH VI, 301, 371.
125. R. Levy, *The Social Structure of Islam*, p. 131.
126. AbH VI, 96, 150, 218, 238, 259, and others.
127. AbH I, 20.
128. AbH VI, 173, 179, 267.
129. e.g. IS8, 5.
130. e.g. IS8, 59.
131. e.g. IS8, 17, 51, 53.
132. e.g. IS8, 89.

133. e.g. IS8, 27.
134. IS8, 73.
135. IS8, 62 ff.
136. R. Levy, *The Social Structure of Islam*, p. 126.
137. Cf. *Islamic Review* (1952), vol.40, no. 8, pp. 3-4.
138. Nazira Zayn al-Din, *al-Sufur wal-Hijab*, p. 227.
139. id., pp. 223 ff.
140. id., p. 214.
141. id., p. 219.
142. id., pp. 214-215.

BIBLIOGRAPHY

1. Abbreviations

AbH Ahmad ibn Hanbal
The Roman figure represents the number of the volume, the second figure the number of the page according to the edition of the *Musnad*, Cairo 1313, 6 vols.

AD Abu Da'ud
The first figure represents the number of the *kitab* as indicated in A.J. Wensinck, *A Handbook of Early Muhammadan Tradition* (Leiden: 1927), p. XIII. The second figure represents the number of the *bab* according to the edition of the *Sunan*, Cairo 1292, 2 vols.

Bu al-Bukhari
The first figure represents the number of the *kitab* as indicated in A.J. Wensinck, *A Handbook of Early Muhammadan Tradition* (Leiden: 1927), p. XIf. The second figure represents the number of the *bab* according to the edition of the *Sahih* vols. I-III by L. Krehl (Leiden: 1862-1868) and vol. IV by Th. W. Juynboll (Leiden: 1907-1908)

IS Ibn Sa'd
The first figure represents the number of volume, the second figure the number of page according to the edition of the *Tabaqat* under the direction of E. Sachau (Leiden: 1904-1908)

2. Works Consulted

Abu Da'ud, *Sunan*. Cairo: 1292
Ahmad ibn Hanbal. *Musnad*. Cairo: 1313
al-Baydawi, Nasir al-Din Abu l-Khayr 'Abd Allah ibn 'Umar. *Hashiyat al-shihab 'ala tafsir al-Baydawi*. Beirut: nd
Beeston, A.F.L. *Samples of Arabic Prose*. Oxford: 1977
Bellamy, J.A. 'Sex and Society in Islamic Popular Literature'. *Society and the Sexes in Medieval Islam*. Ed. Afaf Lutfi al-Sayyid Marsot. Malibu: 1979, pp. 21-42
al-Bukhari. *Sahih* (Le receuil des traditions mahometanes par el-Bokhari), vols. I-III, ed. L. Krehl. Leiden: 1862-1868. Vol. IV, ed. Th. W. Juynboll, Leiden: 1907-1908

van Ess, Josef. *Zwischen Hadit und Theologie.* Berlin, New York: 1975

Freyer, Barbara. *See* Stowasser-Freyer, Barbara

Goldziher, Ignaz. *Muslim Studies.* Ed. S.M. Stern. Vol. I, London: 1967; Vol. II, London: 1972

Harrison, Paul W. *The Arabs at Home.* New York: 1924

Ibn Sa'd. *Kitab al-tabaqat al-kabir* (Biographien Muhammeds, seiner Gefahrten und der spateren Trager des Islams), Bd. VIII, ed. C. Brockelmann. Leiden: 1904. Bd. IX Indices Teil III, ed. E. Sachau. Leider: 1940

al-Khafaji, Ahmad ibn Muhammad. *Hashiyat al-shihab 'ala tafsir al-Baydawi.* Beirut: n.d.

Levy, Reuben. *An introduction to the Sociology of Islam.* London: 1933

Levy, Reuben. *The Social Structure of Islam.* Cambridge: 1969

Pickthall, M.M. *The Meaning of the Glorious Koran.* New York: n.d.

Roberts, Robert. *The Social Laws of the Qoran.* London: 1925

Smith, Jane L. 'Women in Islam: Equity, Equality and the Search for the Natural Order'. *Journal of the American Academy of Religion,* 47, no. 4 (1979), 517-37

Spencer, Robert F. 'The Arabian Matriarchate: An Old Controversy'. *Southwestern Journal of Anthropology,* vol. 8 (1952): 478-502

Stowasser-Freyer, Barbara. 'Former des geselligen Umgangs and Eigentumlichkeiten des Sprachgebrauchs in der fruhislamischen stadtischen Gesellschaft Arabiens (Nach Ibn Sa'd und Buhari)'. *Der Islam,* Vol. 38 (1962): 51-105, vol. 42 (1965): 25-57, vol. 42 (1966): 179-234

al-Tabari, Abu Ja'far Muhammad Ibn Jarir. *Jami' al-bayan fi tafsir al-Qur'an.* Beirut: 1392/1972

Van Nieuwenhuijze, C.A.O. *Sociology of the Middle East.* Leiden: 1971

Von Grunebaum, E.G. *Medieval Islam.* Chicago: 1956

Wellhausen, Julius. 'Die Ehe bei den Arabern'. *Gottinger gelehrte Anzeigen.* Gottingen: 1983.

Wensinck, A.J. *A Handbook of Early Muhammadan Tradition.* Leiden: 1927

Wolf, Eric R. 'The Social Organization of Mecca and the Origins of Islam'. *Southwestern Journal of Anthropology,* vol. 7 (1951): 329-56.

Zayn al-Din, Nazira. *al-Sufur wal-hijab (muhadarat wa-nazarat).* Beirut: 1345/1928

Chapter 2

THE ISLAMIC REVOLUTION AND WOMEN:
QUEST FOR THE QURANIC MODEL

Freda Hussain and Kamelia Radwan

The Islamic revolution in Iran was a unique event for both the Western and non-Western world. How could a traditional society erupt in a mass revolution? What ideologies had been instrumental in activating the Iranian middle classes and masses against the Pahlavi regime? The Muslim world in particular, wondered at the active role played by the Iranian women in this revolution. In a traditional Islamic society, where segregation of sexes was strictly practiced and women had hitherto been confined to their homes, emerging only when draped in a chador - the revolution saw them as part of the massive demonstrations in the streets alongside the men. Not only did they join in the public demonstrations, but were also involved in active struggle against the authorities through underground guerilla movements.

Some died in gunfights while others were captured, imprisoned and tortured in SAVAK prisons. According to one account:

> There are thousands of people in the streets. You can see the women: in one hand they hold up banners and flags; in the other, they carry children. Their belief in the ideology has brought them out. It is morning. People are going out to demonstrate. An old woman is sending her children out one by one - to go and become martyrs - because she cannot go herself. The masses in the streets are faced by soldiers and U.S. weapons. A blind woman is standing on the edge by a phone booth with a bowl of two rial coins. They are for the people to use if they need to make a phone call. People do all they can.

> It is Black Friday (September 8, 1978) when the regime's attack on demonstrators led to some of the heaviest casualties of the revolution. Soldiers are surrounding the people. Women in Islamic clothing say 'If we surround you they will not kill us, and all will be saved'. Moments later the street is full of their bodies on the ground.

> A woman is lying on an iron bed with a fire beneath her. She says only 'Allah O Akbar, God is Great'. She is tortured till she dies. This is the women that Islam builds.[1]

Another account relates the torture suffered by a guerilla fighter inside a SAVAK prison:

> The whip goes from hand to hand, they take turns striking the soles of my feet . . . . the pain grew more excruciating, more and more difficult to endure. There were moments when I really wanted the whipping to stop . . . . I was like a mother delivering a baby. The pain is there and goes on. Nothing can be done but wait for the birth of the child. And in that situation; the birth of the child was the arrival of death. I had to wait for that . . . . Then the others came . . . . torture starts again. This time they take a cattle prod for torturing . . . . they undress me . . . . they bring the prod close to the sensitive spots of my body . . . . Niktah . . . . then comes into the torture room . . . . He ties me on my stomach on the bench, he lets down his pants sordidly before his colleagues and lays on me. He rapes me to humiliate me and crush my spirits. I'm enraged to madness, but I try to look calm and indifferent so that they may be the ones who feel humiliated and vile, not me . . . . they lay me on my back again . . . . they hang my arms on each side of the bench towards the floor. Then they place my arms around the two legs of the bench and they put handcuffs on my wrists and all leave the room. The bones of my back are harshly compressed on the wood and I feel like they are going to break. The pain is more intense than that of the whip. Moreover there are no torturers around me and I cannot distract my attention from the pain by shouting slogans and insults at them. I recite a poem from comrade Mao . . . . the poem is finished but the pain still remains.[2]

Both these accounts help to dispel the myth that women are frail creatures. These are just two instances that came to light while countless others went unrecorded and can only be discovered from the tales of horror told by the families of these women. The two women in the above accounts gained their strength and inspiration from widely different ideologies. Would they have been able to participate in the revolution without such ideologies? In this paper we would like to analyse these divergent ideologies which were espoused by the women of Iran and which in turn activated them into political participation. Although Iran has been used as an example, such behaviour is not restricted to Iranian women alone as it is relevant to Muslim women the world over. The latter part of the paper will therefore deal with lessons drawn from it in the wider context.

The two diverse ideologies that manifest themselves in Iran were those of Islam and Marxism and these in turn had been drawn from original Islamic sources or the works of Karl Marx. They were projected through varied interpretations and shades of opinion and in order to understand them it is necessary to survey the written works of their exponents and practitioners.

THE ULEMA'S VIEW OF MUSLIM WOMEN

In Iran, the Ulema have traditionally been the interpreters of Islam. Through a lifelong religious training in various madrassehs and other religious institutions, they gain an extensive knowledge of Islam and after achieving the status of Mujtahid their credibilty for the interpretation of Islam is enhanced. Their views of the Islamic role of women have exercised a considerable influence on the minds of the masses. In this section we shall briefly outline some of the interpretations given by Mujtahids like Ayatollah Yahya Nuri, Ayatollah Morteza Motahhari and Ayatollah Khomeini. Their interpretations did not show much variation and could therefore be considered as being representative of the religious establishment in Iran.

Ayatollah Nuri published his book *Hughughe-Zan Dar Islam va Jahan* (Women's Rights in Islam and the World) in 1964 and in it he contended that in Islam women are inferior to men because biological differences have determined this status for them. He argued that since women and men have different biological functions to perform they are also psychologically equipped with different natures. Child bearing and child care are the important functions of women. The female has a strong maternal instinct and consequently women are psychologically emotional creatures. Furthermore, men have more biological freedom and are endowed with more physical strength and in their struggle to provide for their families, they are equipped with reason rather than emotions. Reinforcing his arguments further, Nuri points out the differences in male and female physiology as manifested in the size of the female heart, brain and skull and considers them affectionate and lacking in strong nerves to withstand hardship.

According to Nuri, Islam has recognised the biological nature of women and, as such, lifted them from an inferior position in which they were living in pre-Islamic times. Islam raised their status by giving them rights and discouraging old customs relating to female infanticide, marriage and divorce. Women's rights in Islam are suited to their biological natures and, as such, there cannot be any equality of rights between women and men. They are the child bearers while men are the bread winners and since they lack reason and are emotional, they should not be given the right to divorce because 'its great impediment is women's special mentality which like spring weather and infantile temperament is in a state of constant fluxion. She falls in love at the slightest sign of affection and at the slightest sign of bad temper starts a bloody feud. Its great impediment is women's limited mentality. She screams at the slightest misfortune, pours buckets of tears and seeks protection. Its great impediment is the pride, conceit and selfishness of women which knows no bounds. She is ostentatious, full of affection and pretension and constantly inclined to show off. She is never able to use a power like the right to divorce at the necessary time and the slightest pretext is enough for her to display her pretensions to power without any deliberation or hesitation'.[3] Such a perception of women clearly betrayed Nuri's deep distrust of a woman's nature. He did not consider a woman to be of any use other than reproduction.

Ayatollah Motahhari's book *Nezam Hughughe Zan Dar Islam* (The System of Women's Rights in Islam) was published in 1974. According to Motahhari, the institution of marriage is a natural one, for both men and women have sexual desires. The man desires to possess the women while the woman tries to be coy and coquettish and ensnare him through her charms. Man is considered to be 'the slave of his passions' while the women 'desires of affection'.[4]

Based upon this bond, 'the natural mechanism of marriage upon which Islam has based its laws is that the woman should be loved and respected within the family, that if she is no longer desired and loved by the man then the foundation of the family is shaken .... From the point of view of Islam the greatest insult to a woman is for her husband to say I do not love you, I hate you'.[5]

The stability of the marriage depends upon the man and not the woman. Man's love gives and women's love receives and in any marriage if the man is loving the woman cannot but love him. As such 'nature has given the key of the natural dissolution of marriage to the man. It is the man who by being unloving and unfaithful makes her cold and unloving. Contrary to the women whose indifference has no effect on the man and even increases his desires. Therefore man's lack of love results in both sides not loving each other but women's lack of love does not have any effect. The extinction of man's love results in the death and end of a marriage whereas extinction of a woman's love simply turns the marriage into a sick being who is incurable'.[6]

Since a man is a 'slave of his passions' the institution of polygamy is justified. If a woman is pregnant or menstruating or has reached menopause and the man desires to have children, what should he do? He can of course marry another woman, provided he can deal with his wives with justice and not discrimination. Polygamy is also justified by citing examples of European societies after World War II in which the ratio of women was greater than that of men. In such a case, if a man remained married to only one woman, many other women would be deprived of marriage. This would lead them to have illicit affairs with men.

On the question of veiling (*hedjab*), Motahhari holds that it is necessary for women to cover themselves or else the temptations for women could lead to adultery, premarital sex, rape, prostitution, etc. in society. Although the Qur'an enjoins men to lower their gaze and constrain their libido (Sura 24: xxx) their uncontrollable passion could lead to the molestation of women. The word adornment (*Zinat*) which the Qur'an uses is interpreted by Motahhari as referring not only to ornaments but also to parts of the body. As such Motahhari 'holds that the only parts of a woman's body which do not need to be covered are the two hands and the oval of the face'.[7]

Although man is considered to be very susceptible to passion, Motahhari argues that Islam accepts women's sexuality and does not consider it a sin. He contends that women's sexuality should be satisfied and if it is not, it can form the grounds for divorce. A man has less control over his passion than the woman, who often seeks love in a sexual relationship and, as such, has more control over herself.

Both sexuality and motherhood are considered important for women but each has to be satisfied within the sphere of marriage. Marriages can be of two types, permanent and temporary. Temporary marriages (*muta*) are permissible and are good for young people who have sexual urges but cannot enter into permanent marriages because they have not acquired the ability to become breadwinners. Such temporary marriages are contractual and can be terminated when mutually agreed by both parties, thus avoiding homosexuality, adultery, prostitution in society.

A woman's disposition to love and strong emotions disqualify her from taking part in activities like war (*Jihad*) or from occupying judicial positions. She can, however, work for social and economic reasons in jobs such as nursing, medicine and teaching, etc. provided she retains her veil and avoids close interaction with men. Sexual activity outside marriage is not permissible and, as such, it is restricted to the family and separates it from civil society. But as Yeganeh points out, that 'Motahhari is not advancing the argument of the separation of the 'public' and 'private' spheres where women and men respectively belong, which is well documented by anthropologists and used in the most generalised form as the basic characteristic of Islamic society. The differentiation into family and civil society is constructed in terms of the activity rather than gender'.[8]

While Nuri had stressed the differences of the sexes on a physical basis, Motahhari emphasised the natural differences which divided their sphere of activities. On this basis, the latter argued, that equal rights for the sexes were not possible, and dismissed them as misplaced Western notions. Islam gave women their rights 14 centuries ago, while economic and other rights were obtained by Western women only after industrialisation led to the demand for cheap labour. Concepts such as human rights, too, emanated from Western societies where freedom of the individual was considered above that of society. In Islam, societal rights were considered to cater to the needs of all, while in Western societies, women were struggling for equal rights to the males.

Khomeini's views on women are widely scattered in his speeches and in his book, *Tozilolmassael* (Explanation of Problems). In this book he has expressed views on various problems emanating from the sexual relationship between the sexes. These were problems concerned with menstruation, copulation, sodomy, incest and child marriages, etc. In various male-female interactions male superiority is manifested for 'a woman who has entered into a permanent marriage is not allowed to leave the house without her husband's permission. She must submit herself to any pleasure he desires. She may not refuse herself on any grounds other than religious ones .... If a woman does not obey her husband according to the manner set out in the previous problems she is then sinful and is not entitled to food, clothes, housing or intercourse. But she is entitled to her Mehr'.[9]

Temporary marriage is permissible 'even though it may not be for pleasure'.[10] Details of *Hedjab* are set out in the book, and he also states that only the oval of the face and hands should be uncovered; while in divorce, males have more powers than the female. Polygamy

is also permissible only if equality can be maintained in dealing with
the wives. But he comments that 'try as you may you cannot treat all
your wives impartially' and so men should 'marry one only'.[11]

The view that emerges from Khomeini's writings is one that
defines the role of women as mothers and educators of children. The
family is considered as the fundamental unit in an Islamic society and
women are considered as 'the pillars of the nation', as 'strong forts of
virtue and chastity' and 'raising brave and enlightened men and weak
and united women'.[12] Motherhood bestows on women 'a special rank in
society which is not less than a man's if not greater' for it is 'a task
nobler than all other tasks' and because 'child rearing is the most
difficult, the most challenging but one of the sweetest ordeals. This
crucial responsibility is exclusively reserved for women'.[13] A woman's
status is increased if she fulfils her task of motherhood.

No less importance is given to the task of raising children for
women are considered as 'a source of support for the country in future;
in your care, great men and women will be brought up and you are the
foundation of the nation'.[14] Such care in the rearing of children is
imposed on the 'committed and believing women who have taken part
in the upbringing of children, the education of illiterates and the
teaching of social sciences and our rich Quranic culture'.[15] In fact,
this role is considered to be so important that women are considered
to 'comprise half of our nation who are entrusted with the task of
giving an education to the other half'.[16] They were considered to be
the 'instructors of the society' for 'from the lap of woman human
beings emerge. The first stage of being true men and women is the lap
of the woman. The happiness and wealth of the country depends on
women . . . . It is woman who with her correct education, produces
humanity, who with her correct education, cultivates the country'.[17]

In Khomeini's view the Pahlavi regime had not raised but lowered
the status of women. They had perceived the 'woman as a charming
being' and 'brought down the woman from her human position to the
status of an animal, and the pretext of creating a status for her . . . .
He lowered woman from her position. He made women like dolls'.[18]
The Shah's rule 'corrupted men and perverted the youth. They created
prostitution centres for our youths under the pretext of freedom and
progress, in the name of civilisation'.[19] All this led to a sexual
corruption in Iranian society. Khomeini therefore warned women to
'wake up, be careful, do not be deceived by these devils who want you
to come to the streets'.[20]

The education of youth by women should, as stated earlier, be
along Islamic lines. One of the important tasks of their role as
teachers 'in the school of family' was to 'raise their youth to send them
to the front'.[21] In this way women were entrusted with the task of
raising their sons as soldiers for Islam for 'blessings be upon those
mothers who committed their mighty youths to the fields of defending
truth and take immense pride in their splendid martyrdom'.[22] Such
statements were obviously made to encourage the recruitment of
young men for the battlefields of the Iraq-Iran war.

Khomeini was aware of the sacrifices women had made during
the revolution. He thanked the women for coming 'to the streets with

your little children and supporting Islam with your enthusiastic demonstrations. We are all indebted to the braveries of you lion-hearted women .... Just as you had a fundamental role in the movement you must also have a share in the victory .... you must reconstruct the country. In early Islam women would participate in wars alongside men. We see and we saw that women alongside men and even in front of them stood against death, sacrificed their lives and the lives of their children and youngsters, and were still resisting. We want women to reach the high position of humanity. Woman must have a say in her fate'.[23] Such statements raised the expectations of Iranian women.

But, as Yeganeh has correctly noted, that 'there is a deep discrepancy between the content of Khomeini's speeches addressed to women and his teachings on women in his book *Tozilolmassael*'.[24] This misperception by Iranian women was caused by Khomeini's statement before he came to Iran in which he had promised that 'women, like men, will participate in building the future of Islamic society. They will have the right to vote and to be elected. Women have contributed to the recent struggles in Iran alongside men. We will give all kinds of freedom to women. But, of course, we will put a stop to corruption. In that, there is no difference between men and women'.[25] This statement was perhaps due to political expediency but his considered opinion as a *Marja-e-Taqlid* was expressed in his *Tozilolmassael*. One would be mistaken if one expected him to negate his own views. Iranian women read too much meaning into his political statements and although the rights to vote, to stand for election or work were never withdrawn they were to be practiced within his interpretation of Islam.

In the Constitution of the Islamic Republic of Iran, the family was considered to be 'the fundamental unit of society' and within such a unit it was considered necessary to deliver 'woman from being regarded as an object or as an instrument in the service of consumerism and exploitation. Not only does woman recover thereby her momentous and precious function of motherhood, rearing alert and active human beings, she also becomes the fellow struggler of man in all the different areas of life'.[26]

The Constitution further safeguarded 'the rights of women in all respects, in conformity with Islamic criteria, and accomplish the following goals: (a) create a favourable environment for the growth of women's personality and the restoration of her rights, tangible and intangible; (b) the protection of mothers particularly during pregnancy and child rearing and the protection of children without guardians; (c) the creation of a competent count to protect and preserve the family; (d) the provision of special insurance for widows and aged and destitute women; (e) the granting of guardianship of children to their mothers whenever suitable in order to protect the interests of the children, in the absence of a legal guardian' (Article 21).[27]

Khomeini was against Westernised women whose ideology indoctrinated them to 'discard their primary responsibilities to their families and cast off their children in unsuitable places where all deprived offsprings were gathered to grow up into irresponsible and corrupt people'.[28]   The decades of Pahlavi rule with its strong American influence had produced a significant number of middle class women who interpreted freedom in the Western sense rather than the Islamic one. But this segment of women was not in the majority and it was not surprising to find that 'the bulk of Khomeini's support is found amongst the poorest women who welcome his dictum that the husband should feed, house and clothe (his obedient wife) whether he has the means or not . . . . these are the women who have been politicised by Khomeini to take to the streets in support of the clergy, and who are hailed as virtuous examples to all Muslim women'.[29]

When Khomeini called for wearing of *chador* by all working women on March 7, 1979, there was a wave of massive protests by Iranian women. But these were not the poor women who formed the majority, but from the middle class women who were Westernised or followed other ideologies. To quell them one of the most progressive members of the Ulema, Ayatollah Taleghani, was asked by some to express his views on *Hejab*. He considered *Hejab* as 'a question of history and of tradition . . . . in the depths of our history . . . . of preserving their purity, dignity and personality in Iran and in other Eastern countries both Islamic and un-Islamic countries . . . . the perfect symbol of Eastern progressive women, and a competent politican, is Mrs. Gandhi . . . . I have rarely seen her picture in the newspapers without a scarf, and she is not even a Muslim . . . . So what I want to say is that it is a mistake if our women think having a scarf on their head is an insult to their dignity and personality. No, regardless of being Muslim it will preserve an Eastern tradition . . . . If a country wants to be independent, it does not mean it should close its borders, but it should preserve its tradition, its culture, its characteristics. This is the meaning of real independence . . . . on this Islamic *hejab*, that is, *hejab* of dignity and character, that is not invented by me or other clergymen, it is the Quranic text. Neither we nor women who believe in this great holy book can step outside the borders set in the Qur'an'.[30]

The Ulema's view, in general was conservative and subscribed to the functionalist construction of society. Society was considered to have two components, a structure and its function. When the structure and its functions worked smoothly, the societal system was in harmony.

The flaw in this outlook was that the whole system was structured according to the patriarchal-feudal norms which prevailed predominatly in Muslim societies, and to which Iran was no exception. The patriarchal-feudal norms prescribed a strict division of labour between the sexes. The male role was that of the breadwinner while the female role was restricted to reproduction and child-rearing. Such patriarchal-feudal norms pre-dated Islam. In fact Islam had attempted to destroy them and liberate women from their sanctions but they had not been eradicated from Muslim societies. The Ulema themselves were influenced by them and had interpreted Islam in a manner which maintained and reinforced the patriarchal-feudal structures in which women were placed under the control and domination of males. Their interpretation of Islam legitimised such a structure and had distorted

51

Islam itself by making it an instrument of oppression rather than liberation in the hands of chauvinist males. Where women deviated from such norms, dysfunction set in society and disequilibrium disturbed the vested interests of males. Such conservative interpretations by the Ulema had made Islam static. They had ignored the fact that social, political, economic and sexual realities were interconnected and not divided into air-tight, separate compartments. Since they were static and not dynamic, Islam became vulnerable to attacks from external ideologies which began to penetrate Muslim socieites. The Ulema were placed in a defensive situation and functioned as guardians of a feudal structure using Islam to legitimate it. They forced many Muslim women in Iran to seek and choose alternative ideologies, such as those of Marxism.

THE MARXIST VIEW OF MUSLIM WOMEN

There were a number of Marxist womens' organisations in Iran with different shades of opinion. All of them were united on one point: that Iranian women instead of being liberated had lost their freedom in the Islamic Republic of Iran. Many reasons were given for this state of affairs - religion being one of the most important factors contributing to it.

An analysis of the socio-economic status of Iranian women done by the National Union of Women considered that the plight of women was a result of the dominant mode of production and its cultural and supra-structural effects on Iranian society, in particular, on women. During the Pahlavis reign, the feudal mode of production was largely replaced by dependent capitalism, as foreign powers infiltrated Iran in alliance with its ruling elite and laid the foundations of an exploitative economic system. Such exploitation cut across sexual and class barriers as all Iranians were subject to its negative consequences. They were all marginals because of being on the fringes of social production. The peasant women suffered from religious and cultural norms predominant in the rural areas due to the feudal rule which had not been completely eliminated. In spite of working in the fields to supplement her family income, the peasant woman was still in a state where her economic and material condition was pitiful. The bourgeoisie woman, on the other hand, was exploited as dependent capitalism emerged in Iran and transformed it into a consumer society. These women were given 'freedom' and 'emancipation' through the legal sanctions prescribed by the 'White Revolution' ushered in by the Pahlavis. The leaders of this movement were members of the Shah's family, and included Ashraf Pahlavi (the Shah's sister) and Farah Pahlavi (the Shah's wife) who sponsored many women's organisations. In reality they were agents of Westernisation and advocates of the capitalist system. Dependent capitalism needed the participation of women in factories, offices, educational institutions. It facilitated their travel to Europe and the U.S. to import Western culture into their ranks and at the same time women's magazines like *Zan-e Rouz* (Today's Women) and the mass media projected images of women which introduced 'the Western women as the ideal symbol for Iranian women'.[31] Women were sucked into the dependent capitalist system to become consumers of its products and agents of its ideas.

The petit bourgeois women emanated from the middle and lower middle classes and belonged to both the traditional and non-traditional cultures. Since they had not been absorbed in the processes of social production, they were under the control of men who imposed the cultural and feudal rule over them which had in turn 'deprived them of the relative freedom of peasant women and turned them into dull housewives'.[32] Another segment of the petit-bourgeoisie had absorbed new ideas from colonial culture and through 'their social life and relative active participation in the cultural and the political questions of the day, these women are relatively progressive'.[33] Working class women, on the other hand, had to struggle for survival like the male members of their class. They had to endure the exploitation at work and oppression at home. They could not evolve a separate identity for themselves which was determined by the working class culture and their own working conditions. Those most afflicted by conditions of poverty and economic deprivation were often forced to work as prostitutes for survival.

The Iranian revolution raised high expectations for women who considered that it would guarantee their rights. However, the Assembly of Experts devised a framework in which the Islamic rules were vague and not in favour of women. It abolished the Family Protection Law, imposed the chador, gave men the unconditional rights to divorce and to marry more than one woman without justifying its need; limited their right to work or adopt a profession without permission from their husbands and could even deprive them of the right to custody of their children after a divorce - if they were not found 'deserving'.[34]

Another Marxist organisation of Iranian women considered that the Iranian revolution had brought about political but not social changes as the relationship between labour and capital, or worker and the capitalist, had not been altered. Islam in fact had not posed a threat to the capitalist system. The working class women and those from the lower and upper strata had accepted the veil as a reaction for they believed that the West and Western culture was pernicious and believed that their position would be salvaged by religion.[35] But the Islamic system had suppressed the democratic rights of women for 'compulsory veiling, preventing women from holding judicial posts, sexual segregation of swimming areas, execution and the flogging of women on charges of prostitution and adultery, re-establishing polygamy and temporary marriage, practically annulling the Family Protection Law and the recent segregation of all schools - these are but some of the measures of the ruling class against half the population of the society, women. These measures aim, step by step, to eliminate women from social and productive life, to push them back from positions that have been gained through long struggles, and to limit them to the four walls of patriarchal household. These reflect the reactionary outlook of the people in power today. Today our problem is not simply that the people in power and the powerful clergy prevent the development of half the productive forces of society but that they are trying to throw women back fourteen centuries'.[36]

Other Marxist organisations though not directed by women as the above two have also attacked the conservative views of the Iranian Ulema. They believed that the traces of feudalism had not been eradicated from Iranian society and that even members of the Assembly of Experts have expressed views in the name of Islam which reflect the justification of a feudalist system. One member of the Assembly of Experts voicing his views on Iranian women stated: 'Have you ever heard of a woman participating in one of the holy wars or being appointed as the governor of a town or a province? .... A friend suggested that by the same principle by which a woman can become the guardian of an under-aged person so she can become the President too. Just because a woman can wash, change and breast-feed a baby so can she become a President or a Prime Mininster .... From the first moment of the foundation of the world all the irrigation systems, all the inventions have been introduced by men .... how, then should women have the right to a desk but not be obliged to do heavy works! .... Imagine that you appointed a competent woman as a president or prime minister. One morning we go and see that prime minister's office is closed. Why? Because she was in labour the previous night. This is a shame, a source of shame for us'.[37]

Such feudal ideas are untenable, as they show how the feudalist-Islamic thinking was out of touch with reality. In the present age, when the world's largest democracy comprised of some 600 million people is being run by a woman (Indira Gandhi), and one of the most modern Western countries like Britain has a woman Prime Minister, why was the Muslim woman so underdeveloped that she could not be considered the equal of these women? And what was shameful about pregnancy? If male Prime Ministers can be indisposed due to illness - why can't women perform a natural function? It could not be sinful to be legitimately pregnant.

In capitalist societies, women were given a lower role in the production, the family was made into a consumer group and marriages a trade, where exchange took place with emphasis on dowries etc. In Iran, although capitalism was introduced by the Pahlavis, feudalism still remained strong. Both capitalism and feudalism found in *Hejab* (veiling) the best means of oppressing women. In fact the Mujahidin-e-Khalq considered that: '*Hejab* was under no circumstances the outcome of the Quranic laws and genuine Islamic traditions but rather was imposed in its name through outlooks which were essentially the remains of feudal societies - like the Sassanids in our culture. This kind of *Hejab*, which has as its outcome the absolute separation of women from social life, was, among the feudal lords, the product of their effective ownership of their many wives; similarly the protection of the ownership of harem women in case of them contacting others. And among the lower classes too, partly because of the influence of the upper classes and partly because of social insecurity initiated by feudal lords and the reign of feudalism, a *hejab* had been propagated. Since the feudal lords (Khans) were able, because of their absolute power, to possess by force any beautiful women they desired, *hejab* was a way of hiding women from them. But many still think that the forms of *hejab* which are current by tradition were initiated by Islam. And it is because of this that, in our society at present, even after the Revolution, social and political activities of women meet with much resistance.[38] Views akin to these were also expressed by the Fedayeen-e-Khalq in that although the active political participation of Iranian women during the anti-imperialist struggle in meetings, street demonstrations, building street barricades, etc. cannot be denied but the Islamic Republic has taken 'new steps in the direction of further political and social inequalities among men and women'.[39] In fact, the Islamic Republican Party, it asserted, had tried 'to push women out of the arena of production as well as political and social activities. Basing itself on the religious emotions of the masses, it tries to portray compulsory veiling as a step towards fighting imperialist culture. The IRP pretends that one of the causes of the current chaos is women going unveiled .... But our toiling masses know well that many women with the Islamic veil propagate imperialist culture and corruption in their daily behaviour and actions, in their consumption of imperialist luxury goods while many women who will not tolerate the compulsory veiling have fought and continue to fight the imperialist culture and the realities that have turned women into commodities.[40]

Another faction of the Fedayeen-e-Khalq was also critical of the approach of the Islamic Republic towards women. In their words: 'The balance sheet of the Islamic Republic of Iran contains nothing hopeful in this field; giving the right of polygamy to men, barring women from judiciary, recognising temporary marriages, creating tremendous limitations for women employees and experts etc. are amongst measures that make our toiling, militant, conscious women pessimistic towards the Islamic Republic. American imperialism, particularly supporters of Bakhtiar have tried to benefit from the implementation of compulsory Islamic veil. These events have shown once again that one must see the class interests in conflict behind any struggle, even apparently cultural struggles, and take positions beneficial to toilers and to anti-imperialist struggles with such consideration in mind'.[41]

The position of all these organisations and parties is summed up by the Socialist Workers Party by calling upon women to wage their struggles for the following rights:

1. Total equality in legal, social and political spheres. Any kind of prejudice against women, even sanctioned by law or religion, should be made illegal. All religious and civil laws which in any way specify special punishments for women should be abolished, a clear example of this is the Retribution Bill which is in the process of becoming law. According to this Bill, women are considered half the worth of men. When it becomes law it will bring more oppression for women. All laws that treat women as mentally incapable, emotional and weak should be abolished. Women should be able to choose where they want to live and what kind of work they want to do, nor should the way they dress

be decided by their husbands, fathers or the government.

2. Women should have control of their bodies. The decision to become pregnant or to terminate a pregnancy should be exclusively that of women themselves . . . .

3. All reactionary family laws, which in one way or another promote the inferiority of women, should be abolished. All compulsory marriages should be terminated. The law allowing polygamy should be nullified. The right to divorce, unconditionally and on demand, should be granted to both parties. The government should undertake the welfare of divorced women and their children.

4. Women should enjoy full economic independence and receive equal wages for equal work with men.

5. Free educational facilities should be provided for men and women equally. Current prohibitions of women from entering into a number of educational fields and learning particular skills should be removed.

6. Society should be reorganised to bring women's domestic slavery to an end . . . . [42]

IMPLICATIONS FOR MUSLIM WOMEN

The Marxist view of women was strongly opposed to the Islamic view which had limited the role of women to the home and sexual reproduction. These two major views held by Muslim women were not peculiar to Iran - but to most Muslim countries. The case of Iran was discussed, as stated earlier, merely as an example, for such views emerged clearly in that country during and after the Islamic revolution.

The Marxist view was grounded in economic foundations of society while the Islamic view was grounded in the spiritual and cultural context of Muslim society. Both focussed on various problems confronting Muslim women and the important question which poses itself at this juncture is: which one was right and which one was wrong? Before one can answer this question, certain related issues need to be examined.

The transition of Muslim socieites from feudalism to capitalism has not been completed in Iran nor in any other Muslim country. Remnants of the former's patriarchal and the latter's exploitative control over women had victimised them. The result was that the fedualist-conservative mode of Islamic thinking had turned women into a property while the capitalistic-Westernised mode of thinking had turned her into a commodity. Both ideologies did not treat them as persons. In Muslim societies which are predominantly agricultural, the feudalist system still prevailed. Two examples of this will illustrate how it related to women and treated them as a property. The first was the obsession with the virginity of females. The preferences for a virgin bride indicated a way of looking at females as the acquisition of a piece of property. In many Muslim societies the custom still prevails where they have to show the proof of virginity after the first night of marriage. In some cases this practice of ensuring a girl's virginity is carried out before consummation by a daya (midwife). According to el-Saadawi 'in many villages this ritual ceremony in honour of virginity is performed by an ugly old crone, the daya who earns her living by amputating the clitoris of children and tearing open the vagina of young brides. The father of the bride then holds up a white towel stained with blood and waves it proudly above his head for the relatives assembled at the door to bear witness to the fact that the honour of his daughter and of the family is intact .... On one occasion the daya embedded her long nail in the hymen, but only a few drops of scanty blood were forthcoming. To my horror she pushed her finger up the vagina and the blood welled out in a steady stream. The white towel bathed in crimson flopped out over the father's head, the drums beat and female voices emitted the long drawn out shreiks of joy. I realised that she had cut through the walls of the vagina. At the end of the night, in answer to my questions, she explained to me that on marriage nights she was very much in demand. Her fame, built upon her capacity for bringing forth a vigorous flow of blood in the process of defloration, had earned her an unusual popularity and a steady income from such auspicious occasions'.[43]

If the girl was found to be a non-virgin she was considered to have brought dishonour on her family and was discarded by the bridegroom as damaged property. According to Mernissi 'the concept of honour and virginity locate the prestige of a man between the legs of a woman. It is not by subjugating nature or by conquering mountains and rivers that a man secures his status, but by controlling the movements of women related to him by blood or by marriage, and by forbidding them any contact with male strangers'.[44]

El-Saadawi also observes that 'Arab society still considers that the fine membrane which covers the aperture of the external genital organs is the most cherished and most important part of a girl's body and is much more valuable than one of her eyes, or an arm, or a lower limb. An Arab family does not grieve as much for the loss of a girl's eye as it does if she happened to lose her virginity. In fact if the girl lost her life, it would be considered less of a catastrophe than if she had lost her hymen'.[45] But few people have stopped to consider that virginity can be damaged due to many reasons other than coitus. What then is the marital future of such a woman? What if the blood stained bed sheet cannot be produced to prove her virginity? What fears must she undergo before marriage thinking of the consequences should she be discovered to be a non-virgin on the nuptial bed by her husband?

The problem of virginity in Muslim societies focusses on the woman's physical chastity rather than on the chastity of her mind. It is not surprising then to find why female gynaecologists do well in charging parents who want certification of their daughter's virginity before marriage or from the latter who want it to be restored in any way so as to pass detection on the first night.

The morbid obsession with virginity has led to the enforcement of a number of practices which are rigidly enforced. Often parents want to get their girls married as soon as possible to get them off their hands. The segregation and veiling of women impose separation and seclusion from the sight and reach of males. These are all social control mechanisms to safeguard the property from being damaged. Above all Islamic sanctions are brought to justify such actions. However, Islam does not allow women to be treated as a private property, but as a person. In fact, as Mernissi correctly states 'Of what national plan is virginity a part? Does it just float, artificial and venal, in the mine of a disordered morality, without any coherent direction or aim? Religion lays down that both sexes should be virgins at marriage, and this one fact reminds one how much Islam is flouted every day by men who claim to adhere to its principles. Respect for religious law would therefore require a fundamental change in men's mentality and personality, a complete re-evaluation of their relations with the opposite sex, and the acquisition of sound and consistent principles upon which to build their life'.[46] But in reality this is hardly the case. If anything the reverse is true for 'the picture of a male virgin trembling with purity and innocence on the eve of his wedding is, for the Arab man, the height of absurdity. This, however, is what he wishes to impose on the Arab women'.[47]

Another example of how women have been treated as a property is through the practice of female circumcision. This takes various forms, from an incision of the clitoris, its removal, to the total cutting away of the labia minora and the sewing up of the genital organs leaving only a small aperture for urination. The custom has been practised in Egypt, Sudan, Yemen, the Gulf States and a number of African countries. Our concern here is mainly with Muslim women who have to undergo this brutality to safeguard their virginity before marriage. In the words of Nawal el-Saadawi 'the importance given to virginity and an intact hymen in these societies is the reason why female circumcision still remains a very widespread practice .... Behind circumcision lies the belief that, by removing parts of the girl's external genital organs, sexual desire is minimised. This permits a female who has reached the dangerous age of puberty and adolescence to protect her virginity and therefore her honour, with greater ease .... Female circumcision is meant to preserve the chastity of young girls by reducing their desires for sexual intercourse'.[48] Where is the sanction for this in Islam? In fact it was practised in ancient Egypt and for this reason has been labelled 'Pharaonic' circumcision. But feudalist thinking has dominated Islam and the Ulema have not objected to it in spite of its being legally banned in Sudan.

The other side of the picture is not illuminating either. Western capitalism has converted women into commodities to be exploited. Their western image is based on beautifying themselves and becoming the consumer of Western products. It has, on the other hand, stressed their freedom so that they can discard their veils and display themselves as attractive objects with the aid of cosmetics, elaborate hairstyles and fashionable clothing.

Doctrines of emancipation and feminism have sought to transform Muslim women into Westernised women - alienating them from their own cultures to the extent that they become strangers in it and cannot relate to their past and present heritage. They have developed a low self-image of themselves because in order to reach the ideals of femininity - they must reach the ideals of Westernisation and not

Islam.

The Marxist view of Muslim women has developed as a reaction to the doctrines of capitalism and not Islam. Before Karl Marx the doctrines of Marxism and socialism were not articulated as they are done today. Such views have originated not in Muslim societies but in Western societies as Marx's writings reacted to the oppression of the Western masses from feudalist and capitalist mode of productions and the social formations emanating from them. Such alien views too, like those of Western capitalism have been imported into Muslim societies and have alienated women from their cultures.

All such views of emancipation imported from the Western doctrines of capitalism and Marxism tried to shift the foundations to materialist and economic foundations. The spiritual foundations of Muslim societies which had crystalised into an Islamic culture, have been eroded by feudalism, capitalism and doctrines of Marxism. They have given a false authenticity to the social, political, economic and legal aspects of Muslim societies and have resulted in a false culture consciousness that distorts the principles of Islam. It is not within the realm of this paper to delve into these distortions which have taken place over the centuries. Suffice to state that after the Quranic revelations were completed during Prophet Muhammad's lifetime, there was no control over various interpretations of the Quran. After his death, the power struggle which started from the ascension to the caliphate by Abu Bakr, led to split between the Shias (Partisans of Ali, the son-in-law of the Prophet), and the Sunnis, and each sought to justify their position through Islamic legitimation.

At this juncture, when Muslim women are faced on one side with alien ideologies of capitalism and Marxism and, on the other hand, with feudalistic distortions of Islam, their dilemma lies in which path to follow. Who should they follow? What should be the role and status of Muslim women in their own societies?

In order to resolve this dilemma it must be pointed out that the future path for Muslim women will be strewn with numerous obstacles. They will not gain any concessions without a struggle. The global spread of capitalism will attempt to reduce their role into that of commodities. Hence the first struggle of the Muslim women will have to be against the anti-imperialist doctrines. The struggle of the Iranian Muslim and Marxist women has been in this direction and to this extent the objective of both women with different ideological orientations have been similar. But while this struggle will lead them to the consciousness that they are not commodities, the feudal interpretations of Islam by the conservative Ulema have imposed sanctions that result in making women into a man's property. Their doctrines have expanded man's role at the expense of women, who have come to be used as chattels for reproduction and sexual pleasure. Muslim women, therefore, have to struggle against the feudalists who have infused gross misinterpretations into the Islamic faith until it has become difficult even for followers of the creed to recognise their religion.

Women have to seek salvation from the authentic Islam for it is both anti-imperialist as well as opposed to the feudal oppression of women. If the call for the emancipation of women is directed at Islam, there is no need for it, since emancipation presupposes a condition of slavery and a woman is definitely no slave in Islam. Not only is she an equal but has almost more than equality, from the importance given to her role. However, there are those, who imitating the Western call for emancipation in this area, would actually forego some of women's rights under Islam. But the true need for emancipation is from the rigidity and the over-masking effect of false cultures and ignorant attitudes which have been woven into the basic teachings of a liberating religion.

The value of Islam lay in the type of man or woman it set out to create. If there was nothing to admire in the product, then either the religion was wrong, or indeed it was not being truly allowed to influence society. There must be a breakdown in interpretation and where can this breakdown be more disasterous than at the point where women as mothers control and teach the generations of tomorrow? This is where a woman's role is so effective and important and places a man's role in a secondary position. Where women's liberationists have had an adverse effect is in diminishing the importance of a woman's biological and sociological role and exaggerating the attraction of a career woman, severed from family ties and isolated in a new arena - calling this independence. No member of society was meant to be independent of the other. There has to be a new interpretation of Islam to establish that the basis for success in this life is as the Qur'an advocates in mutual co-operation and love. The whole purpose of the creation of the two sexes was to allow people to 'know one another' and co-operate in unity and partnership.

As stated earlier, Muslim women have to brace themselves for the struggle with the retrogressive forces in their societies. But their struggle will not be successful if they espouse Western ideologies of feminism or Marxism. These are transplants which will be rejected by their societies and will only alienate them from their cultures. Western women themselves have struggled to gain freedom in their societies not by following alien ideologies but through the evolution of their own cultures. Likewise Muslim women should evolve their ideologies from their own religion which is the foundation of their cultures and belief system. But this does not mean following the feudal interpretation of Islam. The forces projecting such views have to be eliminated and this should not be done by confronting them with alien ideologies but with Islam. In this struggle the Muslim women have to liberate themselves from the yoke of feudalism in their societies and place themselves under God. According to Islam, both men and women are equal in the sight of God and each will be judged according to his or her depth of religiosity. Thus, contrary to what is thought in Muslim society, women are not under the control of men. They enjoy a separate but equal status. If they were under the control of men - then women would not be able to determine their actions and, as such, before God only men and not women would be accountable. But both are accountable for their own actions and not for those of the others. In achieving this goal, Muslim women will require the help of Islamic intellectuals. The example of Iran is again relevant here for it did produce one such person by the name of Ali Shariati, who died in 1977. His influence in turning the minds of both young men and women against the Pahlavi regime cannot be measured and in fact the role of the intelligentsia was crucial to the Islamic revolution. Shariati's Islamic views of Muslim women applied not only to Iran but across its borders and affected all Muslim women.

Shariati began by calling for the search of true Islam which neither exists in Iran nor anywhere else in the Muslim world. In fact, what existed in the Muslim world were pre-Islamic practices and local customs which had been confused with Islamic principles. As stated earlier, in Muslim societies the predominant mode is still feudalistic – in which patriarchy reigns supreme, and such an interpretation of Islam had distorted it out of all proportion. Shariati therefore strongly criticised the Ulema, the 'timeless ones' who had emphasised veiling and seclusion but not education and enlightenment of women. Women had been kept in ignorance and in Iran, they were expected to attend the *rauzeh khani* (religious recital) to hear the Mullah's speeches regarding Hussein's martyrdom and they were 'the producer of tears in these religious recitals and the producer of children in the society'.[49]

Muslim women therefore have to break the hold of these men over their societies. Since the majority of the population of Muslim countries is illiterate, these men enjoy considerable powers. They do not like intelligent or educated women who can expose their ignorance. The Ulema, therefore, have deliberately kept Muslim women in ignorance in the name of Islam so that their own powers are not undermined. Shariati advised women to seek education and become socially responsible. He urged 'Muslims to distinguish religion from social customs, holding that many of the general beliefs about the role and rights of women practised in Iran are based only on traditional customs and values predating Islam which are imposed on women by the ignorant and irresponsible clergy. He attacks these traditionalists for opposing equal opportunity for women in education and the professions; traditionalists object when a male doctor examines a woman or delivers her baby, never asking why female doctors are not available to offer these services'.[50] The traditional Ulema have defined woman's role and prescribed her destiny according to their feudalist interpretations of Islam. Women have to resist falling into the trap set for them by the men and define their own role. This can be done by studying the Qur'an and Islamic history for themselves. They have to acquire Quranic knowledge in order to free themselves and to exercise their will to change their own situation rather than be steeped in ignorance. Muslim women have to understand that the Qur'an is a book of religious symbolism and, as such, open to interpretation in and by every generation. The religious authorities had negated its dynamism but the truth is that 'yesterday must be examined and evaluated in the light of yesterday's environment and circumstances and today must be looked upon from today's perspective'.[51] Women have to pick up the Qur'an and interpret it themselves without following the biased interpretations of men.

Some of the sanctions of the Qur'an were given for the Arab society as it was at the time and were meant to change it. The injunctions regarding polygamy were not to encourage it but to constrain the Arabs from female infanticide which was practised by them at the time. Also, constant feuding among Arab tribes had led to a surplus of women and polygamy was permitted and restricted to four women - in those circumstances. Today, such a situation does not exist and so the practice of polygamy has become degrading for women. Similarly the custom of veiling had its relevance in those times and according to Shariati's interpretation the *chador* (body veil) 'has become accepted as an Islamic uniform. This has replaced the concept of hejab (modesty in dress) in Islam, which takes different forms in different societies and periods in history. He feels that by equating the chador and hejab, both opponents and defenders of the chador are in a fundamental error. Those intellectuals who find the chador disguising mistakenly attack the concept of hejab, while those who defend the chador falsely believe they are defending Islam'.[52]

In order to defend themselves from these retrogressive interpretations of Islam by the Ulema, women have turned to Western ideologies. Shariati attacks both the Marxist, and capitalist roles as well as the conservative-Islamic. He recommends that they should follow the third alternative by suggesting the model role of Fatima, the daughter of the Prophet and wife of Ali - the fourth Caliph of Islam.

Shariati selected a role model of an Islamic woman so that Muslim women could imitate and follow her rather than imported models from the West. In his opinion an Islamic role model was the best solution and 'the most effective weapon to confront Western dominating values and the most important factor for creating a conscious struggle within the new generation of our Islamic societies against the West's invitation is by having very high, distinguished and characteristic symbols, real personalities in Islamic history'.[53]

The conservative perspective had never presented these figures of Islamic history in a correct dynamic manner. It was the imperative need for young women that such Islamic personalities 'be known accurately .... be revived and introduced properly, scientifically, consciously and with new scholastic cognition, their character, personality and mission be described and announced in our societies, the young and new generation will sense that there is no necessity in adhering to and giving positive answers to the imitations of the West to decline, in the guise of modernism. Rather, they will sense that there are very high, elevated symbols in their own history and culture to be followed and to be considered as a scale for self-reconstruction. And Hazrat Fatima stands at the top of all these personalities, figures and high symbols'.[54]

Fatima was selected because during her lifetime she had many roles to play. As the daughter of the Prophet she took care of her father in times of hardship. As the wife of Ali, she had many political enemies. But she confronted them herself without fear for her life. As a mother she gave birth to sons like Hassan and Hussain who lived up to Islamic role expectations. The Islamic education inculcated in them by Fatima was such that Hussain preferred to die and become a martyr rather than compromise or surrender. The Karbala tragedy is remembered every year and Hussain's spirit of bravery is recounted. Thus Shariati argues that when 'we describe the biography of Fatima, as one of the members of the Prophet's family, we must learn lessons from her personality, her role, her social, mental, political and social parts and use them as a guide in our lives, in our groups and in our societies'.[55]

Shariati's reconstruction of Fatima's life in his book *Fatima is Fatima*, portrayed an ideal Islamic woman who knew her direction in life and did not despair over the harsh realities of life but with a strong faith in her heart learnt to cope and confront the most dangerous situations which dogged her all her life. As a role model she was ideal not only as a daughter, but as a mother and wife and a courageous woman who could hold her own and articulate her views against the opponents of her husband.

In the title of the book itself Shariati had a message for the Muslim woman. He could only entitle it as *Fatima is Fatima* for she was not like any other woman. In others words 'Shariati's text stresses the liability of a woman to 'make' herself, to 'create' herself. It is only in Shariati's work that the dimension of women being responsible for their society can be seen. That is why he feels the need to construct a model and defines Fatima, at the end, as a woman in her own right, more than a mere daughter, mere mother, mere wife'.[56]

Shariati's progressive view of Islamic womanhood, as stated earlier, had influenced a significant number of Iranian women. Some of them like Shahin Tabatabai, Fereshti Hashemi absorbing his views have articulated their views and further reinforced the role of Muslim women.

Tabatabai subscribes to Shariati's view in that there are two forces operating in the world: the forces of *Shirk* (polytheism) and those of *Tawhid* (monotheism). Man is therefore considered to be a 'bi-dimensional being' and, as such, he is a 'creature with a dual nature according to the symbolic language of the Qur'an, he is created from sedimentary mud and the spirit of God. This means that he has the potential of deciding either to descend towards the pole of sedimentary clay or ascent towards the pole of the spirit of God. One drags him down to stagnation, death, lowliness and ugliness and the other enables him to fly toward the absolute, towards God and the divine character. Between these two absolute possibilities he has the free will to choose for himself'.[57]

Whichever path man chooses, he tries to mould history according to it. From this perspective the flow of history shows that there has been a constant conflict between the just and the unjust and, as Muslims believe, that in the end the just forces will triumph then they should 'move forward with history in order to accelerate its determined course with the force of knowledge and science, otherwise if they stand in the face of history with their ignorance, egoism and opportunism, they will be crushed'.[58]

Within this general perspective as projected by the Qur'an, one cannot pick out the issue of women and isolate it. An isolated piece out of a jigsaw puzzle would not make any sense unless it is seen as part of the whole. In the same manner, the issue of women is an intergral part of the Qur'an. The Qur'an deals with many issues but these are all interrelated with an overall world view and individual issues cannot be isolated from it. The Qur'an 'deals with the liberation of women in the framework of the liberation of oppressed people, then the issues concerning those people, their inner relations in the society where they live, their relations with the oppressors gives them guidance how to overcome the oppressors and establish a just social system where there will be no justice towards any member of society, including women and children. The Qur'an's approach is that making an issue of the women's problem is an ignorant or deliberate deviation from the main issue – the oppressed people. This would mean dealing with a superficial contradiction rather than the basic conflict and contradiction'.[59]

Both men and women have to struggle in order to redress the grievances of the oppressed people in an Islamic society. Woman should neither turn to the Western nor Communist models for both have exploited women. The forces of *shirk*, on the other hand, have distorted Islamic history and which has to be rectified through struggle for the liberation of Muslim womanhood within her own culture.

Such a struggle for women's rights and particularly equality should not be confused with the feminist struggle in the West. In the West, the struggle for equality has often become confused with the issue of women acquiring similar roles to those of men. The women's struggle ends up with them trying to become like the men – which in turn brings a host of new problems through capitalist exploitation. But 'Islam sees the roles of men and women as completing roles, not competing roles'.[60] Equality is being a woman within her own province of freedom and not by taking on the role of men.

Fereshti Hashemi too believes that traditional Islam, deviatory Islam, colonised Islam have distorted the Islamic world view and specially the role of women in the Islamic society. The only course left for women was in 'awakening of the Muslim woman, to procure her Islamic rights .... But if the Muslim woman does not know her Islamic rights .... how could she take the smallest of positive steps forward?'[61]

Since Islamic thinking has been deviated from its true path by those in power, Muslim women have lost their true direction. Two kinds of Muslim women are found in Muslim societies. The first group consists of committed women but those 'who are not familiar with genuine Islamic rights. They are conscious of the fact that the present implementation of the rules threatens the fate of Muslim women: yet they try to justify them. Their problem is that while they are deeply attached to Islam, they are ignorant of the genuine roots of laws in the Qur'an and the Fiqh (the body of theological rules and edicts). They thus defend traditional Islam and the current deviations regarding women's rights instead of defending the real Islam'.[62] These women, Hashemi argues, feel the injustices perpetrated on them by a male dominated society but silently suffer rather than actively struggle against them.

The other group of Muslim women is comprised of those who are 'either not so attached to their faith, or else they are more conscious of their rights. They bravely protest, but since they are not familiar with genuine Islam in the field of women's rights, they cannot substantiate their voice of protest and they expose themselves to cries of heresy . . . .'[63]

How should these Muslim women then go about remedying their situation? The only criteria would be to 'evaluate the status of the Muslim women in true Islam by looking at the early years of Islam and the practices of true Muslims. Muslims who have been guided and enlightened by the sources of revelations and prophecy for 23 years and every man and woman among them knew the meaning of being a Muslim and acting as a Muslim'.[64] This criteria takes one back to the early period of Islam and look at the role models of men and women who were close to the Prophet and lived the Islamic life. If they did not, the Prophet was always there to guide and censure them.

In the current context in Iran, women's problems and issues relating to family still have to be restored according to the rules and regulations of true Islam. This has been delayed due to three reasons. First, due to the Iran-Iraq war, other political and economic problems have been given priority over women's rights. Secondly, the 'prevailing views in society towards women' are such that 'a lot more time is needed to eradicate these conceptions from every pore of society at all levels'.[65] Thirdly, the women themselves are to blame for, as stated earlier, women are not conscious of their rights and 'either try to justify the existing laws, or raise cries for our rights without any valid backing'.[66] Hashemi therefore hopes that the more Muslim women become aware of their rights the more the chances of leading a struggle for acquiring it.

CONCLUSION

The implications of the Iranian revolution for Muslim women the world over cannot be ignored or underrated. The social conditions in which the Iranian women have lived under feudalist oppression, capitalist exploitation and Marxist reaction are similar to those in other Muslim societies. The lesson to be learnt from them is that Muslim women have to struggle against both the internal forces (feudal) and external forces (Western and Marxist) which have infiltrated their socieites. This struggle has to be waged from the platform of interpreting the true Islam themselves and following of ideal role models of Islamic women like Fatima. If they have suffered, they themselves are responsible for it, and in the words of Ali - the fourth caliph of Islam: 'Two are responsible for tyranny. The tyrant and the one who submits to tyranny'.

REFERENCES

1.   Pamela Haines, Women in Today's Iran, in David H. Albert (ed.) Tell the American People: Perspectives on the Iranian Revolution.   Philadelphia, PA: Movement for a New Society, 1980, pp. 99-10.

2.   Ashraf Dehqani - a Marxist woman guerilla fighter. See Ali

Reza Nobari (ed.), Iran Erupts, Stanford, CA: Iran-American Documentation Group, 1978, pp. 161-162.

3.   Cited in Shireen Mahdavi, Women and the Shii Ulama in Iran. Middle East Studies, Vol. 19, No. 1, January, 1983, p. 19.

4.   Ibid., p. 19.

5.   Ibid., p. 19.

6.   Ibid., p. 20.

7.   Ibid., p. 20.

8.   Nahid Yeganeh, Women's Struggles in the Islamic Republic of Iran, in Azar Tabari and Nahid Yeganeh (ed.), In the Shadow of Islam: The Women's Movement in Iran, London: Zed Press, 1982, p. 47. This is an excellent reference work on Iranian women.

9.   Quoted in Shireen Mahdavi, op. cit., p. 23.

10.   Ibid., p. 23.

11.   Haleh Afshar, Khomeini's Teachings and their implication for Iranian Women in Azar Tabari, op. cit., p. 82.

12.   Ibid., p. 77.

13.   Ibid., p. 78.

14.   Ibid., p. 78.

15.   Ibid., p. 78.

16.   Ibid., p. 78.

17.   Kohmeini's speech on 19th May, 1979. Quoted in Azar Tabari, op. cit., p. 101.

18.   Ibid., p. 101.

19.   Ibid., p. 101.

20.   Ibid., p. 101.

21.   Quoted in Haleh Afshar, op. cit., p. 78.

22.   Ibid., p. 78.

23.   Khomeini's speech on 4th March, 1974, in Azar Tabari, op. cit., p. 99.

24.   Nahid Yeganeh, op. cit., p. 81.

25.   Khomeini's speech on 23rd January, 1979. Quoted in Azar Tabari, op. cit., p. 98.

26.   The Constitution of the Islamic Republic of Iran. Quoted in Tabari, ibid., p. 93.

27.   Ibid., pp. 93-94.

28.   Nahid Yeganeh, op. cit., p. 81.

29.   Ibid., p. 80.

30.   Ayatollah Taleghani, On Hejab in Azar Tabari, op. cit., pp. 104-105.

31.   National Union of Women, An Analysis of the Socio-Economic Status of Women in Iran, in Azar Tabari, ibid., p. 148.

32.   Ibid., p. 149.

33.   Ibid., p. 150.

34.   National Union of Women, Message to the Solidarity Conference, ibid., p. 154.

35.   Emancipation of Women, the Veil and the Question of Women in Iran. Ibid., pp. 166-67.

36.   Emancipaton of Women. Women in the eyes of clerics of the Islamic Revolution. Ibid., p. 168.

37.   Mujahidin-e-Khalq, Women on the Path of Liberation, ibid.,

p. 120.
38. Ibid., p. 122.
39. Fedayeen-e-Khalq (Minority), Compulsory Veiling under the Pretext of Fighting Imperialist Culture, in Azar Tabari, ibid., p. 127.
40. Ibid., pp. 128-29.
41. Fedayeen-e-Khalq (Majority), Women's Rights and Islamic Hejab in Tehran, ibid., p. 137.
42. Socialist Workers Party of Iran, The Necessity for Women's Unity and Organisation in Tabari, ibid., p. 133.
43. Nawal el-Saadawi, The Hidden Face of Eve: Women in the Arab World. London: Zed Press, 1980, p. 29.
44. Fatima Mernissi, Virginity and Patriarchy, Women's Studies International Forum, Vol. 5, No. 2, 1982, p. 183.
45. Nawal el-Saadawi, op. cit., p. 26.
46. Fatima Mernissi, op. cit., p. 187.
47. Ibid., p. 185.
48. Nawal el-Saadawi, op. cit., p. 33.
49. Ali Shariati, Fatemah Fatemah Ast (Fatima is Fatima), Tehran: Hoseinah Ershad, 1971, p. 79.
50. Adele K. Ferdows, Women and the Islamic Revolution, International Journal of Middle East Studies, Vol. 15, No. 2, May, 1983, p. 285. This paper gives an excellent exposition of Shariati's view on Muslim women.
51. Ali Shariati, Islam Shenasi (Knowing Islam), Vol. 7, Solon: Ohio: Muslim Students Association, 1979, p. 87.
52. Adele K. Ferdows, op. cit., p. 285.
53. Ali Shariati, What the Contemporary World expects from the Muslim women, Mahjubah (Tehran), Vol. 1, No. 11-12, February-March, 1982, pp. 12 and 58.
54. Ibid., p. 58.
55. Ibid., p. 58.
56. Nahid Yeganeh, op. cit., p. 51.
57. Shahin Eetezadi Tabatabai, Understanding Islam in its totality is the only way to understand women's role, in Azar Tabari, op. cit., p. 172.
58. Ibid., p. 173.
59. Ibid., p. 174.
60. Ibid., p. 174.
61. Fereshti Hashemi, Women in an Islamic versus women in a Muslim view, in Azar Tabari, p. 178.
62. Ibid., p. 178.
63. Ibid., p. 179.
64. Ibid., p. 179.
65. Ibid., p. 183.
66. Ibid., p. 183.

Part Two:

ROLE CHANGES

Chapter 3

ROLES IN TRANSITION: THE EVOLVING POSITION OF WOMEN IN ARAB-ISLAMIC COUNTRIES*

Debbie J. Gerner

In most of the Western world, the phrase 'Arab Islamic women' conjures up a vision of heavily veiled, secluded women, whose lives consist of little more than their homes, their children, and the other females in the harem or immediate kinship circle. As recently as fifty years ago, this kind of image had a great deal of validity, at least in the urban centres, and in some areas it is still an accurate portrayal. Increasingly, however, it no longer reflects reality. This essay surveys the changes in the legal, political, economic and social laws and norms governing the status and roles of women in the Arab world which have occurred in the past 50 years.

This approach is somewhat controversial, for clearly there is a great deal of diversity in the historical and contemporary experiences of women in various nations, and thus differences in their status. There are also variations based on the socio-economic class to which a woman belongs and whether she lives in an urban or rural area. These must be taken into account whenever generalisations are made. Nonetheless, there are reasons for considering Arab women as a unit. First is the underlying influence of Islamic law which governs, or at least affects, the legal codes of personal status in virtually all Muslim countries. More generally, Arab societies share a common heritage, common culture and common traditions. From these come the societal expectations for women. Finally, 'the policy concerns of women themselves transnational .... population control, education, health care, and so forth – are almost always approached by women themselves on a transnational basis'.[1] For these reasons, it is useful to look generally at the lives and roles of women who share both a culture and a religious tradition; that is the purpose of this article.

I

A major debate exists among scholars as to whether Islam improved the status of women or is responsible for keeping them oppressed now, or both. One difficulty in settling this debate is that it is not clear what position women actually held in the early years of Islam, or how this differed from their status in the *Jahiliya*. Indications can be seen through examination of the Qur'anic teachings, along with the *sunnah* and *hadith* of the Prophet, but it must be recognised that these, like religious writings in all traditions, represent precept, not necessarily practice. Interpretations of the Qur'an by different religious traditions have been at least as important in determining patterns of acceptable behaviour as the actual writings.

Evidence does seem to indicate that Islam was initially far ahead of other religious and cultural traditions in its recognition of women as independent persons with rights and obligations. However:

> Arabs stopped at this magnificent beginning and did not develop that situation as time passed. Nor did they make any attempt to conform their spiritual and social values with the changing of the circumstances of life. .... The result was that the procession of civilisation passed us by ....[2]

In some nations, the interpretation of Islamic law has been such that women have been denied even those basic rights traditionally granted them. What are some of these?[3] First, the Qur'an gives women explicit economic rights, though they are not identical to those of men. According to the Qur'an, a woman is entitled to a portion of any inheritance - her share is half that of a boy or man of equal status in the family. Women are partially compensated for this smaller portion by having no legal responsibility to spend their personal income on the support of their children or the household in general. It belongs exclusively to them and can be passed on to heirs of their own choosing.[4] Women also have the right to buy and sell property and the right to hold a job and be involved in trade and commerce without the influence or permission of husband, father, or other male guardian.

Polygyny, which had been common prior to Muhammad's time, was not abolished by the Prophet. It was limited, however; according to the Qur'an a man may have no more than four wives, and he is charged to limit this still further if he feels he will be unable to treat each wife equally. This is understood by some scholars as a compromise solution which avoided the major social upheaval which might have followed the total elimination of polygyny. This interpretation is consistent with what is known about early Islam, particularly its relative lack of demands for fundamental lifestyle changes on the part of new converts and conquered people. Others argue that it was simply a way of legitimising a practice which is oppressive to women. In contemporary Arab society, polygyny is no longer common. Less than ten percent of marriages in most areas are polygynous and the majority of these involve only two wives.[5]

Under traditional Islamic law, divorce (in particular, *talaq*, divorce by unilateral repudiation) was and is fundamentally a right pertaining to the husband, to exercise as he pleases, without explanation or justification, and without the decision being reviewed by a court or judge. Furthermore, a man has no financial obligations toward his former wife and receives total custody of their children over seven years of age. Certain provisions limiting these rights can be written into the marriage contract at the woman's insistence, but in the past fear of antagonising a future husband and his family prevented many women from utilising this prerogative. The Qur'an also specifically prohibits forced marriages. In practice, however, this has also proved difficult to implement as girls and young women are reluctant to speak up against their father's or guardian's choice of a husband for fear of incurring their family's anger.

As adults, Muslim women in the early Islamic State took an active role in the religious, political, economic and social life of the community. Women owned property, were involved in the politics of caliphate succession and were active with men in the public obser-vance of religious rituals and obligations.[6] The Islamic ideal of women and men as equally valued and important, with complementary status and rights, did not last, however, if it ever existed. Much of this appears to be related to the interplay of Islam with the indigenous Arab culture and with the cultures of those areas which were conquered by the Muslims:

> Islam operated on a principle of toleration and absorption of a vast diversity of cultural patterns and social practices. With the subjugation of highly civilised peoples, the Arab conquerors freely melded diverse elements from local cultures into their own institutions and laws. At the same time, they impressed upon everything they acquired the unmistakable stamp of Islam.[7]

In some instances this resulted in the enrichment of both cultures; however, it did not result in an improvement in the position of women. Elise Boulding comments:

> One could interpret the history of women in Islam as one long struggle on their part to maintain the rights enunciated by Mohammed in the face of a series of traditions hostile to women's rights in the various Mediterranean countries conquered by the Moslems.[8]

The pre-Islamic Arab world also had its own customs and attitudes which were hostile to women. One of these was compulsory veiling which in some parts of the world dates back to at least the first century A.D.[9] In the cities it was used to differentiate free women, who wore the veil, from slaves. Thus, both men and women considered it a mark of honour, modesty and respectability for a woman to veil. Village and desert women, whose work made heavy veiling difficult or impossible, were less affected, and generally only put on the veil when they had to go into the city or when they knew there were male strangers in their village.

A related custom, also required through association with other cultures, was the seclusion of women. Although it is not known when the harem system and the seclusion of women began to be widespread, 'one-and-a-half centuries after the death of the Prophet, the system was fully established . . . . (that) amongst the richer classes, the women were shut off from the rest of the household'.[10] Thus purdah became another symbol of male prestige and prosperity, as well as a way to distinguish and set apart upper class women from peasants.[11]

TABLE 3.1

The Basis of the Legal Systems of Arab States

Shari'ah	A Combination of the Shari'ah and Secular Law	
Libya	Algeria*	Mauritania*
Oman	Bahrain*	Morocco*
Qatar	Djibouti	P.D.R. Yemen**
Saudi Arabia	Egypt**	Somalia*
United Arab Emirates	Iraq	Sudan**
Yemen Arab Republic	Jordan	Syria**
	Kuwait	Tunisia**
	Lebanon**	

*   More conservative
**   More secular and liberal

Additional freedom was lost once the Islamic State fell under foreign domination. Although 'there was a great variety in the patterning of women's life depending on the mix of pre-Islamic traditions and the character of the Moslem colonial occupiers',[12] on the whole, the status of women was much lower than it had been in the first years of Islam. A woman's role in the world came to be narrowly circumscribed - home, children and private relationships with other women.

At present the Arab world can be divided into two general categories[13] (see Table 3.1). The first is composed of countries where the *shari'ah* remains the basis of the legal system and is rigidly applied more or less in its entirety across the range of human relationships. In these countries, located primarily on the Arabian Peninsula, women have few, if any, rights. It is difficult for women to move constructively toward changing their situation since the structure of society is not receptive to mass movements, even at an elite level, of the kind which were important for reforms in Egypt and Tunisia.

The second category is illustrated by most Arab nations: a combination of religious and secular law. In the past there was a clear-cut dichotomy between the two forms of law: political and legal affairs were governed by Western-inspired secular law, while the *shari'ah* remained the unchallenged guide for personal status and family laws:

> .... although in theory all parts of the divine law rest equally on revelation, in practice a certain distinction can in fact be made. It is the personal and family law that, together with rules of ritual and religious observance, has always been regarded as the very heart of the *shari'ah*. The public law, on the other hand, although in theory equally based on divine authority, has been much less meticulously observed down through the centuries.[14]

More recently, however, this distinction has been fading. In some nations, government leaders are realising they can reinterpret *shari'ah* law broadly enough to deal with all aspects of modern life, rather than accepting wholesale major portions of the Western legal structure as they have done in the past. Other countries are moving closer to complete secularisation (e.g. Tunisia); in these cases *shari'ah* law has only a minor role in the legal system, specifying religious observances and other aspects of life not generally governed by secular law. There is a great variation in the way secular and *shari'ah* law interact in these countries. In some (e.g. South Yemen), women are for all practical purposes free from legal restraint, while in others (e.g. Morocco), the freedom is more in name than in actual fact.

A third option, not chosen by any of the Arab nations, is the complete elimination of religious law as a basis for civil law. This was the course taken by Turkey under the leadership of Mustafa Kemal.[15]

II

In many parts of the Arab world, early feminist movements were tied to the nationalist movement and the most progress toward emancipation was made in those situations where the two were closely united. Initially, both were heavily influenced by increased contact with European nations and an ensuing awareness of the political and economic reforms which were changing European society. Many people who were most supportive of women's rights during this period did not identify themselves primarily as feminists, but rather saw themselves as following in the European tradition as crusaders for nationalism and modernisation. The majority of these individuals came from Egypt, the Arab nation with the greatest opportunities for contact with the rest of the world.[16]

Among the first leaders were Muhammad 'Abduh and Jamal-ud-al-Din Afghani. Although few of the reforms advocated by these men, such as expansion of the educational opportunities for females and elimination of compulsory veiling, were instituted, the intellectual underpinnings necessary for future reforms were established. Through their writings and teachings, Afghani and 'Abduh paved the way for the feminist movement in the Arab world by attempting to free Islam from the rigid orthodoxy into which it had fallen.[17]

The first Arab to be identified specifically as a feminist was Egyptian Kasim Amin who transformed the women's cause into a full-blown feminist movement. Two of his books, *Tahrir-al-Mara'h (The Emancipation of Women)*, published in 1900, and a later volume, *Al-Mara'h-al-Jadidah (The New Woman)*, caused him to be vigorously attacked by religious authorities, as did his support of higher education for females, the elimination of the abuses of polygyny and divorce, and the removal of the veil. Like Afghani and 'Abduh, Amin felt that the emancipation of Muslim women did not require the reform or rejection of Islam itself, but rather bringing practice in line with doctrine, a task that could be accomplished within the framework of the *shari'ah*.[18]

A number of upper-class women participated in the early

feminist movement. Among these was Malak Hifni Nasif, known also by her pen name, Bahithat al-Badiya. A contemporary of Amin, Malak Hifni Nasif was active both in teaching and writing, and designed a ten-point plan to improve the status of Egyptian women which she presented to the first Egyptian Congress of 1911. Included in her demands were primary and secondary school opportunities for females, freedom for any girl or woman to study whatever interested her, and the institution of civil marriages.[19] Although there was 'no intention to lead the woman out of her traditional realm into a more public arena of positions and professions'[20] through these proposals, they were considered too revolutionary and threatening to society and were unanimously rejected by the Congress.

Arab feminism was given a strong push during the post-World War I years by another Egyptian woman, Huda Sh'arawi. At first, Sh'arawi restricted her activities to teaching and operating a girls' school, the first in the country to offer general rather than vocational training for young women. Soon however, she became involved in political activism – in the nationalistic demonstrations against the British in 1919, and as head of the Women's Executive Committee of the Wafd party. When the Committee was dissolved in 1923, it was replaced by the Egyptian Feminist Union for Women's Suffrage, a combination school, workshop and club.[21] During the mid-1920s, Sh'arawi established the first secondary school for young women. She also had a role in opening Cairo University to women in 1927, and in the 1940s assisted in the organisation of the All-Arab Federation of Women.[22]

The linkage between nationalism and women's rights in evidence in the years before World War II has become even more striking since then, without, however, the ties to European expectations and norms which had characterised the earlier period. It is a natural linkage, for a woman is 'subjected to a double exploitation (in pre-revolutionary societies): she is exploited by those who exploit the man and is then exploited by the man himself'.[23]

The three nations most often mentioned as places where women have played an important role in the liberation movements are Algeria, Palestine, and Oman/Dhofar; however, women were also instrumental to varying degrees in the Sudan, People's Democratic Republic of Yemen, Somalia, Iraq, Lebanon and elsewhere. In Algeria, women began their resistence to French colonialism in the 1930s when they participated in public demonstrations against the French. Fannon points out that during this period, one of the colonian political doctrine stated:

> If we want to destroy the structure of Algerian society, its capacity for resistance, we must first of all conquer the women; we must go and find them behind the veil where they hide themselves in their houses where the men keep them out of sight.[24]

So wearing a veil became a symbol of resistance to colonialism. Once women became more actively involved in the revolution, they wore or dropped their veils as the situation demanded to make their participation most effective. Women were involved in both the urban and rural phases of the fighting: as couriers and messengers, spies, combatants, terrorists, etc. Ultimately, however, this extensive participation did not result in an improved situation for women. Although the new Algerian Constitution guarantees full equality of the sexes, the reality is much different (see note 57). Once the war ended, women were put back in their place.

In Palestine and Oman, the revolutions continue, so it is impossible to determine what effect women's participation will finally have on their position in society. In both revolutions, women have been involved from the very beginning, and now serve both behind the scenes in medical and social support positions, as participants in covert operations, as organisers and leaders of demonstrations and as combatants. Yet among many of these women is the apprehension that once the revolution has been won their contributions, like those of Algerian women, will be forgotten.

III

In education, despite rapid advances made in the past twenty years, opportunities for girls and women still lag far behind those for men. Initially, this wide discrepancy did not exist; until the mid-1800s, schools for either sex were rare. The wealthy were educated at home or sent abroad, while the majority of the population remained illiterate.

The first girls' schools were started in the 1840s by Christian missionaries.[25] These were followed by schools run by upper-class educated women (such as Sh'arawi), and, much less frequently, by the government. Those schools which did exist, such as the Teacher's Training College in Jordan, were far apart, usually located only in major cities, and required the payment of a fee to attend. A family with few resources, or one which did not have relatives in the city with whom to house their daughters, inevitably sent the boys to school and kept the girls at home. The decision was, perhaps, of little significance at the time. For a number of years, the curriculum of the girls' schools was extremely limited, and was at least as concerned with socialising girls into Islamic social structure as with teaching them to read, write and think.

In the past forty years, changes have occurred. Compulsory education laws have been enacted in nearly every country, and in urban areas are beginning of have an effect on the literacy rates of girls and women. Implementation and enforcement continue to be major problems particularly in the rural areas where a majority of the Arab population lives.[26] Among traditionally oriented families, extended education for females is not perceived as serving any useful purpose. It takes girls away from the home, so that their labour is temporarily lost to the family unit, and it is associated with modernisation, which threatens the traditional ways of life. Furthermore, it is feared that too much education will hinder a young woman's chance for a good marriage, as many men still believe educated women make poor wives.

The problems caused by the attitudes of rural and nomadic Arabs are complicated by the continuing severe shortages of schools outside the urban areas. A small village finds it difficult to afford one school for boys, let alone a separate one for girls, as is required by the prevailing understanding of traditional Islamic laws. Thus, rather than integrating the single school or building two schools, education is simply not provided for girls. Egypt, Iraq, Jordan and Syria are among the countries which have confronted this problem directly by emphasizing the acceptability and advantages of co-education, at least at the primary level. This has greatly expanded opportunities for girls. Nonetheless, many families remain reluctant to allow their daughters to attend, disapproving of the free exchanges between males and females which take place in such a setting. As co-education becomes more common, it may cease to be seen as a threat to Islamic values.

The fact that a girl is allowed to enroll in school does not mean equal educational opportunity is assured. In many places, a different curriculum is still used for females, particularly at the lower levels:

> (In Egypt) the stated intention of the school curriculum is to prepare women to improve living conditions within the family, to help increase incomes, and to enlighten women sufficiently for them to understand the outlines of the country's developing plans. Thus, the Egyptian educational system theoretically provides equality of opportunity for Egyptian girls, but does not attempt to prepare women for the same role as men.[27]

The pattern is even more evident in Saudi Arabia where girls are taught virtually no maths or science, and are not allowed to participate in physical education classes. There is strict sexual segregation in classes and all teachers are female, except for occasional male professors who lecture and answer questions via closed circuit television and telephone.[28] Those who aspire to further education (perhaps abroad) find themselves poorly prepared unless they have had private tutoring at home, a privilege of only an elite few.

As a result of all these problems, women still lag far behind men in their literacy rates and in participation in education at all levels. In Egypt, for example, illiteracy dropped from 98 percent in 1917 to 79 percent in 1966. However, male illiteracy fell much more rapidly, leaving the relative position of women worse than before. This pattern is evident in a number of other Arab nations as well. In the least developed countries, the illiteracy rates are extremely high (i.e. over 90 percent in Oman), but the gap between the rates for men and women is minimal.[29] As a country begins to make education a priority, there is a differential change in the literacy rates over time. Literacy increases among both sexes, but much more quickly among men. Eventually, women 'catch up' so that in highly developed nations the large majority of both men and women are educated and literate.[30]

In recent years, there have been a growing number of girls and women attending school at all levels; eventually this will also result in higher literacy rates. In Libya, for example, girls comprised 21

TABLE 3.2

**Male and Female Literacy Rates
of Selected Arab States***
(15+ years of age)

Country	Year	All Males	Rural Males	All Females	Rural Females
		%	%	%	%
Algeria	1971	42	34	13	6
Bahrain	1971	49	–	29	–
Egypt	1976	54	45	22	13
Kuwait	1975	65	–	34	–
Lebanon°	1970	79	–	58	–
Libya° //	1973	68	–	27	–
Morocco	1971	34	22	10	1
Saudi Arabia	1980	30	–	2	–
Somalia	1980	10	–	1	–
Syria	1970	60	–	20	–
Tunisia	1975	51	38	25	11
United Arab Emirates°	1975	60	–	44	–
P.D.R. Yemen°	1973	48	46@	8	3@
Yemen Arab Republic	1980	16	–	1	–

Source: UNESCO, Statistical Yearbook (London: UNESCO, 1981): Table 1.3

Notes: * Percentage rounded to nearest whole number
° 10+ years of age
// Libyan population only
@ excluding nomads

percent of the total primary school enrollment in 1960. Eighteen years later, this had improved to 47 percent,[31] and secondary enrollment had jumped to 39 percent from (18 percent in 1970). Morocco has experienced a similar increase: the number of girls in primary schools has risen from 15,080 in 1947 to 702,231 in 1978. However, this still only represents 36 percent of total enrollment.[32]

It is not clear what level of commitment to education for women exists in the Arabian Peninsula. In the past, this stronghold of conservative Islamic practice paid little attention to providing educational opportunities for either sex, particularly females, as evidenced by the extremely low female literacy rates (in relative as well as absolute terms). In some states, the increased availability of economic resources has resulted in an increased enrollment of female students: in Kuwait, Qatar, the United Arab Emirates and Bahrain primary and secondary school enrollment is nearly equally divided between girls and boys. In others, however, this has not occurred. In

TABLE 3.3

**Adjusted School Enrollment Ratio
in Selected Arab States, 1978***

Country	Primary		Secondary	
	Male	Female	Male	Female
Algeria	114	82	36	22
Egypt	88	58	60	35
Iraq	130	103	68	31
Jordan	86	80	63	49
Kuwait	110	98	79	69
Lebanon@	127	109	47	32
Libya	128	119	80	54
Mauritania+ //	34	17	9	1
Morocco	90	54	25	15
Qatar@	123	101	59	15
Saudi Arabia//	74	44	33	19
Somalia//	57	32	6	2
Sudan	58	42	20	11
Syria	105	78	60	35
Tunisia	117	83	30	18
P.D.R. Yemen//	92	51	42	15
Yemen Arab Republic°	50	7	8	1

Source: UNESCO, Statistical Yearbook (London: UNESCO, 1980): Table 3.2. Data for Lebanon and Qatar from International Bank for Reconstruction and Development, World Tables, 2nd edition (Baltimore: Johns Hopkins University Press, 1980); 455–459.

Notes: * Adjusted school enrollment is the enrollment of all ages as a percentage of the school age population (primary: 6-11 years; secondary: 12-17 years). Numbers may exceed 100 because some pupils are above or below the official school age.
@ 1970: Calculated from total enrollment figures, assuming a 50:50 sex distribution in the population
+ primary: 6-12 years; secondary: 13-19 years
// 1977
° 1975

North Yemen, only 11 percent of the primary students are girls, while in Oman there were no schools for girls until 1970, and females still only comprise 32 percent of primary school enrollment (although they are a much higher percentage of secondary enrollment). Similarly, in Saudi Arabia, which has a female literacy rate of well under 5 percent, government schooling for girls has only been available since 1960.[33] In

TABLE 3.4

**Female Primary and Secondary Students
in Selected Arab States**
(as a percentage of all students)

Country	Primary		Secondary	
	1970	1978	1970	1978
	%	%	%	%
Algeria	38	41	28	37
Bahrain	42*	45	41*	47
Djibouti	30	35//	-	-
Egypt	38	40	32	37
Iraq	29	43	29	30
Jordan	44	47	34	43
Kuwait	42	47	43	46
Lebanon	45	-	-	-
Libya	37	47	18	39
Mauritania	28*	34@	-	-
Morocco	34	36	28	37
Oman	14	32	21	47
Qatar	45	49	32	47
Saudi Arabia	31	37@	20	33@
Somalia	25	36@	10	10@
Sudan	38	41	28	34
Syria	36	41	26	35
Tunisia	39	40	28	36
United Arab Emirates	38	48	33	43
Western Sahara	31	-	-	-
P.D.R. Yemen	20	35@	20	26@
Yemen Arab Republic	9	11//	5	11//

Source: UNESCO, Statistical Yearbook (London: UNESCO, 1980):
Tables 3.4, 3.7

Notes: * estimate
// 1975
@ 1977

the past five years there has been a major government effort in Saudi Arabia directed at improving the educational level of both boys and girls. It remains to be seen whether this substantially improves the situation for females in the coming years.

Also noteworthy is the increased participation in higher education. There are now co-ed or women's universities in at least twelve Arab countries,[34] and women make up a substantial portion of their enrollment. At Baghdad University, women comprised less than

TABLE 3.5

Women University Students in Selected Arab States
(as a percentage of all students)*

Country	1970	1978
	%	%
Algeria	21	24//
Egypt	26	31
Iraq	22	30
Jordan	29	38
Kuwait	48	57
Lebanon	23+	–
Morocco	17	25
Qatar	–	58@
Saudi Arabia	8	25
Somalia	13	11°
Sudan	12	23
Syria	19	24
Tunisia	21	32//
United Arab Emirates	–	42
P.D.R. Yemen	27	30°
Yemen Arab Republic	3	12°

Source: UNESCO, Statistical Yearbook (London: UNESCO, 1981):
Table 3.11.

Notes: * These figures do not include students studying abroad.
// 1979
+ estimate
@ 1976
° 1977

2 percent of the student population in 1936, the first year they were
admitted. By 1956, this had increased to 24 percent[35] and in 1978
women comprised 30 percent of Iraqi university students. Nearly one-
third of the students at the University of Jordan at Amman are now
women, and women students outnumber the men at the University of
Kuwait and in Qatar. This is partially due to the high percentage of
men who study outside the country, but also reflects real increased
opportunities.[36] Women are still handicapped by family attitudes,
early marriage and motherhood, but it is more acceptable for a woman
to be both a wife and a student now than twenty years ago,
particularly among professionally oriented families.

Although these opportunities represent major advances for
women, it must be reiterated that in most countries only a miniscule
group of elite women and men are able to continue their education at
the secondary level, let alone attend the university. For that reason,

the most important and fundamental changes are those which occur at the primary school level, the level at which the majority of females are likely to be affected.

IV

It has been assumed by most scholars that the level of development in a country is a major determinant of the extent to which women are engaged in non-agricultural economic activities. In the Arab world, this does not appear to be the case - women have not responded to increased development with a proportional increase in the wage-labour force. Instead the 'official' involvement of Arab women in both the agricultural and non-agricultural work forces is low in absolute numbers, low as a percentage of the total work force, and low when compared to women from non-Arab countries at similar levels of development. There are, however, major problems with using these official figures as actually indicative of female economic participation rates:

> One recurrent problem in the discussion is that most statistical information omits the subsistence activities which are largely women's work. Food production and processing for home and local consumption, or the fetching of water and fuel are often time and energy consuming tasks which should, but do not, appear as productive work.[37]

This reflects the tendency of Western industrial societies to define work as only that which is directly paid, creating an artificial distinction between household chores and economic activities, which makes little sense in non-industrial nations. In addition, much of the work in which women are engaged is seasonal, which further exacerbates the problem of undercounting working women. Similarly, the pronounced reluctance of Arab men to admit that females in the family unit are employed reduces the accuracy of these figures.

The inaccuracy of both the method of defining employment and the actual data collection process causes particular problems for data on rural and nomadic segments of the population. In Bedouin and nomadic societies, women are considered integral members of the household in its division of labour, their work respected and regarded as essential to the continued maintenance of the economic unit. In fact, females begin working at a younger age, and often work harder and for longer hours than do the men in the family unit. It would be misleading to view their contribution as subordinate or supplemental. In describing one nomadic society, the Kababish, Talad Asad wrote:

> Wherever labour requirement is heavy, such as the annual migration cycle, women do men's work .... There is no male task that a woman may not perform .... but men almost never perform women's tasks.[38]

This is consistent with the pattern in other areas of the world:

poor and agricultural families have always needed the productive labour of all their family members, and women have traditionally worked alongside men. Yet when a family is engaged in subsistence labour, census figures include only the work activity of the men, implying that women are idle or that their efforts are of a secondary importance. These problems are complicated by the fact that women who are not involved in agriculture-related subsistence work are often engaged instead in home and cottage industries which are also not considered worthy of reporting.

Despite these caveats, it is true that Arab women have not traditionally taken an active role in the non-agricultural, non-home-based paid labour force. The two major inhibitors of female wage-labour activity are traditional family and societal attitudes, and low literacy and education rates. Both factors limit the occupational opportunities available to women. A third depressant is the high level of male unemployment and underemployment in many countries. For example, the 1967 census in Algeria revealed that 45 percent of the active male population (ages 15-65) was unemployed.[39] Governments and male dominated trade unions are unlikely to actively support and encourage increases in the female working population when insufficient jobs exist for men; however, it should be emphasized that even when a need does exist, women are often not encouraged to participate in the work force. In Saudi Arabia, less than 1 percent of the paid non-agricultural work force is female, despite a great need for additional workers. According to the Manchester Guardian, Saudi Arabia 'has been forced to import nearly 1.5 million foreign workers and another 500,000 or more are likely to be recruited in the months and years ahead'.[40] Yet there are no plans to bring larger numbers of women into the wage-labour force.

In terms of traditional attitudes hindering female employment, many of the same fears which were operative in a family's reluctance to allow its girls to attend school are important in this context as well. Some people still believe a working woman is exposing herself unnecessarily to men, becoming uncomfortably close to a prostitute. Families are afraid that by working a daughter or sister will destroy her chances of marriage and ruin her reputation. For many, there is shame associated with employment - it implies that her husband and other male kin are unwilling or unable to provide adequately for the family. It must also be acknowledged that there are are few incentives for a woman to work unless she is internally motivated as her economic support and well-being is assured within the kinship structure, and she gains few if any personal freedoms by seeking outside employment.

Attitudinal changes are slow in coming. A 1968 study of United Arab Republic male youth indicated that even among a sample of well-educated, elite boys, nearly half (45.6 percent) did not want their future wives to work at any time during their marriage. An even larger number (57.6 percent) did not believe women should receive equal wages for doing the same jobs as men.[41] This is despite the fact that the National Charter, which is carefully studied by all students, explicitly states a government commitment to female emancipation in all areas of life and indicates, at least by implication, that women should receive equal pay for equal work. Clearly these youths had not internalised the official government position. It would be expected that those boys would have been more liberal than the majority of Arab young men because of their higher education level and higher social class relative to the general population. If this is the case, total economic freedom for women is in the very distant future.

Although it is not determinant in and of itself, education remains an important factor in determining both attitudes toward work, and the types of jobs held by women. Education is closely associated with upper-class status, which in turn is linked to more liberal ideas about the appropriate roles for women[42] and with the ability to hire domestic help to assist with traditional women's work. Since there is an inverse relationship between education and fertility, highly educated women are also less likely to be constrained by heavy child-rearing responsibilities.[43] Furthermore, because upper-class women do not need to work, their holding a job represents less of a threat to the honour of the men in their families than if employment were an economic necessity.

Educated women in the Arab Middle East have a very high propensity for paid employment, particularly in professional fields. In Egypt in 1978, literate women made up nearly half the paid non-agricultural female labour force, although they comprised less than a quarter of the female population. Furthermore, women held 26.3 percent of the scientific, professional and technical positions in the country, although they represented only 8.8 percent of the total paid work force (see Table 3.6). These jobs include teaching and medicine, the two fields which have traditionally been considered acceptable for females because of the possibility of continued sex-segregation while in the working world. In Syria, Libya and Egypt, teaching absorbs nearly 40 percent of the female professional workers, and teaching and nursing together account for 96 percent.[44] Only slowly are women entering other professional fields in larger than token numbers.

The specific wage-labour occupations of non-professional, less well-educated women vary among countries; however, some generalisations can be made. Relatively few women are active in the domestic service occupations which are a major source of employment for women in other developing societies. Egypt is an exception, with women comprising 18.7 percent of the workers in this category.[45] Home crafts and cottage-type industries are particularly popular among the rural women because they, like teaching and nursing, reflect traditional feminine roles, involve only infrequent public exposure and association with non-family men, and can be combined with family responsibilities. Thus they do not result in a substantial lowering of the family's status. Those women who cannot find this type of work must resort to low-status, low-paying jobs such as waitressing, factory work, or field work on a non-family farm.

In a few countries the government has made a concerted effort to bring a greater number of women into the active wage-labour force, through legislation supporting equal pay for equal work, free child care services, etc. In Sudan a number of special provisions were instituted

TABLE 3.6

**Structure of the Economically Active
Female Population in Selected Arab States**

Occupation*	Egypt (1978)	Tunisia (1975)	Bahrain (1979)	Syria (1979)	United Arab Emirates (1975)
	%	%	%	%	%
Professional, technical and related workers	30	5	9	15	43
Administrative and managerial workers	2	1	4	1	1
Clerical and related workers	18	6	10	7	20
Sales workers	4	1	8	1	1
Service workers	8	9	9	2	29
Agriculture, animal husbandry and forest workers, fishermen and hunters	10	23	4	58	1
Production and related workers, transport equipment operators and labourers	7	43	53	13	1
Workers not classified by occupation	23	14	3	3	4
Total number economically active females	858,500	303,510	12,600	342,853	9,961
% of female population	6.0%	3.5%	8.6%	9.4%	8.0%
% of total male and female economically active population	8.8%	18.7%	9.3%	15.8%	3.4%

Source: International Labour Organization, Yearbook of Labour Statistics (Geneva: International Labour Organization, 1980): 3-31, 80-111, Table 2.

Note: * Numbers may not add to 100% due to rounding

in the early years of the Nimeri regime, including a three-month maternity leave with half-pay, government pensions for women, and a guarantee of equal pay for equal work. Recently, Nimeri has become much less progressive in his attitude toward the demands of Sudanese feminists, and working women are concerned that these provisions not be revoked.[46] Similar benefits exist for women in Egypt:

> The Labour Code of 1959 stipulated that women be provided with social services by the employer: seating accommodations were appropriate; two ½ hour breaks per day for mothers of infants during the 18-months following delivery, without any deductions in pay; delivery leaves not to exceed 50 days during which time women are to receive 70 percent of their wages; that women cannot be dismissed from work as a result of pregnancy or delivery for any ailment connected with them so long as their absenteeism does not exceed 6 months; and that all establishments employing over 100 women are required to provide day-care centres.[47]

There are two difficulties with such regulations. First, they are often not followed or enforced. Second, they make it more expensive to hire women, and thus less likely that women will be given employment so long as men are available to fill the positions.

A third example of government effort to raise female employment is Jordan, where a Department of Women's Affairs was recently created as part of the Ministry of Labour.[48] Its goals include modernising the laws relating to working women, abolishing tax discrimination against families with two working adults, acting as a clearing-house for women's concerns, setting priorities for the national government, and accelerating in any way possible the political and economic advancement of women. Particular emphasis is being placed on educating and encouraging women in the poorer and more conservative parts of the country.

By and large, these government efforts, while representing a beginning point for increasing female participation in the paid labour force, have proved of little value to the bulk of the population which is poor, rural or small and town, and uneducated.[49] These women have neither knowledge of, nor access to, the increasing non-agricultural employment opportunities available to their urban counterparts and remain untouched by the advancements in employment rights.

V

Although there is no Qur'anic text which denies full political equality of women and men,[50] the societal prohibitions against active political participation by women are still high in many Arab-Islamic countries. Since political strength is one of the few ways a group can effect socioeconomic change, this lack of participation is highly detrimental to the cause of women's emancipation.

One of the first and most basic political rights is the right to vote and stand for election. In only one nation in the Arab world is

TABLE 3.7

Political Status of Women in Selected Arab States

Country	Granted Suffrage	Stand for Political Office
Algeria	1958	1962
Egypt	1956	1956
Iraq	1967*	1967
Jordan	1973	1973
Kuwait	o o	-
Lebanon	1953	1953
Libya	1963	@
Oman	++	-
Qatar	++	-
Saudi Arabia	++	-
Somalia	1958	1958
Sudan	1964	@
Syria	1954//	@
Tunisia	1956	1959
United Arab Emirates	++	-
Yemen Arab Republic	++	-

Sources: Baer, 1964; Fluehr-Lobban, 1974; Gordan, 1968; Heggoy, 1974; al-Marayati, 1968; Minces, 1978; Women in Developing Countries, 1974; American University Press's Area Handbooks (Somalia, Iraq, Algeria, Libya, Jordan, Egypt, Saudi Arabia, Iran)

Notes: * A 1958 constitution amendment gave women with a primary school education the right to vote.
o o Only men have the right to vote
@ Information not available
++ This state has no elected legislature
// Initial election rights were granted in 1949 to women with an elementary school certificate.

this right granted to men and not to women: Kuwait. Several other countries, such as Saudi Arabia, grant suffrage to no one, and in others, notably Jordan, the right to vote is meaningless because of a non-legislative form of government (see Table 3.7). Although in the rest of the Arab world women are allowed to vote, few do. A 1972 UNICEF study found that in Egypt's 1971 elections, only 10 percent of the voters were female, despite the fact that women have been franchised since 1956.[51] Modesty is a factor in the low female voter turnout, as are family prohibitions, ignorance, and a cultural framework which suggests that women ought not to be concerned with politics. Those women who do vote often follow the lead of their male kin rather than choosing candidates independently.

In most nations, the right to stand for election was granted to women in the same year as the right to vote. As is true in the United States and much of Western Europe, however, the right and the reality are vastly different matters. For example, the first year women could stand for election in Egypt, they won only two of the approximately 350 seats in the National Assembly. That number increased to four in the following election, and in 1975, eight women sat in the Assembly. However, women still only comprise 2 percent of the total membership in that body. In both Syria and Tunisia, women held only 4 percent of the seats in Parliament in 1973, and in Lebanon, despite a tradition of female political activism, only one woman has ever been elected to Parliament. Sudan has one of the highest participation rates in the Arab world, with women holding 6 percent of the Parliament positions in 1975.[52]

Another indication of political emancipation and power is the number of appointed positions held by women. At the highest levels of government, very few women occupy such positions, and those who do seem to be token symbols of a policy of equality which the government only half-heartedly supports. This is not to imply that these women are not competent in handling their responsibilities, only that their numbers are so limited that one must question whether the official commitment to non-discrimination in political affairs is more than surface deep. Little is known about whether, and to what extent, the political nature of the government (e.g. semi-secular monarchy, religious dictatorship) predicts to its real or stated support for women. Such research would add greatly to the understanding of women's present and potential political power in the Arab world.

The pattern of low female participation and impact in formal politics in Arab countries is echoed by both major non-Arab Middle Eastern nations, Iran and Turkey. A study of political elites in Turkey reveals that the thirty-eight women who were members of the National Assembly from 1938 until the early 1960s were usually from the elite classes, were younger than their male counterparts, and were generally well-educated professionals from urban areas. In few ways did they reflect the majority of the female population. Despite their election in (relatively) high numbers, these women did not have a significant impact on the political system in Turkey. They remained peripheral members and were rarely re-elected:

> This accords with the repeated finding in other countries that women, if they do not get into the national legislature, tend to be less active than men, tend to be found in activities related to health, education and welfare (the legislative matters most proximate to the traditional female role), and tend to be rarely if ever in important positions of political leadership.[53]

Despite this, it would be inaccurate to understand women as having no political role or influence. Particularly in village and nomadic communities women are involved, often informally and behind the scenes, in political decision-making and dispute adjudication. Furthermore, women have an important place in religious rituals, and are generally responsible for keeping trace of, and making decisions about, gift-giving, a ritual which reflects status relations within the community. Both activities have major political implications.

Once a woman has passed her child-bearing years, her potential power increases greatly. She is allowed to argue with the men of the community on a more or less equal basis, and has a great deal of control over her family, especially her male children and their wives. In nomadic communities, a woman who exhibits particular leadership among other women may be called *aq birchek,* a title of honour and respect. This designation, given only to old or barren women, implies power and influence among both men and women. The power of the *aq birchek* is not formalised, however, and depends on the willingness of the men of the community to acknowledge her special role and importance.[54]

Thus, women in the Arab world are involved in political issues and do wield varying amounts of power at the lower levels of social organisation; however, by and large they do not take an active role in national political activities, nor do the results of their involvement at the local level extend beyond their own community group. A woman may be able to better her own life and that of her kin through acquiring political status within this small unit, but she has little political power to improve the status of all women.

VI

In most of the areas under discussion women have made a great deal of progress in the past fifty years. New opportunities have opened up, and women have been allowed, and occasionally even encouraged, to take a more active role in the life of their community and their nation. But the one area where women have made very little progress is a most crucial one: the personal codes and family laws which deal with marriage and divorce, inheritance, etc. and are at the root of Arab-Islamic traditional life. In only a few countries have these laws kept pace with the reforms in economic, political and educational affairs. 'It is hard for the mind to connect these two situations: the home and family situation, in which Arab woman's position is very weak, and the public and social situation, in which she has achieved so many victories'.[55]

As long as marriage and divorce laws and other regulations dealing with personal status continue to favour men, and to give them control over their wives, daughters and sisters, full emancipation cannot take place, no matter how great the progress in other areas of social and political life. Eventually this progress will be stymied unless fundamental changes are made in the family laws. Only when women are given control over their personal lives will they be able to take their full share of responsibility for the growth and development of their country. Equally important, women must be informed of the rights that they already have, and encouraged to exercise them.

Table 3.8 presents a ranking of Islamic countries by the degree

TABLE 3.8

Reform in Restrictive Laws Affecting Women's Status
(to January 1974)

		Minimum Marriage Age	Marriage Registration	Dissolution of Marriage	Inheritance Reform	Polygamy Regulation	Abolition of Talaq	Abolition of Polygamy	Secular Inheritance Law	Civil Code Replacing all Religious Law
10.	Albania	+	+	+	+	+	+	+	+	+
10.	Soviet Central Asia	+	+	+	+	+	+	+	+	+
10.	Turkey	+	+	+	+	+	+	+	+	+
8.	Tunisia	+	+	+	+	+	+	+	–	–
6.	Syria	+	+	+	+	+	–	–	–	–
6.	Morocco	+	+	+	+	+	–	–	–	–
6.	Iraq	+	+	+	+	+	–	–	–	–
6.	Iran*	+	+	+	+	+	–	–	–	–
5.	Egypt	+	+	+	+	–	–	–	–	–
4.	Pakistan	+	+	+	–	–	–	–	–	–
4.	Jordan	+	+	+	–	–	–	–	–	–
4.	Indonesia	+	+	+	–	–	–	–	–	–
4.	Algeria	+	+	+	–	–	–	–	–	–
4.	Sudan	+	–	+	–	–	–	–	–	–
3.	Libya	+	+	–	–	–	–	–	–	–
3.	Mali	+	+	–	–	–	–	–	–	–
1.	Afghanistan	–	–	–	–	–	–	–	–	–
1.	Saudi Arabia	–	–	–	–	–	–	–	–	–
1.	Mauritania	–	–	–	–	–	–	–	–	–
1.	Somalia*	–	–	–	–	–	–	–	–	–
1.	Yemen Arab Republic	–	–	–	–	–	–	–	–	–

Source: Elizabeth White, 'Legal Reform as an Indicator of Women's Status in Muslim Nations' in Women in the Muslim World, edit., Lois Beck and N. Keddie (Cambridge: Harvard Press, 1978), p. 60. Reprinted by permission of Harvard University Press.

Note: P.D.R. Yemen (South Yemen), not listed, is now among the most progressive of the Arab nations, due to extensive reforms in the family laws in the past five years.

* Reforms since January 1974 change the place of Somalia and Iran in this table.

of reform. As it illustrates, in all Arab countries, some remnants of the traditional Islamic laws which apply to personal status remain in force. For some nations, this remnant is small. The Tunisian Constitution declares the equality of men and women before the law, and the Code du Status Personnel forbids polygyny and arranged marriages (the former punishable by mandatory prison sentence), defines a minimum age for both women and men, and gives women equal divorce rights with men. Only in the matter of inheritance when there is no will is the Qur'anic ruling enforced.

P.D.R. Yemen (South Yemen) has made tremendous progress in the past five years. Their 'Law number 1 Concerning the Family' was formulated after a group of researchers spoke with women and men in all parts of the country to determine what the citizens felt the law should contain. Among its numerous provisions, the law gives both women and men the right to choose their own marriage partners, and defines marriage as a contract 'between men and women equal in rights and obligations, based on mutual understanding and respect'. Unilateral divorce is outlawed, but their partner can seek a divorce through the courts.[56]

However, in other countries, women are much more restricted, and in some instances, rights previously held by women are now being taken away.[57] Saudi Arabia has often been mentioned as an example of a less progressive state in its treatment of women, and nowhere is this more evident than in the area of personal freedoms. Women are rarely allowed to go out unless accompanied by their husbands, they are almost always heavily veiled, and seclusion is still a very real part of their lives. They are not allowed to participate in the community prayers which form the foundation of the society and are taught that their role in life is to marry well and serve their husbands.[58]

This pattern is echoed in the other nations of the Arabian Peninsula, but is not limited to them. For example, in Libya any form of female liberation (e.g. freedom of movement, not veiling, employment) is equated with a low standard of morality. 'The current government's attitude to women's emancipation, as one might expect, is hardly progressive. Qadafy let it be known himself, by denouncing the Tunisian women's liberation movement as a cheap legalisation of prostitution for the tourist market . . . .' [59]

In Morocco, inequality is institutionalised in the family law which sets up very different rights and responsibilities for men and women in a marriage. In particular, husbands are entitled to fidelity, obedience, deference by the wife toward all close relatives of the husband; wives have no similar rights regarding the behaviour of their husbands.[60] Instead, they are granted 'rights' of dependence, such as support in the form of food, clothing and housing, and permission to visit and receive visits from family.

Many of the personal status laws stem from the idea of *al-sharaf* (honour) which symbolises the ideal character of males as strong, authoritative, powerful, and women as submissive and weak, unable to protect their sexuality or the honour of their families. This is the responsibility of the males in the family:

The double standard of sexual behaviour is inextricably imbedded in this concept of extended honour, since the concept poses an impossible dilemma. How can a 'keeper' preserve his honour when it does not reside in his own actions . . . . but resides rather in the behaviour of related females? How else, indeed, except to control the females. This brings us back to veiling. But veiling is only a shorthand glass for sex segregation achieved through various forms of female seclusion . . . . The real point is that seclusion-segregation of women (through purdah, through restricted movement, through modesty or concealment) is necessary for the protection of men. Economic and ecological differences may yield actual variations in the degree to which seclusion is achieved, but they do not eliminate the reason for its desirability. Nor do they obviate its consequences.[61]

This attitude is perhaps the greatest factor working against the emancipation of women. The loss of control which must necessarily be experienced by men as women are given an increasing number of rights and freedoms is threatening in fundamental ways, not all of which are clear or obvious.

The roles of Islamic women in the contemporary Arab world are complex. In many cases they are still bound, legally or emotionally, to traditional patterns of behaviour. At the same time, there is movement toward women taking a freer and more active position in society:

Thus, one of the most important challenges facing the Arab women today is that of trying to equate her inner self, her thoughts and attitudes and feelings, with the contemporary social reality about her. It is not easy to resolve the contradictions, both personal and societal, which are bound to occur between the old inherited traditions and the new currents of thought.[62]

The status of women is undergoing rapid transformation in many parts of the region and not even in the most traditional societies is the position of women remaining completely stagnant. The greatest advances have occurred in the area of education. Less progress has been made in the economic and political spheres; however, often legislation is on the books and only requires a government commitment and some degree of modified societal attitudes to be fully implemented. Education, as the chief mechanism for translating the legal structures for society into social reality, will become increasingly important in initiating this process. Again, the stumbling block for furthering the emancipation of women remains the family laws, which are used to keep women in a submissive and subservient position by denying them the freedom to make basic life decisions and thus keep their status dependent on factors beyond their control. Yet even here there are encouraging signs in the examples of Tunisia and South Yemen. With the Arab world changing rapidly, the next fifty years will be at least as significant in establishing new roles for women as the previous fifty have been.

NOTES

* This is a slightly revised version of an article which was originally published in *Arab Studies Quarterly*. Thanks are due to the editors of the *Quarterly* for allowing its reproduction here. The author would also like to thank Sarah Sherwin, who guided me through the Women's Ephemeral Collection at the Northwestern University Library, and Ibrahim and Janet Abu-Lughod, who read and critiqued an early draft. The essay is stronger due to these three people, though they are, of course, not responsible for its contents.

REFERENCES

1. Nancy Adams Shilling, 'The Social and Political Roles of Arab Women: A Study in Conflict', in *Women in Contemporary Muslim Societies*, ed. Jane I. Smith (London: Associated University Presses, 1980), p. 105.

2. Aminah al-Sa'id, 'The Arab Woman and the Challenge of Society' in *Middle Eastern Muslim Women Speak*, ed. Elizabeth Warnock Fernea and Basima Qaltan Bezirgan (Austin, Texas: University of Texas Press, 1977), p. 377.

3. For a more detailed analysis of the legal status of women, either now or in the past, see J.N.D. Anderson, *Islamic Law in the Modern World* (New York: New York University Press, 1959); Noel J. Coulson, *A History of Islamic Law* (Edinburgh: Edinburgh University Press, 1964); Noel Coulson and Doreen Hinchcliffe, 'Women and Law Reform in Contemporary Islam', in *Women in the Muslim World*, ed. Lois Beck and Nikki Keddie (Cambridge: Harvard University Press, 1978); John Esposito, 'Women's Rights in Islam', *Islamic Studies* 14 (Summer 1975); 99-114; Ronald Jennings, 'The Legal Position of Women in Kayseri, a Large Ottoman City, 1590-1650', *International Journal of Women's Studies* 3 (November/December 1980): 559-582; T. Mahmood, *Family Law Reform in the Muslim World* (Bombay, India: Tripathi PVT, Ltd., 1972); Josephine F. Milburn, *Cross National Comparisons of Women's Legal Status* (Washington, D.C.: American Political Science Association, 1973); Elizabeth White, 'Legal Reforms as an Indicator of Women's Status in Muslim Nations', in Beck and Keddie.

4. Among Bedouin communities, the status of women as possible heirs is generally ignored. Emrys L. Peters ('The Status of Women in Four Middle East Communities', in Beck and Keddie, p. 324) explains this to be a result of the male-headed family corporation serving as the property-owning group. 'Since women are free to be married by men outside their natal corporations (nearly half their marriages are of this sort), female inheritance would mean an uncontrolled run on corporate resources. This would be serious enough if only mobile property were involved, but if land were threatened in this way also, the entire basis of corporate life would collapse'.

5. White, p. 58.

6.   Parveen Shauket Ali, *Status of Women in the Muslim World* (Lahore: Aziz Publishers, 1975); Elsie Boulding, *The Underside of History: A View of Women Through Time* (Boulder, Colorado: Westview Press, 1976), p. 387;   Reuben Levy, *The Social Structure of Islam* (Cambridge: The Cambridge University Press, 1974), p. 126.
      In a study of one 17th century city governed by Islamic law, it was found that women often had extensive property holdings and 'a clearly defined legal position within which they inherited and made bequests, bought and sold houses, fields, gardens, and vineyards, and brought legal claims against men. The court consistently upheld their rights'. (Jennings, p. 55).

7.   Nadia H. Youssef, *Women and Work in Developing Societies*, Population Monograph Series 15 (Berkeley: University of California, Institute of International Studies, 1974), p. 95.

8.   Boulding, p. 386.

9.   Lois Beck and Nikki Keddie, 'Introduction', in Beck and Keddie, p. 25.   Although veiling is often referred to as a religious responsibility of great importance, there are only brief references to veiling in the Qur'an: 'Prophet! Tell thy wives and daughters, and the believing women that they should cast their outer garments over their persons (when abroad)' and 'And say to the believing women that they should lower their gaze and guard their modesty; that they should not display their beauty and ornaments except what (must ordinarily) appear thereof;   that they should draw their veils over their bosoms and not display their beauty except to their husbands, their fathers, their husbands' fathers, their sons, their husbands' sons, their brothers or their brothers' sons . . . .'

10.   Levy, p. 127.

11.   Beck and Keddie, p. 8 point out: 'Recently, veiling and seclusion have become much more complex social phenomena.   While the wealthier classes educated in Western ways have increasingly abandoned veiling and seclusion, these practices, ironically, have spread among the lower-middle and lower classes'. The veil has also become, in some circles, an affirmation of nationalism and a rejection of western culture and society, further complicating interpretation of its use.

12.   Boulding, p. 718.

13.   Since countries rarely fall neatly into categories, it might be more appropriate to view the Arab world as on a continuum, with North Yemen and Saudi Arabia at the most conservative end, and Egypt, Tunisia, South Yemen and Lebanon at the other extreme.   An example of this, applied only to the status of women in personal and family matters, is seen in Table 3.8.

14.   Anderson, p. 15.

15.   With the adoption of the Swiss Civil Code in 1926, Turkey completely secularized its judicial system, and eliminated all legal distinctions between men and women. This included the elimination of polygyny, equality of divorce rights, obligatory civil marriage, and the right of a Muslim woman to marry a non-Muslim man. Although no Arab nation has completely followed this path, an awareness of Turkey's example (and a variety of reactions to that example)

permeates the rest of the Arab world.

16.   In her book *The Hidden Face of Eve: Women in the Arab World* (London: Zed Press, 1980) Nawal El Saadawi devotes an entire chapter to 'Arab Pioneers of Women's Liberation' which is a more elaborate treatment of this topic.

17.   Ali, p. 38.

18.   El Saadawi, pp. 171-72;   Nadia Abbott, 'Women', in *Mid-East: World Center Yesterday, Today and Tomorrow*, ed. Ruth Nanda Anshen (New York: Harper and Brothers, 1956), p. 207;   Gabriel Baer, *Population and Society in the Arab East*, trans. Hannan Szoke (New York: Praeger, 1964), p. 45.

19.   Charles C. Adams, *Islam and Modernism in Egypt* (New York: Russell & Russell, 1933), p. 237; Baer, p. 43.

20.   Thomas Philipp, 'Feminism and Nationalist Politics in Egypt', in Beck and Keddie, p. 286.

21.   The Union, which published *The Egyptian Woman* to acquaint women with its goals, focused its attention on education for women, raising the minimum age for marriage, equality of job opportunities, the abolishment of prostitution, and the establishment of orphanages, women's centres and workshops where unemployed women could earn wages.   The Union also engaged in social and political activism, and was instrumental in facilitating the passage of the Family Law of 1929 which, although it made no fundamental changes in the social structure of Egypt, rectified many of the worst abuses of polygyny and divorce (al-Sa'id, p. 382; Abbott, p. 208).

22.   Aziza Hussein, 'The Role of Women in Social Reform in Egypt', The Middle East Journal 7 (#4 1953): 445;   Elizabeth Warnock Fernea and Basima Qaltan Bezirgan, 'Huda Sh'arawi: Founder of the Egyptian Women's Movement', in Fernea and Bezirgan;   Joseph Graziani, 'The Momentum of the Feminist Movement in the Arab World', *Middle East Review* 2 (Winter 1974): 27.

23.   Laila Khaled, 'Women's Liberation', *Funny Farms* (1974): 2. See also Carolyn Fluehr-Lobban, 'The Political Mobilisation of Women in the Arab World', in Smith; El Saadawi, pp. 169-183; David Gordan, 'Women of Algeria: An Essay on Change', *Harvard Middle East Monograph Series* 19 (Cambridge: Harvard University Press, 1968); and Committee for the Revolution in Oman and the Arabian Gulf, 'Women and the Revolution in Oman', *News from Oman and Southern Arabia* 36 (November 1980):   entire issue.

24.   Frantz Fannon, *A Dying Colonialism* (New York: Monthly Review Press, 1965), p. 38.

25.   Peter C. Dodd, 'Youth and Women's Emancipation in the United Arab Republic', *Middle East Journal* 22 (1968):   160.

26.   For example, in Tunisia, the 1975 census data indicated that 38 percent of women in urban areas were literate, while only 11 percent of rural women were able to read and write.   Similarly, in Egypt (1976), 48 percent of urban women were literate, compared to only 13 percent of rural women.   The overall literacy rate for women which is usually reported (in these cases, 17 percent and 22 percent) does not reveal these geographic differences.

27.   Audrey Chapman Smock and Nadia Haggag Youssef, 'Egypt:

From Seclusion to Limited Participation', in *Women: Roles and Status in Eight Countries*, ed. Janet Zollinger Giele and Audrey Chapman Smock (New York: John Wiley, 1977), p. 51.

28.   Kamla Nath, 'Education and Employment among Kuwait Women', in Beck and Keddie, p. 177. It is interesting to reflect on the importance of oil wealth and modernisation in enabling Saudi Arabia to educate females in this way - a true merger of traditional and modern ways of life.

29.   Smock and Youssef, pp. 41, 53; *National Basic Intelligence Factbook* (Washington, D.C.: U.S. Government Printing Office, 1978). Estimate assumes a 50:50 sex distribution in population.

30.   I appreciate Janet Abu-Lughod for pointing this out to me.

31.   Richard Mead and Alan George, 'The Women of Libya', *Middle East International* 25 (1973): 20.

32.   Fatima Mernissi, *Beyond the Veil: Male-Female Dynamics in a Modern Muslim Society* (Cambridge, Massachusetts: Schenkman Publishing Co., 1975), p. 92; UNESCO, *Statistical Yearbook* (Geneva: UNESCO, 1980), Tables 3.2, 3.4, 3.7.

33.   Ann Deardon, ed. *Arab Women* (London: The Minority Rights Group, 1975); *The Middle East and North Africa 1979-80* (London: Europa Publications Ltd., 1979), p. 619.

34.   *Random House Dictionary of the English Language* (New York: Random House, 1973), pp. 1691-96; *The Middle East and North Africa*.

35.   Abid al-Marayati, *A Diplomatic History of Modern Iraq* (New York: Robert Speller and Sons, 1961), p. 70.

36.   The large attendance of both men and women at the Universtiy of Kuwait is made possible by tremendous oil wealth. Not only is education at all levels free (and considered socially desirable for both sexes), but high wages and a commitment by the Kuwaiti government to provide jobs to all who wish them means young people can be spared the necessity of working until their studies have been completed, secure in the knowledge of a well-paying position once they are out of school (Nath).

37.   Judith Tucker, 'Egyptian Women in the Work Force', *MERIP Reports* 50 (August 1976): 5.

38.   Talad Asad, *The Kababish Arab: Power, Authority and Consent in a Nomadid Tribe* (London: C. Hurst and Co., 1970), cited in Cynthia Nelson, 'Women and Power in Nomadic Societies of the Middle East', in *The Desert and the Sown*, ed. Cynthia Nelson (Berkeley: University of California, 1973), p. 44. See also Lois Beck, 'Women Among Qashaq'i Nomadic Pastoralists in Iran' in Beck and Keddie; Ester Boserup, *Women's Role in Economic Development* (London: St. Martin's Press, 1970); and Paters in Beck and Keddie.

39.   Juliette Minces, 'Women in Algeria', in Beck and Keddie, pp. 166, 170.

40.   Richard Harwood, 'The Stern, Man's World that is Saudi Arabia', *Manchester Guardian*, 5 March 1978.

41.   Dodd, pp. 163-4.

42.   Dodd (p. 171) found that the educational level of a boy's mother was more important in determining his degree of support for,

or opposition to, female employment in the public sphere than either social class or geographic location.

43.   Youssef, p. 42.

44.   Youssef, p. 35.

45.   Smock and Youssef, p. 59.

46.   Carolyn Fluehr-Lobban, 'Women and Social Liberation: The Sudan Experience', in *Three Studies on National Integration in the Arab World* (nc: Association of Arab-American University Graduates, March 1974), p. 74.

47.   Mona Hammam, 'Women and Industrial Work in Egypt: The Chubra El-Kheima Case', *Arab Studies Quarterly* 2 (Winter 1980): 59.

48.   Penelope Turing, 'Women in Jordan: Progress and Participation', *Middle East International* 60 (June 1976): 21; Charis Waddy, 'Egypt's Modern Woman - the First Fifty Years', *Middle East International* 24 (1973): 29.

49.   According to al-Sa'id (p. 387) approximately 60 percent of Arab women live in rural sectors and an additional 25 percent live in small towns. This leaves only 15 percent of Arab women in the urban areas where the greatest reforms have occurred.

50.   Jean Paul Charnay, *Islamic Culture and Socio-Economic Change* (Leiden: E.J. Brill, 1971), p. 62.

51.   Kathleen Newland, 'Women in Politics: A Global Review', *Worldwatch Paper* 3 (Washington, D.C.: Worldwatch Institute, 1975), p. 7.

52.   Ali, p. 139; al-Sa'id, p. 386; Dearden, pp. 7, 17; Newland.

53.   Frederick W. Frey, *The Turkish Political Elite* (Cambridge: The M.I.T. Press, 1965), p. 155.

54.   Nancy Tapper, 'The Women's Subsociety among the Shahseven Nomads of Iran', in Beck and Keddie, pp. 383-388.

55.   al-Sa'id, p. 385.

56.   Tabitha Petron, 'South Yemen Ahead on Women's Rights', *Middle East International* 48 (June 1975): 25.

57.   Algeria is one such nation. In 1970, divorce by repudiation was reinstated, and many of the anticipated legal changes have not materialised, despite the egalitarian words of the Algerian Constitution (Baols and Steihm 1974:76). This illustrates a theme which has run through this essay: As long as rights and opportunities for women remain a commodity which the male half of the population can grant or withdraw at will, women cannot and will not achieve complete emancipation. Only when women have political, economic and personal power and have taken control over their own lives will they be able to assure that their rights are upheld.

58.   Conversation with an anonymous Saudi women.

59.   Elizabeth Davies, 'Lifting the Veil', *Middle East International* 44 (1975): 29.

60.   Fatima Mernissi, 'The Moslem World: Women Excluded from Development', in *Women and World Development*, ed. Irene Tinker and Michele Bo Bramsen (New York: Overseas Development Council, 1976), pp. 35-36.

61.   Janet Abu-Lughod, 'Book Review', *Arab Studies Quarterly* 1 (Fall 1979): 377.

62.   al-Sa'id, p. 380.

Chapter 4

THE LITERARY TREATMENT OF WOMEN IN THE MAGHREBIAN NOVEL IN FRENCH

Anne-Marie Nisbet

The novel is a relatively new and 'foreign' genre in Maghreb. Encouraged by French writers (like Camus, Audisio, Robles), it arose from the wars of independence as a product of historical and social factors. It is at once a portrayal of society, an investigation of the hidden aspects of economic, cultural and psychological experience. As years went by, the novel went hand in hand with a new aesthetic approach, specifically Maghrebian.

Since independence (1957 in Tunisia and Morocco, 1962 in Algeria), literature has seen distinct stages of development. Between 1962 and 1968, few works appeared. During the post-colonial period, social structures underwent profound changes. Novelists were analysing and interpreting the new social order in an attempt to identify its essential elements.

In 1968, writers started questioning their relation to authority. They found themselves in a dilemma: was it true, as the authorities claimed, that the novel failed to meet the aspirations of the people, did it ignore the need for social realism? Or was it a political threat because it was too critical, too daring or too bourgeois? Certainly, the majority of novels written in French challenged a socio-political system deemed to be inadequate. This was especially so in Algeria and Morocco. In Tunisia, it was notably the short story written in Arabic which played this role. *issues*

Among the fundamental questions with which the new generation was grappling, two predominated: the quest for identity and the liberation of women. I propose to provide an introduction to the literary treatment of the latter.

The question of the liberation of women is important for two reasons: it illustrates the traditional dependence on men and it is at the heart of the quest for personal, cultural, linguistic and national identity.

One point must be emphasised from the start. In Western literature women enter the capitalist arena not as men's equals but as their adversaries. This is not at all the case in the Maghrebian novel. Tunisian, Moroccan and especially Algerian women have had the chance of taking part directly in the struggle against colonisation on an equal footing with men. However much ethnic and socio-political conditions may differ in the three countries, their family and cultural structures have a common basis, namely the Islamic-Arab tradition. As far as social structures are concerned their 'evolution' followed different paths, as it does still, in the three countries.

Tunisia took the lead with President Bourguiba's *Code du Statut des Personnes* in 1956. The *Majalla* took effect from 1957 despite some opposition from irate religious figures who reproached Bourguiba for trying to 'parfaire l'Islam deja parfait en soi'.[1] In Morocco, various decrees amended laws dealing with inheritance, divorce and polygamy. In Algeria, reforms came more slowly because the reaction to colonisation brought about a distortion of certain religious practices. As a result, Algerian novels place far more emphasis on the condition of women and their importance in the evolution of social structures.

The treatment of women characters in the Maghrebian novel has seen several stages of development. Djamila Debeche and Assia Djebar were the first to introduce them. Until then, women had been absent from novels because

> Cela correspond a la realite et a la faible place que les hommes leur laissent dans la vie du pays.[2]

The new image of women, free from all constraints, did not correspond at all, according to the critics, to the traditional image of the Arab or Muslim woman. However, the movement had begun.

In the second stage women formed an integral part of the novel's structures, thus reflecting and challenging the existing social structures which were thought antiquated. Women had become a divisive force in a system where the decision-making powers were restricted to men.

In *Le Scorpion*,[3] Albert Memmi insists on the vital need to achieve a synthesis of the traditional and the modern. Tahar Ben Jelloun, in his poetic novel *Harrouda*,[4] questions the established tenets of order and history while Aicha Lemsine in *La Chrysalide*[5] presents the ideal (and very romantic) metamorphosis of the 'modern' woman, thus attracting justifiably bitter criticism.

At the third stage, women, now considered as an 'exorcised evil', becomes the catalyst in the process of releasing the forces of the unconscious. The function of the dream, which she consistently dominates, is no longer the expression of man's conscious goals but of his unconscious desire, which must surface if he is to be free. The dream quest exposes at best a divided self as in Rachid Boudjedra's *L'Escargo entete*,[6] but more often a fragmented self as in Mohammed Khair-Eddine's *Une Vie, un reve, un peuple, toujours errants*.[7] For other authors, like Mohammed Dib in *Habel*,[8] love is the only healing force. In every case, however, this neo-mythical figure of the woman is used to revive the aborted revolutionary ideal through the power of fantasy.

NARRATIVE STRUCTURE

Despite the differences which exist in the three countries (Morocco, Algeria and Tunisia), the social context of the Maghrebian novel in general bears the marks of alienation and depersonalisation. Any alteration to the status of women triggers a total upheaval, for she is the central 'pillar'. She dramatises the clash between two cultures (modern and traditional) and two universes (real and imaginary). This confrontation, in its turn, creates a dynamic social force in which she, together with the people, contributes to the making of history.[9] She connects several levels of meaning: social, political and psychological. In each case, she is the pivot of the forces in conflict: the individual and society, the people and power, the ideal and reality. The crises of civilisation are linked to those of the female condition. This is what Driss Chraibi exposes in two of his novels, *La Civilisation, ma mere!* .... [10] and *Un Ami viendra vous voir.*[11]

The female character is more or less 'real' according to the authors and the country (or even the area) to which they belong. However, the more she is depicted as being despised or ignored in real life, the more the woman appears in the hero's dreams (mostly nightmares). At any rate, whether it be in real life or in dreams, she is never considered as a person or spoken to as an equal.

Desipte the severe criticism of certain customs and practices, the image of the woman and the various ways in which she is presented in the novels show that her fate is closely linked to and dependent on the male. Either he possesses the authority and uses it, or he wavers between the attitude which traditionally has been his and the new necessity of personal as well as social progress.

I must emphasise that the Maghrebian novel in French is not at all 'feminist'. The exploitation of women (whether real or fictional) is denounced because it is felt to be the cause of the evils which beset society. However, the social criticism is only a step towards a more comprehensive denunciation. The woman, with her plight, her struggle, her metamorphosis, her hopes, is an example to follow, the model of a synthesis of conflicting elements of a 'productivite mythique et une situation existentielle'.[12]

In the novels, the female character cannot be explained, interpreted or understood except in terms of authority and privilege. As a divisive force, the female character destroys the traditional relationship which grants privileges to a man. However, a more difficult task is to grant her some of these privileges: for example, the right to education, the right to speak, the right to participate in social and political life.

In Maghrebian fiction, this total destructuring of society does take place although the main 'active' hero is always a male: the father, the son or the brother. The woman (mother, daughter or sister) is represented, however, as being also invested with power. Therefore, the man who has liberated her must confront her at a later stage. 'Privileged' in turn, this new female social being destroys the myth of economic success linked to masculinity. As she threatens this myth, so she becomes the source of anguish and phantasm. Therefore, the male must now exorcise this anguish of the devouring female, of incest and androgyne which is 'tapie un coeur meme de la personnalite individuelle et collective'.[13]   This male-female relationship must progress from rebellion to exchange because the woman is an important element in the dynamics of self-realisation through self-discovery.

The authors emphasise particularly the need to demystify sexuality. Male and female share in the sexual misery which leads to submission and exploitation, a situation aggravated by the traditional acceptance of Fate in the societies involved. On one hand, man must not consider himself as only a sexual being; on the other, he must exorcise the inhuman image of the woman and of the mother that tradition, taboos and society force upon him. The woman, as she appears in dreams, is a source of anguish because she destroys desire. Man must now conquer the dynamics of desire if he is to exercise power. This is why the woman is the main agent of liberation. She is the one who, traditionally, introduces the male and the child to the world of the irrational. In return, she allows them to exorcise the phantasms which annihilate them. This aspect is particularly strongly presented by authors like Ben Jelloun and Boudjedra.

Analysis of the novels reveals the use of a common narrative structure: the female character condemns personal and social failure, demystifies history and originates the liberation of man through the power of fantasy. She is therefore represented as a paradigm of the revolutionary ideal which must remain alive if man wants to be free.

At the end of the process is self-realisation or, in Rachid Boudjedra's terms, the 'therapeutical catharsis'. The function of the female characters is to contribute to a new ontological definition of man because, through the process of dreams, she helps him conquer space and time and master his destiny.

For certain writers - Nabile Fares, for example, and particularly Mohammed Dib - the woman in the novel is above all a mediator between man and the universe. Love is the only way to the discovery of the self, of the other and of the world. For other writers, like Mohammed Khair-Eddine, Rachid Boudjedra and Tahar Ben Jelloun, she is always associated with delirium, wounds, blood.

In every case, however, she is the paradigm of the people, submitted to exploitation and deprivation. Therefore, her function goes beyond exposing the problem of emancipation. As presented in the novels, the female character is meant to implement as well as represent a total and revolutionary process by which existing social, political and psychological conditions are overthrown. This implies a revolutionary reorganisation of society from its economic structures to its grammar, as Fatima Mernissi puts it.[14]

THE NEED FOR COHERENCE

The Maghrebian novel in French has taken various forms, from folkloric description to the 'poetic novel', each step being a little more critical about a more and more complex social structure. The female character reflects this movement: rebellion against authortiy, regression and progression, and concomitant dangers of remaining static. She is the symbol of a dynamic society of all the various cultural elements which are, if not contradictory, at least controversial. This dynamic process can be analysed, as we have seen, on the syntagmatic level of the narrative structure.[15] However, this process repeats itself at every level of analysis, and we can summarise it as follows:

MYTH	SACRED (Closed)	PROFANE (Open)
Mythical space	Nature	Culture
History	Independence	Integration to the world
Time	Past–Present	Future
Woman as a metaphor	Divisive force	Agent of liberation
Society	Authority and Privileges	Opposition to the system through sexuality
Psychology	Project and incestuous desire	Purified desire Triumph of the self
BALANCE	IRRATIONAL	REASON

The dynamic synthesis should generate the reconciliation of the two poles of conflict in order to create a coherent and balanced world. This is the ultimate aim, inasmuch as the situation of the woman is closely linked to the economic, political, cultural and religious conflicts.

It is possible to reconcile the opposites as Aicha Lemsine proposes in *La Chrysalide*? It seems particularly doubtful, for she presents a ready-made society, a very stable situation which, to a large extent, does not correspond to reality. On the contrary, is everything chaotic in the Maghreb, as Mohammed Khair-Eddine suggests in his novels, particularly *Une Vie, une reve, un peuple, toujours errants*? Between these two extremes, we find Albert Memmi's heroes, depicted as the products of a specific socio-political situation and as trying to find a way to escape death. Rachid Boudjedra's heroes unleast their fantasies to escape petrification. Mohammed Dib isolates his from the world and makes them consume themselves in a mystical flame. Nabile Fares' characters run the risk of remaining 'performing myths', as Jamal E. Ben Cheikh puts it.[16]

If the authors do not offer any solution, as the critics constantly point out, it is because there is no immediate or ready-made response to the problem. The point is not to choose one or other political orientation, but to integrate them so as to create a third, specific answer which would satisfy the specific demands of authenticity, progress, legitimacy without the author's becoming a 'fonctionnaire de regime'.[17]

The attitudes of the writers may vary, but they are all derived basically from the common situation of being trapped between two systems (if not exposed to cross-fire). The conflicting elements of the systems are determined as follows:

TRADITION AND CONTINUITY

To a certain extent, the 'mobility' of the female character is all the more important since the authors want to stress the dangers of petrification. The woman refuses inertia, traditional fragmentation, discontinuity. She offers the possibility of continuity. However, this continuity does not mean tradition, as Jacques Berque explains:

> La continuite n'est pas la tradition. La personnalite collective est a revendiquer non pas en terme de tradition, mais de possibilite de se reconstruire elle-meme.[18]

The true debate is not, or is no longer, between tradition and modernity, but between tradition and traditionalism. As we often find in the novels, one must go back to the sources to 'recover memory', that is to establish necessary links with one's past. In contrast, traditionalism denies tradition, because it 'substitue le dogme a la question ontologique: primaute d'un Etant Immuable et eterne'.[19]

This attitude implies calling into question the theological structures from which the social institutions derive. If the forces of the past are so strong as to prevent any possibility of balance, as is the case in Rachid Boudjedra's *L'Escargot entete*, then society at large is threatened because the individual cannot communicate with the present and is, therefore, doomed to a symbolic confinement.

MODERNISM AND SPECIFICITY

No longer is there any question as to whether or not the Maghrebian woman should 'copy' the Western woman. Very often, discussions about modernity take place in the context of criticism of service imitation of exogenous elements. However, this is quite different from modernism, which implies a social dynamic involving the re-arrangement of endogenous elements. This attitude has been attacked, however, as an ideological manifestation of reformism and liberal intellectualism because, as a result of Maghrebian society's contact with industrial civilisation, its deep structures are not always clearly perceived.[20]

Here again, specificity is not the end result of an a priori definition. It must take into account the concepts of identity and personality, with the subsequent trial and error they imply. This is precisely what the female characters reflect in their search for 'affinity' rather than 'altercation'.[21] This attitude is sometimes presented with humour as the novelists scoff at the accepted 'wisdom' which forbids a critical approach to the problem of identity. However, it is again revolutionary because it implies a reconsideration of Time and History.

TIME AND DURATION

One of the aspects of this new collective identity in the making is its relationship with time. Again, the diversity of female characters in the Maghrebian novel reflects the multiplicity of time within the same civilisation.[22] First, as the origin of rebellion, comes the woman's defiance of determinism. She does not correspond at all to the traditional, never-changing image nor to reality because this image is precisely what the authors refute. The various aspects of the character represent the end of the 'eternal return' and the refusal of a cultural conformism which is felt to be artificially imposed. The woman is depicted as belonging to a hypothetical future which she herself helps create. Second, she facilitates a double regressive process. From a sociological point of view, regression implies a return to the past and social sclerosis, often described in terms of 'petrification'. From a psychological point of view this return to an earlier stage is a process necessary for self-discovery. It 'unveils' the unconscious and reveals definite situations resulting in an alternative. Either man locks himself in his traumatic past and, like the hero of *L'Escargo entete*, falls back into fatalism, which renders his future development impossible. Or he comes to terms with his past and assesses his present situation, thus making his way in History.

The woman, who is very often openly identified with the memory of the Maghrebian people, destroys the all-embracing concept of historical time. Her history, like that of the people, consists of breaks, ruptures, failures, wanderings, differences, etc. As woman/memory, she links the various stages together. She questions the concept of duration: the past does not mean the nostalgic memory of bygone days. The historical pessimism of certain authors derives less from a metaphysics than from a fundamental humanism. Man is his own enemy. A critical look at oneself and the past shows that colonisation alone is not responsible for the evils which beset society. The basic problem is to be found in man and in his relationship with the world. What is needed is a balance between the acceleration of history on one hand and the evolution of values on the other. Regression, therefore, is both historical and personal. The hero of *L'Escargot entete* is a 'man of the Third World'; Mohammed Khair-Eddine's hero is a representative of 'les pauvres paumes'[23]; Tahar Ben Jelloun's Harrouda is the people at large. Thus the liberation of the individual's unconscious forces is the only way to the people's liberation.

To question duration is also to repudiate fatalism, which puts man into God's hands and takes away from him any historical initiative. To denounce 'le Destin fourbe'[24] is a necessary condition for the decolonisation of history. However, man makes history at the same time as history makes him, and the Maghrebian novel denounces through the woman a 'lay transcendance' which endows History with an absolute primacy. Yet when man assumes God's initiative and responsibility, he risks being trapped in a circle of purely theoretical values (reason, progress, history, science, etc.) which would expose him to new forms of exploitation. The irrational, timeless, even disorderly aspects of the female character are symptomatic of a 'free' historical being who is not always able to master his or her destiny. None of the female figures presented in the novels could be considered as 'real'. However, all of them belong to a trend of thought which advocates the refusal of pure subjectivity and, at the same time, the refusal of historicism. The phenomenon of 'cultural schizophrenia' which seems to plague the characters indicates the difficulty of forming a collective identity which would be neither totally irrational nor subjected to the sterilising and alien categories of reason. The elusive nature of the feminine being, ambiguous and uncontrollable, which is associated with the collective being, is able to destroy any illusion of 'mastery'. The woman is presented not as an object in the hands of authority, but as the partner of the people in a subversive enterprise.

REASON AND SUBJECTIVITY

The ambivalence of the female character, as presented by Mohammed Dib in *Habel*, dramatises the struggle between an unbounded subjectivity and an unpredictable reality which must be dominated.

The relationship between man and woman, a mixture of horror, fear and desire, parallels that between man and nature. Because of her superiority in the domain of the irrational, woman can cope with the irrational of a world which can never be completely dominated by power or order. After the urgent rejection of a strictly functional relationship between man and woman, an emotional, even sensual relationship becomes necessary. As rationality becomes all-embracing, the forces of fantasy are unleashed. This is particularly so in the case of Rachid Boudjedra's meticulous and paranoiac civil servant. Surface rationality starts to be challenged by all the deep, unconscious and irrational forces. *L'Escargo entete* certainly points out the danger of ignoring the unconscious. However, the hero loses touch with reality as a result of his failure to re-examine his situation in a new perspective.

A balance between reason and subjectivity should have the effect of avoiding two risks: an over-attachment to the past and a rootless modernism. These are precisely the two extremes within which the female character functions. Between these two extremes, one finds a world of possibilities, and it is this world which the novelists explore through their writing.

WRITING AND TREASON

Woman and writing are inextricably linked in the quest for the integrity of the person. From the point of view of the dominant ideologies, both constitute 'une mise en question ou un veritable scandale'.[25]

In fact, the metamorphoses of the female characters do not merely reflect the historical process. They evoke, through the medium of the word, all the problems which the Maghreb must face: under-development, sexual misery, culture, identity, language. Woman and writing call power and privilege into question while proposing a new image of man, defined in terms of his own self. By returning to childhood, to the mother, he can begin to rediscover his self and his consciousness. This journey into the past also brings him to an awareness of the contradiction inherent in the fact that he belongs to both 'la source initiale et le temps fou'.[26] As the poet Nissaboury says in a most revealing way, in the cave you find 'ni pere ni mere'.[27] There, man is alone and naked, but real. Just as woman, in her struggle for progress, demands the right to speak, the novelist, in his struggle for survival, demands the right to criticise.

The female character and writing play the same destabilising role in the same process: 'Lutter contre l'oppression mais aussi demythifier et abattre les croyances venimeuses qui font remper le peuple'.[28] Social criticism implied through the female character is so much more outrageous in that it is expressed in terms which the establishment finds offensive, for 'dans un certain contexte politique, ce n'est pas la verite qui compte mais le souci de ne pas faire le jeu des ennemis du peuple'[29]!

Symbolically unveiled by writing, stripped of mystical interpretation, woman abandons the private, sacred, taboo world for the public, profane one. Thus, she threatens man's very being since she attacks his honour. This scandal makes her a traitor or an outcast.

Finally, we can say that the function of the female characters is linked to all the other upheavals in the Maghreb, but can offer only hypotheses and strategies.

And the writers? Because they defy the Church by refusing to write mere parables lauding the doctrines of Islam; or because they resist the State by ignoring the dictates of social realism; or because they deny an illusory uniculture by insisting on writing in the language which in itself demonstrates the very contradictions they are striving to resolve; because of these stands, will they be treated as pariahs? 'Coupee de ses racines, que peut dire cette litterature maghrebine sinon son erance et sa deraison sur un sol qui l'engloutira?'[30] Abdelkebir Khatibi's question finds a response in Jamal E. Ben Cheikh's declaration:

> Nous decouvrirons la science et l'amour. Nous fonderons la science de l'amour. Les hommes sont reduits a aimer ou a se demettre. Et si cela s'appelle utopie, et si cela s'appelle mensonge, et si cela s'appelle delire, dites-moi ou est l'arme qui aneantira cette race de fous.[31]

REFERENCES

1.   .... 'perfect an already perfect Islam'.
2.   'This corresponds to reality and to the insignificant role men grant them in the life of the country'. Mammeri, M. Interview, *El-Moudjahid*, 10 December, 1967. For a more detailed analysis of the Maghrebian novel in French see: Nisbet, A.-M. *Le Personnage feminin dans le roman maghrebin de langue francaise. Representations et fonctions.* Sherbrook, Naaman, 1982.
3.   Memmi, A. *Le Scorpion*, Paris, Gallimard, 1969.
4.   Ben Jelloun, T., *Harrouda*, Paris, Maurice Nadeau, 1973.
5.   Lemsine, A. *La Chrysalide*, Paris, Editions des Femmes, 1977.
6.   Boudjedra, R. *L'Escargot entete*, Paris, Denoel, 1977.
7.   Khair-Eddine, M. *Une Vie, un reve, un peuple, toujours errants*, Paris, Denoel, 1978.
8.   Dib, M. *Habel*, Paris, Seuil, 1977.
9.   The woman and the people follow the same stages of development. After independence, the people rebuild their forces and enter the world scene. The 'new woman', on the other hand, breaks free from the old structures, becomes a persona and then finds her place in a new social system.
10.   Chraibi, D. *La Civilisation, ma mere!* ...., Paris, Denoel, 1972.
11.   Chraibi, D. *Un Ami viendra vous voir*, Paris, Denoel, 1967.
12.   A mythical productivity and an existential situation. Fares, N. 'Histoire, souvenir et authenticite dans la litterature maghrebine de langue francaise', *Les Temps Modernes*, No. 375 bis, October 1977, pp. 397-406.
13.   .... 'hidden in the innermost individual and collective personality'. Bouhdiba, A. 'Le royaume illusoire des meres', *Jeune Afrique*, No. 825, 5 November 1976, pp. 66-68.
14.   Mernissi, F. *Beyond the Veil: Male-Female Dynamics in Modern Muslim Society*, Schenkman Press, 1976, p. 108.
15.   As Jacques Berque explains it, societies can only progress as a coherent continuum, that is to say as a syntagm, if they are capable of mastering the substitutions as paradigm.
16.   Ben Cheikh, J.E. 'La litterature algerienne horizon 2000', *Les Temps Modernes*, No. 375 bis, October 1977, pp. 355-377.
17.   .... political civil servant.
18.   Continuity is not tradition. One must assume the collective personality not in terms of tradition but in terms of possibility of reconstructing the self. Berque, J. *L'Orient second*, Paris, Gallimard,

1970, p. 39.

19. .... substitutes dogma for the ontological question: the primacy of an immutable and eternal Being. Khatibi, A. 'Le Maghred comme horizon de pensee', *Les Temps Modernes*, No. 375 bis, October 1977, pp. 5-20.

20. Chelod, J. *Les Structures du sacre chez les Arabes*, Paris, Maisonneuve, 1964, p. 247.

21. Ben Jelloun, T. 'Le sens d'une renaissance culturelle', *Le Monde Diplomatique*, February, 1975.

22. On the various aspects of Time, cf: Chelhod, J. 'L'espace et le temps sacres', in *Les Structures du Sacre chez les Arabes*, op. cit. Charnay, J.-P. 'Temps sociaux et interpretation historique en Islam', *Studia Islamica*, XXVIII, 1968. Hasnoui, A. 'De quelques acceptations du temps dans la philosophie arabo-musulmane', in *Le Temps et les philosophies*, Paris, Paijot, 1978, pp. 55-82.

23. .... the poor wandering bums.

24. .... treacherous Fate.

25. .... a challenge or an outright scandal. Fares, N. 'Histoire, souvenir et authenticite', op. cit.

26. .... primeval source and incoherent time. Khatibi, A. *La Memoire tatouee*, Paris, Denoel, 1971, p. 200.

27. Nissaboury, M. *Plus haute memoire*, Rabat, Atlantes, 1968, p. 13.

28. Struggling against oppression but also demythologising and destroying the insidious beliefs which subjugate and debase the people. Khair-Eddine, M. 'Foncation organique de l'ecriture', in *La Memoire future*, Paris, Maspero, 1976, pp. 50-62.

29. In a certain political context, it is not the truth which matters but rather the refusal to play the game of the enemies of the people. Ahmed Sefrioui, quoted in: Dejeux, J. 'Regards sur la litterature maghrebine d'expression francaise', *Cahiers nord-africains*, No. 61, October-November 1957.

30. Cut off from its roots, what can this Maghrebian literature express if not the insane wanderings in a land which will eventually swallow it up? Khatibi, A. *La Memoire tatouee*, op. cit., p. 12.

31. We will discover knowledge and love. We will found the science of love. Man must love or surrender. And if that is Utopia, and if that is delusion, and if that is delirium, show me the weapon which will annihilate this race of fools. Ben Cheikh, J.E. 'Verset pour une distribution des prix', Numero special 'Litterature algerienne', *Europe*, July-August 1976, p. 137.

Chapter 5

EARLY FEMINIST MOVEMENTS IN THE MIDDLE EAST:
TURKEY AND EGYPT

Leila Ahmed

In her article on Egyptian women in the early nineteenth century Nada Tomiche draws attention to a curious and terrible story. Following Napolean's invasion of Egypt and during the brief French occupation (c. 1800) General Menou married a woman from Rosetta - converting to Islam and calling himself Abd Allan Menou in order to do so. He treated her 'in the French manner':

> .... led her by the hand into the dining-room, offered her the best seat at the table and the tastiest pieces of food. If her handkerchief fell to the ground he would hurriedly pick it up. When this woman had narrated these things at the Rosetta bathouse, the others began to hope for change and signed a petition to the Sultan Kabir (Bonaparte) to have their husbands treat them in the same manner.[1]

It was probably this petition and similar audacities on the part of the women which, Tomiche speculates, led to the carnage which was to follow - again as reported by a French contemporary - 'I have heard Franks who were in Egypt when the French army left this country. They described to me horrible deeds which occurred in harems at the time. Up to several thousands of women were massacred, poisoned or drowned in the Nile'.[2] Not least curious about this story is how it has been allowed to almost completely drop out of history. A shadow of it though appears in the pages of Al-Jabarti (1745-1825) who so voluminously chronicled the Egypt of his day. The last great historian in the ancient tradition, he laments the 'pernicious innovations' and the 'corruption of women' that the French occupation brought about, and he records that the daughter of one of the greatest religious notables, Shaykh al-Bakri, was killed after the French departed because she had mingled with them and dressed like a French woman.[3]

Despite this bloody beginning, change in the status of women in the Muslim world following upon increased contact with and openness to the West most often in fact proceeded smoothly and relatively rapidly. Far and away ahead of other Middle Eastern societies in reforms relating to women was Turkey. The last Middle Eastern peoples to convert to Islam, the Turks were also responsible for developing furthest the institution of the harem: to the point where it most nearly embodied and was even almost militaristically organized around the notion of woman purely as sex-object and reproduction machine. Thus, in addition to 'a multitude of female slaves and eunuch-guards' the Turkish harem contained 'a group of women chosen for their beauty and destined for the pleasure and service of the sultan. They were organized in pyramidical form, at the base of which was the Sagrideler (Novices), from which class, after wholesale eliminations, the most talented in arts and beauty were promoted to Gedikliler (Privileged Ones). It was at this stage that they first came into direct personal contact with the sultan and in accordance with his desires, he chose those who were to share his bed. A girl thus honoured was known as Gozde (In Favour) and if the relationship showed any sign of permanence, she was promoted to the rank of Ikbal (Fortunate)'.[4] Aside from the imperial harem, city women rarely left the house and were hemmed in even when they did by imperial decrees as to which areas they may go, and precisely prescribing their dress and comportment in public places – and even specifying the days of the week on which they might leave the house. But even during the most repressive pre-reform periods, some women were privately educated (daughters of professors, generals, judges) and a few became famous as writers, composers, calligraphers – and one as an astronomer. It was not they however, nor indeed women at all, who first called for reforms regarding women's condition.

The first moves in that direction came about as part of and to begin with apparently as only casually and incidentally a part, of the Ottoman's attempts to modernize Turkey. Already in the eighteenth century as the scientific revolution in Europe and advances in military technology placed Europe clearly in the lead, and Turkey ceased to be able to treat with it as an equal, the need for reform and for learning and adopting Western methods, particularly in military fields, began to be voiced. The influence of Western embassies in the imperial capital now increased, European advisors were sought out and Turkish men were sent to newly opened embassies in Europe, both as diplomats and to learn the languages and arts of Europe. By the 1820s there existed in Turkey a group of Turkish men who were familiar with the European heritage of ideas. In 1826, as a preliminary step to re-organising the army the Janissaries were disbanded and suppressed – a year taken now as marking the beginning of the *Tanzimat* or period of reform. In the following year male student missions were sent to various European countries; in the same year a medical school staffed by Europeans was opened in Istanbul to train doctors for the army; in 1831–1832 two military schools were opened, and in 1838 primary and secondary schools for male civilians, and then in 1842 a school for midwives. Midwives presumably were thus singled out among all women because they constituted a group of women practising what even males had agreed to recognize as a profession; courses were offered, Taskiran informs us, by a European specialist, and 'the government made all practising midwives attend';[5] (it was at about this time too, it will be remembered, that the male takeover of gynaecology was occurring in Western countries). Midwives moreover were evidently of a class of women that even at that early date could be taught by men without any concern for their 'honour'. Not so other Turkish females. An attempt was made to start a girls' primary school in the 1850s – but failed because there were no women teachers and the school had had to be be staffed by elderly males. In 1870 a teachers' college for women was opened, staffed, as its regulations stipulated, 'only by elderly men of good character' and in addition elaborate precautions were taken to ensure that student and teacher were always chaperoned and never met face to face.[6] Fifty places were offered, and 32 women enrolled. In the same year a girls' primary school was also opened.

In the last decades of the nineteenth and early in the twentieth century the emancipation of women and women's education became issues that were much discussed and written about, particularly by the Young Turks and their reformist and nationalist sympathisers – many of whom were graduates of the new schools established earlier that century. Numerous newspapers were established in which, for the first time in Turkey, a wide range of political and social reforms were freely discussed and called for. The new graduates, including graduates of the teachers' college for women, published articles on the need for reform. In 1895 the first Turkish women's weekly began to be published, its contributors were almost all women. It emphasized the need for education for women and 'was successful in serving the three major aims of how to become a good mother, a good wife, and a good Moslem'.[7] Eminent male writers took up the issue. Ziya Gokalp wrote: 'In the future, Turkish ethics must be founded upon democracy and feminism, as well as nationalism, patriotism, work, and the strength of the family'; Ahmed Agaogly stressed that progress in the Islamic world depended upon two factors: literacy and the emancipation of women, and Tevfik Fikret, that 'When women are debased, humanity is degraded' – and this last was adopted by the feminist movement as its slogan.[8] The emancipation and education of women thus became one of the reforms agitated for by the nationalist revolutionary movement and henceforth progress in this area was to be linked to and to follow from the success of that movement and the access of its members to power. Until the end of the First World War and the dissolution of empire the reformers were involved in power struggles with the sultanate. Nevertheless they were able to put through a number of reforms and to make important advances particularly in education. More girls' schools were opened, as were lycees (which allowed for the more extended period of study of ten years) and more women's teacher training colleges. In 1912 the nationalists opened community centres which offered lectures and cultural events which women as well as men were encouraged to attend – and which women did attend, with the result that a charge was brought against the centres claiming that 'Turkish women were being corrupted and incited to revolt, and that they were playing the violin and reading poetry'.[9] In 1914 some lectures at the University of Istanbul were opened to women: and in September of that year a university for women, affiliated to the teacher training college, was established. In 1920 women were transferred to Istanbul University proper, and the following year segregation was formally ended. Over the same years, the war years, the quality and scope of women's lives dramatically changed; because of the War, women worked in government offices, in the post office, and as factory workers, nurses and street cleaners, replacing the men who had gone to war. At the end of the War the Sultan signed a treaty with the European powers agreeing to the dismemberment of Turkey. This was unacceptable to the nationalists and after a rebellion in which Anatolian women played an important part (and in which also Halide Edib Adivar one of Turkey's leading women writers and feminists, took part, serving as corporal, sergeant and sergeant major) the Sultan was overthrown and Turkey was declared a republic.

Kemal Ataturk, the country's new president, argued strongly for women's equality and full participation in labour on the grounds that only thus could Turkey progress. 'A country which seeks development and modernisation must accept the need for change', he said in a speech in Izmir in 1923, 'the weakness of our society lies in our indifference to the status of women'. One of Turkey's major needs he declared was 'the enlightenment of our women in every field. They shall become educated in science and the arts; they shall have the opportunity to attend any school and attain every level of education'. At first Ataturk argued for change in the status of women – as also with other of the government's modernising secularist objectives – while seeking to conciliate and even to strategically invoke Muslim orthodoxies and the values of Muslim orthodoxy (Turkey was the first Muslim nation to broach feminist issues on a national political level, and the attitudes and formulations he made use of were to be repeatedly resorted to this century by other modernising Muslim states – Iran for instance (before, of course, this recent revolution) and Tunisia. Thus, the education of women was legitimized within a Muslim framework by stressing its importance if women were to properly fulfil their 'highest duty' as mothers ('paradise', runs a much-quoted *hadith* – dictum of the Prophet's – 'lies under the feet of mothers'). Furthermore, Ataturk declared in this same speech at Izmir, not Islam but 'distorting customs' originating in corrupt palaces had been responsible for the oppression of women: 'Our enemies accuse us of being under the influence of religion, and they attribute our stagnation and decay to this factor. That is a great mistake, for nothing in our religion requires women to be inferior to men'. On the contrary, he continued – referring here to another popular *hadith* (plaques inscribed with it adorn many an Arab office now, particularly in ministries of education) 'the pursuit of knowledge is a duty enjoined upon every soul'.[10]

This conciliatory line however he soon abandoned. On the issue of women the conservatives were proving too entrenchedly conservative. A committee appointed in 1923 to review Islamic family law and to suggest ways of making it more equitable to women, came up with no significant proposals – so that their review constituted in effect an endorsement of the law as it stood. In the same year the National Assembly plunged into angry debates as to whether a law permitting men and women to sit in the same compartments on public transport (and not as previously required in separate compartments) would be violating the principles of a Muslim republic. Radical reform therefore within the old framework, particularly in relation to women, was evidently highly unlikely: and the old framework was consequently summarily jettisoned. Turkey was declared a laic state, the veil outlawed, and the Islamic family code abolished and replaced by a civil code (1926) modelled on that of Neuchatel, Switzerland. In 1930 women were given the vote.

Thus by 1930 Turkish women had achieved legal and civil status equal to that of women in the more advanced of European countries – and against how different a background, how different a reality. Details such as the debate over sex-segregation on public transport, or the warning issued to women in 1911 by Sheykh-ul-Islam not to wear European dress, or the arrest in 1920 of the first Turkish female actor to appear on stage – simply for appearing on stage – give some notion of how oppressively interfering and restrictive the state had been towards women. And other records of moments in women's lives more sombrely make evident how ordinary and 'natural' a part of the fabric of living was the pain of women, the deprivation of women – and how shot through that reality was with, reduced to its essence, contempt for women, for women's pain, women's lives. The debate on sex-segregation for public transport for instances translates thus into the reality of experience: the law requiring segregation meant that on boats sailing the Bosphorus and running between Istanbul and the islands, women were obliged to stay in closed cabins below deck. 'When women were finally permitted to remain on deck, a female author described her feelings at being able to watch the sea in the open air during the one-hour boat trip with such zest that one would think she was crossing the ocean for the first time'.[11] To cite only one more such record – a description of the deposed Sultan Abdel Hamid's harem – the last imperial harem – in 1909:

> One of the most mournful processions of the many mournful processions of fallen grandeau that passed through the streets during these days was one composed of the ladies of the ex-Sultan's harem on their way from Yildiz to the Top-Kapu Palace .... These unfortunate ladies were of all ages between fifteen and fifty and so numerous that it took thirty-one carriages to convey them .... Some of them were sent to the Old Seraglio in Stamboul, but this old palace of the early Sultans had fallen into such a state of disrepair that it was found to be unsuitable for them and they were sent back to Yildiz. Finally they were collected in the Top-Kapu Palace in connection with one of the strangest ceremonies that ever took place there. It is well-known that most of the ladies of the harems of Turkish sultans were Circassians, the Circassian girls being very much esteemed on account of their beauty and being consequently very expensive .... The Turkish government telegraphed to the different Circassian villages in Anatolia, notifying them that every family which happened to have any of its female members in the ex-Sultan's harem were at liberty to take them home, no matter

whether the girls had been originally sold by their families or had (as was the case in some instances) been torn from their homes by force.

In consequence of this, a large number of Circassian mountaineers came in their picturesque garb into Constantinople, and on a certain fixed day they were conducted in a body to the Old Palace of Top-Kapu, where, in the presence of the Turkish Commission, they were ushered into a long hall filled with the ex-Sultan's concubines . . . . all of whom were then allowed to unveil themselves for the occasion . . . .[12]

This passage, it should be stressed, records a moment in the lives of the women of Abdel Hamid's harem – but also a moment in the lives of all women who witnessed it and all women who heard of it: just as simply the very existence of harems as a 'natural' part of their societal environment must inescapably form part of and inerasably scar the consciousness of every woman and child.

The new laws were to be slow in their impact on rural, as distinct from urban, Turkey. For instance, the law abolishing polygamy gave property rights only to children issued from marriages performed by the secular authorities; despite this, and despite the fact that their children would be considered illegitimate as well as disinherited according to the civil code, men in the rural areas continued to marry more than one wife, performing, only the religious ceremony. By 1950 the Turkish authorities had granted legal status to eight million children (at a time when the population was at the 21 million mark), which gives some idea of the prevalence of the habit.[13] In urban Turkey however the old patterns swiftly disappeared and women entered, and since have been freely entering, the professions (one-third, for instance, of university professors now are women). For the urban Turkish woman the battle for equality is now essentially no different from, and probably no greater than, that of her Western sisters.

In Egypt as in Turkey the advocates of feminist notions, those who most strongly urged upon their society the importance of educating women and of raising their status, were, initially, men. As in Turkey these ideas grew not out of a new concern for women *per se* or a new pressing sense of the wrong done women, but out of the conviction that educating women and raising their status was part, and perhaps even the chief part, of a necessary process of regeneration and transformation that society must undergo for the sake of progress and the advancement of the nation (men). In the centuries immediately preceding the emergence of these ideas, European travellers in the Middle East had regularly commented on what they were alternately fascinated or appalled by, or envious of: the undisguisedness of male control of women in Muslim societies, and the explictness and unequivocalness with which women were regarded and treated as inferior. It was in this respect that Muslim societies most visibly and glaringly differed from Western societies, and as the Muslim world declined in power Westerners contemplating the 'degenerateness', 'despotism', 'vice' and general 'backwardness' of the Muslim East came up with some unanimity with the idea that at the root of these lay the Muslim world's low valuation of and its degradation of women. In perceiving the status of women as perhaps the single most important aspect of their society in need of reform, Middle Eastern thinkers were therefore to some extent accepting and endorsing the diagnosis of their societies arrived at by Western men. Sometimes indeed their self consciousness respecting the condition of women in their societies in the eyes of Western men is transparently present in their declarations, and even the need to appear differently to those Western observers is explicitly given as an incentive for reform. Ataturk for instance declared: 'In some places I have seen women who put a piece of cloth or a towel or something like that over their heads to hide their faces, and who turn their backs or huddle themselves on the ground when a man passes by. What are the meaning and sense of this behaviour? Gentlemen, can the mothers and daughters of a civilised nation adopt this strange manner, this barbarous posture? It is a spectacle that makes the nation an object of ridicule. It must be remedied at once'.[14] Nevertheless it would be erroneous to conclude that in endorsing Westerners' diagnosis Muslim thinkers were simply facilely and uncritically echoing their ideas: on the contrary, their conclusions were often developed from - notably Qasim Amin's in Egypt - a comprehensive and rigorous analysis of their societies and a perfectly lucid sense of the various oppressions operating within them. Similarly, the observation that women were blatantly oppressed in Muslim societies and were conceived of and treated as inferior, cannot be summarily dismissed as invalid because it originated in the West, on the grounds that Western representations of the Islamic world have often been disingenious and often informed (as who would deny) by an explicit or insiduous desire to denigrate it. Distorted and disingenious as Western reflections of the Islamic world may indeed have been, this of course in no way alters the fact that the reality of women's oppression in the Middle East is indeed ugly and unacceptable.

Ideas of reform and feminist notions emerged in Egypt out of a process that closely paralleled that which occurred in Turkey. Egypt was of course at least nominally part of the Ottoman empire, and their societies were sufficiently linked for their rulers and thinkers to be acting out a shared societal experience and a commonality of ideas. In some ways even, it was Egypt, under the more dynamic Mohamad Ali, who led the way. Mohamad Ali had, for instance, sent student missions to Europe the year before Turkey decided to do so. Similarly, the medical school in Egypt was established just before that of Turkey. And in Egypt also, as already implied, it was an openness to Western thought, and among those who set themselves to explore the Western heritage, that reformist and feminist notions were born. (Consequently it is not 'ironical' as many writers like to remark, that it was men who first, in Middle Eastern societies, called for the emancipation of women: since such ideas in every case followed from contact with Western thought, far from being ironical it is entirely unsurprising that it was men, (who to begin with, alone had access to Western thought) who were the first to voice them. And such ideas here even found a champion in a leading Azhar-trained, religious figure - Sheikh

Mohamed Abdou, scholar at the ancient religious university of Al-Azhar and eventually (1899) Mufti of Egypt (head of the whole system of religious law) and one of the most prominent Egyptian reformists. Their more secular exponent, Qasim Amin (1865-1908) published his work on the emancipation of women (Tahrir al-mara'a) in 1899, arousing a storm of protest; in the few months after its publication a series of books and pamphlets were published attacking it - and a very few, supporting it. In reply Amin published a second book in 1900, on the 'new woman' (al-Mar'a al-jadida): these two books are still looked upon in the Arab world as the seminal works on feminism, and can still, so liberal are they seen as being, rouse considerable hostility among conservative and religious elements.

But while the issue of women and the improvement of their condition was thus as live among Egyptian intellectuals as it was among Turkish, no government, party, or male individual with access to power was to adopt it as a central issue, and this was to make a crucial difference to the evolution of the women's movement in Egypt. On education for instance, the government in Egypt made some moves towards making it available for women, but stopped well short of what was done in Turkey over the corresponding period. Thus a school was founded in 1873 which in 1874 admitted 400 girls, but by 1920 there were still only five government primary schools for girls, and the government made no attempt to provide more advanced schooling for girls until 1925, when it opened the first secondary school. Private education by contrast seems to have been thriving[15] so that when the Egyptian university opened its doors to women in 1928, six women were in a position to enrol in the medical faculty, and a number of others in the faculty of arts and science. Privately educated women contributed in the first decades of the century to journals established then in Cairo mainly by Levantine women (who were predominantly Christian, and in one or two cases, Jewish).

Women in Egypt were to be much more actively involved in the fight for their rights than they had been in Turkey; whereas in the latter from the inception of feminist ideas to the granting of new rights to women had in fact been a remarkably swift process, in Egypt many of the rights granted their Turkish sisters in the 20s were not - and still have not - been granted. In the 20s a committee was set up in Egypt, just as one had been in Turkey, to review Islamic family law with a view to revising it towards a more equitable treatment of women: and as in Turkey the committee essentially endorsed the law as it stood in all its male-favouring aspects, and came up with no proposal for any amendments of any significance. But unlike Turkey (and later, in different degree, Tunisia) the government did not see fit, nor has any government since seen fit, to set aside the inevitably conservative findings of conservative religious committees and sever women's civil and marital status from the heritage of Islamic received ideas.

The first political action in which women became involved in Egypt was in 1919, when hundreds of women marched together through the streets of Cairo in support of the nationalists against the British. In the lead were women who were the wives of prominent nationalist politicans - among them Huda Sha'rawi. Although the issue had been a nationalist and in no way a feminist one, nevertheless women's very participation seems to have empowered them to henceforth take a stand on issues relating to the status of women. In 1922 Huda Sha'rawi formed, with her friends, the Egyptian Feminist Union and was from then on throughout the 20s and 30s to be a central figure in the women's movement. In 1923 she led the Egyptian women's delegation to an international women's conference in Rome. It was at this time that she cast off her veil (there are a number of versions of this event: that she took it off on her way to Rome and never wore it again, that she cast it into the sea as she stepped ashore in Alexandria on her return from Rome, etc.) and thus inspired Egyptian women (middle and upper class women) to also cast off theirs. (Much is made at the moment in literature on women in the Middle East of the fact that it was mainly women of the middle and upper classes who wore the veil, and of the fact that the necessities of work meant that working women did not in fact much wear it: therefore, the argument runs, the issue of wearing or not wearing the veil is really of very little significance since only a very small number anyway were affected. It consequently seems necessary here to briefly state the obvious. It is the idea of the veil much more than the veil's material presence that is the powerful signifier; of women's proper seclusion and relegation to a private world, of their proper non-participation, passivity and even invisibility - metaphorically signified by the veil - in the public domain. And so as long as the veil is notionally present in a society (as it is when it is in use among a portion of the society and particularly among the elite, to whose status and mores others aspire) then that society is as surely riven in two, and women - whenever possible in practice, and always, on the ideal plane - are non-participant, passive and invisible).

During the 1920s and 30s Sha'rawi and the group of women she gathered around her were active in seeking to increase education for women and in urging the government (with some success) to provide free public education for girls. It was also partly their efforts which secured women's entry into university. They campaigned too for reforms in Islamic family law - though unfortunately without any significant success (and to this day reforms in this area have been minimal). Thus Sha'rawi delivered a lecture in 1935 at the American University in Cairo, in which she called for 'the restriction or abolition of polygamy'. At this point in her speech, Woodsmall has reported, two white-turbaned sheikhs from Al-Azhar, of whom there were many in the audience, rose up and shouted 'Long live polygamy!'[16]

Sha'rawi's call for 'the restriction or abolition' of polygamy is typical in its cautious conservatism. As Woodsmall observed, Sha'rawi 'carefully based her demands for social reform on the spirit of the Koran and has not promoted reforms which do not have Islamic sanction. For example her claims for equality of education for girls have been based on the teachings of the Koran'; similarly when protesting against polygamy she 'recognised the exceptions for polygamy which are granted by the Koran (adultery, childlessness and incompatibility). One has the feeling', continued Woodsmall, 'that this policy of maintaining a careful balance between Islamic teaching and social reform, which is followed by Madam Sharawi and the Feminist Union is dictated more by political expediency than by religious conservatism'.[17]

No doubt this conservatism, even decorousness, to women's demands and the style of women's demands, was essential to some at least of those demands being granted; and no doubt Woodsmall was to some extent right in seeing it as a matter of political expediency. However this blend of conservatism, decorousness, of zeal in wishing to be seen to be observing the proprieties, even to be emphasizing them, and to be seen to be absolutely and irreproachably 'correct' on one's position with respect to Islam/Arabness is a fundamental trait not only of Sha'rawi's feminism but of feminism and feminists in the Arab world generally. And far from being a matter simply of diplomacy, of astute women practising 'the art of the possible', it is rather, I would argue, a position imposed upon feminism and feminists by the internal needs of the Islamicate civilisation – and it is an imposition that has had the consequence that feminism in the Arab world has never (or never until at least the last few years) seriously challenged that civilisation's conception of the role of women, and has been a matter, when all is said and done, of requesting merely (and often deferentially) that injustice be trimmed a little here and there, and oppression perhaps sugared over a little here curbed slightly there.

Malak Hifni Nassef's famous 'ten points' document beautifully exemplifies both the qualities mentioned above as typical of the history of Arabic feminism, and of how feminism then becomes merely an instrument by which the fundamental assumptions of the culture are reinforced. Nassef, honoured as one of the pioneers and founding mothers of Egyptian and Arab feminism, drew up and presented to the Legislative Assembly in the 1910s ten points that she considered should form the basis of reforms for women; and the document, ostensibly in support of women's rights in fact overwhelmingly endorses the Arabic civilisation's traditional conception of women. Thus its points include: (point One) teaching of true religion for girls – the Koran and the true Sunna; teaching domestic science, theoretical and practical health laws, training of children, etc.; appointment by the government of a certain number of girls to be trained in medicine and education, sufficient to meet the needs of women in Egypt (argued from her stand that it was more suitable for women to be treated by women doctors); the maintenance of the welfare of the country and the refusal, as far as possible, to adopt that which is foreign; and (point Ten) the appointment of men to see the above carried out.[18]

Similarly in more recent times the feminist Doria Shafik, a protege of Sha'rawi's, in her numerous writings advocates quite as carefully as her mentor a balance between Islamic teaching and feminist reform, and like Sha'rawi and Nassef, she remains scrupulously correct and loyal in her attitude to Islam. (Shafik is most associated with the demonstrations she led in the early fifties demanding the vote: at one time provoking al-Azhar to respond (1952) by issuing a declaration prepared by a committee of sheikhs – including, for all one knows, the two who had cheered for polygamy when Sha'rawi spoke in 1935 - stating that women were unfit for the vote on the grounds that they 'are swayed by emotion and are of unstable judgement. Whereas men are impartial and balanced, women stray from the path of wisdom even when they have the advantages of a good education'.[19]

A Middle Eastern historian of the women's movement wrote in 1951, in praise of Sha'rawi, that 'it was extremely pleasant and important' to be able to record that 'this outstanding woman, although profoundly imbued with European culture, never tried to separate her feminist activity from the principles of Muslim religion'.[20]   This, together with the Nassef point quoted above regarding the importance of the refusal to adopt anything foreign, points to an element that is very much at the heart of the matter; the issue of remaining loyal to one's culture, of, although 'modern' and 'European' in one's outlook, not betraying one's society's (and one's own) cultural identity, construed as a matter of remaining loyal to what is seen as being its symbolic core, 'Islam' (and in Arabic societies also 'Arabness'). The stance adopted by the Egyptian women feminists just described, the feminism was essentially in tune with an Islam properly understood, was (as we saw above with regard to Turkey) a stance adopted early on by Muslim reformers when first, under the impact of the West, ideas of the need to reform women's status began to emerge in Islamic societies (the two early Egyptian reformers mentioned earlier, Abdu and Amin, also adopted this stance). But Islam and feminism are naturally incompatible (as Ataturk found) and the literalism of Islamic civilisation and the complete enmeshing of the legal tradition with this literalism means that this incompatibility can only be resolved, if any significant advance is to be made in the status of women, by the complete severance (which Ataturk resorted to) of Islamic tradition from the issue of the position and rights of women. To say that Islam and feminism are incompatible, represent ideologies with irreconcilably conflicting interests, is not to say anythig extraordinary. Feminism is irreconcilably in conflict with all or nearly all currently entrenched ideologies. It is in conflict with the dominant ideologies in the West to more or less the same extent that it is with the Islamic. But Western women can be critical and radically critical of their cultures and prevalent ideologies - although these in the West as elsewhere also exert their pressures, perhaps more subtly than elsewhere, towards conformity and acceptance. For the Islamic woman however there is a whole further dimension to the pressures that bear down on her urging her to silence her criticism, remain loyal, reconcile herself to, even find virtue in the central formulations of her culture that normally she would rebel against: the pressure that comes into being as a result of the relationship in which Islamic society now stands with the West. The Islamic civilisation has a very special, even unique, relation with the West so that the issue of cultural loyalty and betrayal perhaps at issue in any culture in this new age of the simultaneity and accessibility of a range of cultures, is experienced with unique force and intensity in that civilisation. This stems from the unique history of the relationship of the Western and Islamic worlds - for centuries in a confrontational stance in which, in the first centuries, Islam was in the ascendant; and then for centuries, as the balance began to shift in favour of the West, in mutual fear and hostility, each afraid that the infidel power would triumph and the infidel take over. In our case the Infidel has taken over: first gallingly as colonisers and now in the flood of ideas and general appurtenances of Western civilisation abstract and material it is pervasively everywhere. So that the Islamic civilisation is not only a civilisation unambiguously on the defensive, emphasizing and re-affirming old values, but also a civilisation that finds itself re-affirming them the more intransigently and dogmatically and clinging to them perhaps the more obstinately because it is re-affirming them against, and safeguarding them from, and old enemy. It is this underlay that gives the issue of cultural betrayal its particularly disturbing quality for the Islamic and Arabic individual; and this I believe, rather than some inexplicable hold which Islam exerts over members of its civilisation, accounts for the persistence with which reformers and feminists repeatedly try to affirm (with remarkable tenacity and often too with ingenuity) that the reforms they seek involve no disloyalty to Islam, that they in fact are in conformity with it, and if not in conformity with the letter and actual text of the culture's central formulation, then in conformity with what nevertheless is still there somehow, in the spirit not quite caught by the words.

It is only when one considers that one's sexual identity alone (and some would not accept this) is more inextricably oneself than one's cultural identiy, that one can perhaps appreciate how excruciating is the plight of the Middle Eastern feminist caught between those two opposing loyalties, forced almost to choose between betrayal and betrayal.

And this issue is evidently still a live and central one for Middle Eastern women. It is precisely the matter of cultural loyalty that currently skillfully manipulated in militantly Islamic societies is behind such bizarre phenomena as women marching and protesting, in the name of cultural authenticity, in support of the revoking of their own rights.

REFERENCES

1. Nada Tomiche, The Situation of Egyptian Women in the First Half of the Nineteenth Century in W.R. Polk and R.L. Chambers, (ed.) Beginnings of Modernisation in the Middle East. Chicago: University of Chicago Press, 1966, p. 180 (citing Clot-Bey, 1840).

2. Ibid., p. 180.

3. Abd al-Rahman al-Jabarti, Aja'ib al-athar fi'l-tarajim wa'l-akhbar Cairo 1904-1905. This work was written in 1322 A.H. Vol. III, p. 202.

4. A.D. Alderson, The Structure of the Ottoman Dynasty. Oxford: Clarendon Press, 1956, pp. 79-80.

5. Tezer Taskiran, Women in Turkey. Istanbul, 1974, p. 32.

6. Ibid., p. 38.

7. Ibid., p. 35.

8. Ibid., pp. 45, 43.

9. Ibid., p. 44.
10. Ibid., pp. 55-56.
11. A. Afetinan, The Emancipation of Turkish Women. Paris: UNESCO, 1962, p. 42.
12. N.N. Penzer, The Harem. London, 1936, pp. 20-21.
13. Fatima Mansur Cosar, Women in Turkish Society in Louis Beck and N. Keddie (ed.), Women in the Muslim World. Cambridge, Mass.: Harvard University Press, 1978, p. 127.
14. Ataturk's speech at Kastamonu in 1925. Quoted in B. Lewis, The Emergency of Modern Turkey. Oxford: Oxford University Press, 1961, p. 165.
15. Arslam Bohdanowicz, The Feminist Movement in Egypt. The Islamic Review, August, 1951.
16. Ruth F. Woodsmall, Moslem Women Enter a New World. New York: 1936, p. 121.
17. Ibid., p. 404.
18. Charles C. Adams, Islam and Modernism in Egypt. New York: 1933, pp. 235-237.
19. The Muslim World, Vol. 42, 1952, p. 307.
20. Bohdanowicz, op. cit., p. 29.

Part Three:

CONTEXTUAL REALITIES

Chapter 6

TRADITIONAL CEREMONY IN AN ISLAMIC MILIEU:
MELENGGANG PERUT AMONG MALAYSIAN WOMEN

Heather Strange

The Malay women's seventh-month-of-pregnancy ceremony, *lenggang perut* or *melenggang perut* (rocking the stomach) is the subject of this paper.[1] In order to place the ceremony in the religio-cultural context, unity and diversity within Islam and some broad ideas about pregnancy ceremonies are discussed before I turn to the specifics of the Malay example.

I follow writers such as Radcliffe-Brown and Norbeck in defining rituals as customary or conventionalised, collective actions that are repetitive and focus on the supernatural. A ceremony is made up of a specific sequence of ritual acts.

The *lenggang perut*, as I have observed it, has a 'prologue' and three distinct parts, each of which comprises a sequence of ritual acts. It is a type of ceremony referred to as syncretic in that it combines elements from several traditions: old, 'magical' practices (i.e. early problem-solving techniques), later Hindu-Buddhist concepts and, more recently, Islamic components. My observations were made in a cluster of villages in Trengganu, a northeast coast state of Peninsular Malaysia (Malaya). The ceremony is not limited to that state; it is performed in other parts of the country although the details vary. And there is (or at least has been in the past) one major variation: whether or not the expectant father has any ritual role.

My concluding discussion concerns the ceremony in the context of two current and frequently conflicting trends in Malaysia: Islamic fundamentalism and socio-economic development.

ISLAM

The official religion of polyethnic Malaysia is Islam but the Federal Constitution guarantees freedom of religion to everyone - Hindus, Buddhists, Christians, and others. Malays, by Constitutional definition are Muslims.

The basic unity of Islam rests upon 'The Five Pillars of Faith', five prescribed duties. Briefly, they are:

1.   **The profession of faith.** 'There is no God but God; Muhammad is the Messenger of God'.

2. **Prayer.** There are five prescribed prayer periods each day, preceded by ritual ablutions.
3. **Zakat.** The term is usually translated into English as 'alms-giving'.
4. **Fasting.** Muslims must abstain from eating, drinking, and all sensual pleasures between dawn and dusk throughout the ninth month of their lunar calendar, Ramadan. Fasting should encourage reflection about one's personal behaviour and promote self-discipline.
5. **The pilgrimage (Hajj) to Mecca.** The *hajj* is required of all Muslims who are physically and financially able to undertake it. Those who do, acquire the honorific titles, *Haji* (for men) and *Hajjah* (for women).

Like any widely spread religion, Islam is characterised by diversity. Diversity has been discussed and analysed by sect, school of law, degree of orthodoxy, or tendency to reformism;[2] by whether particular groups tend to be militant, bourgeois, reactionary, socialist, and so on;[3] and through time, within particular cultural contexts that a believer experiences and practices the religion.[4] Further, it is generally accepted that, within a cultural context, there is an 'expert', theological level of interpretation as well as local variations. As stated by el-Zein:

> People acknowledge the general concepts dictated by the *Ulama*, but they choose to live according to more particularistic notions of Islam, which conform with the patterns of their daily experience.[5]

The 'particularistic notions' in combination with the 'general concepts' can result in many permutations. Geertz's 1964 study, for example, analyses three distinct variants of Islam in Java.[6] No similar study has been undertaken in Malaysia. However, it can be noted that in Peninsular Malaysia there are two systems of *adat* (Malay customary practices) that modify Islamic law and affect rites of passage in different ways. At both the theological and local or folk levels of Islam there is another dichotomy - by gender.

Islam is egalitarian in that women and men are equally responsible for living according to the basic tenets of the religion. However, the *Ulama* is composed of men; mosque and *shariah* court officials, and other formal leaders are men; and men are acknowledged as being 'in charge of women'.[7] Further, women are forbidden to perform *any* religious act during menstruation; they may not pray, touch the Holy Qur'an, fast during Ramadan, enter a mosque or prayer house, and so on. Thus from menarche through menopause, biological periodicity constrains the Muslim woman from fully practising her religion. There are no parallel limitations upon men. The restrictions are not necessarily negative from a Muslim woman's point of view. Many women enjoy having several days each month that are not structured by religious requirements. Pro or con, however, women's religious rights and obligations are different from and more limited than those of men.

A common western stereotype of Muslim women pictures them as secluded, confined to their homes or permitted to emerge from them only if wearing all-enveloping cloaks and veils. Some Muslim women are secluded and enter the public domain, if at all, only with the protection of veils and cloaks. In Saudi Arabia, these practices are universal; in some other societies they are associated with the elite, showing that a man can afford to keep his wife in *purdah*, as discussed by Cohen,[8] Mernissi[9] and others.

Yet seclusion and veiling are not Islamic requirements. The Qur'an enjoins modesty upon women but it nowhere requires them to be sequestered nor to cover their faces in public.[10] Malay women, unless they are members of one of the small, recently formed, fundamentalist groups, neither live in seclusion nor veil themselves.

Women in Malaysia have access to all levels of education and are represented in most professions; they are under-represented in higher education and in many professions. They have a great deal of mobility as adults, e.g. urban, academic women attend international conferences and rural women, at least in the states of Trengganu and Kelantan, control marketing of most commodities. Women have the same right to vote and stand for election as men; a few serve in Parliament – both Houses – and in the Cabinet.

Under civil law, women have the same contractual rights as men. Muslim law, pertaining to marriage, divorce, inheritance rights and other family or religious matters is not egalitarian. A man can divorce his wife by a simple statement of repudiation; she can divorce him only by appeal to a *shariah* court and then only under specific circumstances. A man has the right to have four wives simultaneously, a wife has no right to protest, and there is a current trend toward revoking state laws that constrained men from polygamy.[11]

Islamic ceremonies associated with marriage and funerals as well as calendrical observations such as those for the Prophet's birthday and Ramadan are essentially male events. An observer is struck by the gender-based and very different forms of participation: women prepare appropriate foods, men pray, perform other rituals, and eat.

Important ceremonies for women appear to be lacking until Malay *adat* practices are examined. These customary practices predate the arrival of Islam in the Malay Peninsular in the fourteenth century and some of their elements are undoubtedly very old. Today, there are two major traditional ceremonies that involve Muslim women: the *bersanding* and the *lenggang perut*. The *lenggang perut* is most clearly a women's ceremony, and a type of ceremony that must be among the oldest known to humanity.

TRADITIONAL RITUALS AND CEREMONIES

Attempts to attract positive forces and ward of negative forces may predate the appearance of our species. But it is among *Homo sapiens* traditions of the European Upper Paleolithic cultures (around 40,000 to 10,000 years ago) with their development of sculpture, bas relief, and cave painting that the abundant evidence allows for diverse and multifunctional interpretations, including the magico-religious.[12]

A fertility focus has been interpreted for many of the ancient symbols painted or incised on the walls of caves and the 'Venus' or 'mother goddess' figures appear to depict pregnant women. Whatever the form of the art, it seems likely that:

> Many of the representations may have had to do with birth ceremonies, to ease the pains of childbirth and ensure safe delivery.[13]

Although this viewpoint may never be proved, it is both likely and logical. Danger and pain have always been integral to pregnancy and childbirth - miscarriage, bearing a deformed child, death of the mother, the infant, or both, are possibilities that every women, her family, and her society must face. A majority of the world's women live within systems that attempt to ward off danger, attract positive forces and reduce suffering by recourse to traditional medical and supernatural means. The argument that many rituals grew out of human feelings of anxiety about aspects of life beyond our control and, coming full circle, that rituals serve to dispel these anxieties and beget confidence among the participants seems especially apt with regard to pregnancy and childbirth.

In his 1908 discussion of pregnancy ceremonies, van Gennep pointed out that it is often difficult to determine 'whether a particular ceremony is a rite of passage (i.e. celebrating an individual's change from one status to another), a rite of protection or a sympathetic rite'.[14] A sympathetic rite is one that symbolically represents the desired reality, the idea being that things and actions that are similar influence one another. Van Gennep also noted that dual purpose of many pregnancy rites: 'to facilitate delivery and to protect mother and child .... against evil forces',[15] particularly during a first pregnancy, thus emphasizing the protective and sympathetic themes of such rites.

It is apparent that the three themes can be encompassed in one ceremony. When danger is obvious, as during pregnancy and childbirth, the protection and sympathetic aspects should be dominant, with the latter including actions to facilitate delivery. The idea that the ceremony gives recognition to a process of status change is not, however, precluded. Van Gennep emphasizes first pregnancy as the one most likely to be celebrated ritually, as in my Malay example, and it is the first pregnancy that normally results in changing a woman's status to mother. The themes may have arisen independently but they are now interwoven by thousands of ceremonial repetitions, each at least slightly different from the one before it, by generations of practitioners.

Ceremonies during the seventh month of a first pregnancy are reported for a number of Asian socieites: the Todas of India, the Melanau of Sarawak, the Malays of southeastern Thailand, the Javanese, the Atjehnese of Sumatra, the Malays in several areas of Malaya.

LENGGANG PERUT IN TRENGGANU VILLAGES

The following description of a seventh-month ceremony as performed in northeastern Malaya (Peninsular Malaysia) is based upon personal observations of *lenggang perut* (or *melenggang perut* according to my informants) and discussions with village women in coastal Trengganu. Some of the details varied, but essentially the ceremonial patterns observed were the same. I write in the 'ethnographic present' although the ceremony that I describe was held in 1966 for Asiah, who was eighteen years old at the time. Asiah's was the first ceremony of its kind that I attended and my field notes about it are the most detailed.[16]

Alleviation of anxiety is one function of the *lenggang perut*: the express purpose of many of the rites is to make the pregnant women's delivery easy and safe. The rituals should encourage confidence in anyone who believes in them. And by performing the ceremony, the *bidan kampung* (village midwife) makes the commitment to be present at the birth. The *lenggang perut* also brings together women of the kin group and friends, often from several villages, and reaffirms reciprocal obligations among them as well as providing an opportunity for socialising.

The Prologue
Around 2.00p.m. on the ceremonial day, seven man known for their piety gather in the front room of Asiah's parents' home to recite verses from the Qur'an. A brass container filled with water to be used in the *lenggang perut* is placed in their midst. The recitations are beneficent and are believed to confer beneficial properties on the water. The recitations continue for approximately half and hour before the men pray. The water is removed. Other men join the seven for additional prayers and all are served a celebratory meal (*kenduri*) before departing around 3.30p.m.

While the men are reciting in the front room of the home, Asiah's mother and kinswomen, under the direction of the *bidan kampung* (village midwife) arrange all of the things needed for the ceremony in the back room.

The Ceremony – Part I
Asiah, wearing one sarong knotted at her waist by her mother, and with another held over her breasts, is led to her parents' bed by the *bidan* who helps her to lie down with her arms at her sides. The women assisting in the ceremony stand in a semi-circle, from the head of the bed, around the right side and the foot. The *bidan* and Asiah's mother are on the left side of the bed (to Asiah's right) and there are two large trays holding an assortment of ritual paraphernalia nearby. The *bidan* straightens the seven folded cloths (*kain lepas*, a large square cloth used for multiple purposes, e.g. making a sling to support an infant close to its mother's body) beneath Asiah's waist, unties the young woman's sarong and folds it so as to preserve Asiah's modesty while exposing her abdomen. Asiah is extremely nervous and discomfitted, her hands grasping the sarong to keep it from slipping

any further. The *bidan* climbs onto the bed and squats next to Asiah.

One of Asiah's kinswomen, Fatimah, a young woman who has given birth to a healthy child and had no miscarriages, is the main assistant. It is she who hands the *bidan* the ritual objects and, throughout the ceremony, sprinkles sweet-smelling herbs upon a container of embers near the bed. Fatimah hands the midwife a small container of coconut oil, some of which is lightly massaged over Asiah's abdomen, an obvious sympathetic rite, for the women say that it will make the womb slippery and the birth easy.

Next, Fatimah gives the midwife a weaving shuttle into which young shoots from the pandanus plant, coconut palm, and areca palm – three hardy plants – protrude. The *bidan* brushes the shoots down Asiah's abdomen and then rolls the shuttle, an implement used only by women, down it. Homemade cloth has been replaced by commercially manufactured goods but there is nevertheless a possibility of sympathetic creation here: as a woman created whole and perfect cloth, so, by the association, she creates a whole and perfect child.

A green coconut is the next object to be rolled lightly down Asiah's abdomen. The coconut is *kelapa sulong* and a person's first-born child is *anak sulong*. The coconut is followed by a hard-boiled egg (a fertility symbol) smothered in *tepong tawar*, a flour paste mixture with mystical properties to ward off evil. The coconut is split over a tray and the water from it is rubbed on Asiah's abdomen.

The *bidan* rubs coconut oil into Asiah's hair and places a strand of the hair in the young woman's mouth, telling her to suck it three times. During the birth, when Asiah is in pain, the *bidan* will pull the same strand into her mouth and tell her to bite on it. Again, there is the idea of slippery oil easing the birth process.

The ends of the top cloth folded under Asiah's waist are grasped by two kinswomen, one of them having moved to the left side of the bed. They use the *kain lepas* to gently rock Asiah's body, thus beginning the process of 'placing the baby properly' for an easy birth, one of the major goals of the ceremony. It must be noted that many women state categorically that such 'placing' is not possible, although they add that 'long ago' people believed it was. Now, they say, the ceremony is to *minta selamat* (ask for safe-keeping) from God.

The first cloth is pulled from under Asiah, from her waist to her feet. One of the women takes it and moves it, draped, up to Asiah's head. Then the woman on the other side grasps two of the corners and the cloth is spread like a canopy and passed from Asiah's head to her feet before it is discarded at the foot of the bed. The same process is followed with all of the cloths.

Beneath the seventh cloth there is a cord made from seven strands of twisted thread which has bits of medicinal roots with pain-killing and 'opening' properties threaded along it as well as a ring brought from Mecca. The cord is tied around Asiah's waits by the *bidan* who tells her to wear it for seven days.

The container of embers and aromatic herbs is passed over Asiah, along the right side of her body from head to toe three times by one woman, then taken by another who passes it along the left side three times, always from head to foot. All of the objects – coconut, egg, cloths, and so on - have been moved over Asiah's body in one direction, from head to feet, the direction the baby must move at birth.

A tray on which there is a large container of unmilled rice (whole, unbroken rice) and a coconut topped by a sopping wad of thick, unbleached thread is passed to the *bidan* who squeezes the water, prayed over earlier by the seven men, on Asiah's face. Then the midwife fixes the sarong around the young woman's waist because Asiah is not allowed to knot the cloth lest she impede the birth process.

The Ceremony - Part II

Asiah rises and is led to the kitchen. Turmeric root, salt, and *asam* are placed on a low stool and covered with a banana leaf upon which Asiah is directed to sit. The *bidan* mixes *tepong tawar* with herbal water in a cup and pours this over Asiah. Next, Asiah is bathed with the water that was prayed over earlier. A third container of water, into which the juice of three limes was squeezed and the fruit added, is given to Asiah who sips from it before it too is poured over her.

The *bidan* picks up three *terlepas* ('escaped'; each is made from two strands of pandanus interwoven into a knot; by pulling on the ends, one opens the knot) that she moves in front of Asiah's face where they are pulled open. She is told to spit on them. Both the opening of the knots and the spitting symbolize Asiah bringing forth her child with ease.

Asiah stands and the wet, unbleached thread squeezed over her face earlier is formed into a circlet that is put over her head, drawn down around her body and, as it reaches her feet, she is told to step out of it, again removing impediments to the birth.

A tray, now holding only the unmilled rice and the burning herbs, is passed around her three times by two co-operating women, standing on each side of her. The banana leaf and other objects on which Asiah was sitting are thrown through the floorboards of the kitchen, expelled to the earth. Asiah is led from the kitchen by her mother who will help her to dress.

The Ceremony - Part III

Asiah, dressed in her best clothes is led into the front room, where the men prayed earlier, to a chair draped with a fine batik sarong. Before her there is a table spread with little dishes holding portions of the *kenduri* foods and an enormous bowl of *nasi semangat* (the rice of the spirit of life) decorated with red-dyed eggs impaled on sticks topped by yellow, paper flowers. On either side of the table there are bottles holding lighted candles.

The *bidan* squats next to Asiah and feeds her mouthfuls from each of the feast dishes, presses a lump of *nasi semangat* to her lips, and gives and Islamic benediction. The ceremony is over at 5.20p.m.

Asiah goes to the porch to chat with her friends, relieved that she is no longer the focus of everyone's attention. Her mother divides the *nasi semangat* and 'flower eggs' among the women who participated in the ceremony. The *bidan* is given a large portion of the former and several of the latter as well as the unmilled rice and some of the *kenduri* foods. At the time she was invited to officiate, she was sent all of the ingredients to make betel quids, the traditional symbol of hospitality and good-will. After the birth, she will receive cloth, money, or both.

Symbolism

Some symbolic interpretations of ritual paraphernalia and actions were integrated into the above description. All of them were provided by informants except the idea about homemade cloth which is mine. Many old meanings have undoubtedly been forgotten. The significance of the numbers seven the three is in this category. Skeat attributes the wide use of seven in old Malay rituals to a belief in 'a seven-fold soul' and also discusses the role of the 'Seven Heavenly Bodies', i.e. sun, moon, and five planets in Malay cosmology.[17] Requests to villagers for the meaning of seven generally elicted an 'I don't know' or 'people long ago said seven was a good number'. When Skeat's ideas were introduced, the typical response was, 'maybe - but long, long ago'.

Three can be interchanged with seven in some instances: if seven men are not available to recite Quranic verses and pray, three are acceptable; the cord tied around the pregnant woman's waist can be worn for three days instead of seven. But the meaning of three is also obscure. Imagination can lead in any direction: there might be an ancient tie to the Hindu 'trinity', or a more mundane concept that the first-born child with its parents creates a new 'family trio' so that emphasizing three gives a strength to 'the third'.

Despite the problem with numbers, it is clear that many of the rituals are sympathetic, carried out to produce a desired effect, and that others avert misfortune or bestow blessings. At the least, that is what 'people long ago' believed. As noted above, there is no concensus among women about the overall effects of the ceremony, whether it 'places the baby properly' for an easy birth or 'asks for safe-keeping' of mother and baby. Even those who make the former interpretation agree that ultimately human beings have no control over such matters. Like the Polish peasants discussed by Thomas and Znaniecki, rural Malays perform traditional rites and ceremonies to the best of their ability and then 'leave the rest to God'.[18]

It is important to remember that all of the participants in the *lenggang perut* are Muslims. They recognise the seventh-month ceremony as *adat* and there is no conflict in their belief system between Islam and *adat*. As the term syncretic implies, fusion of beliefs has occurred.

THE LENGGANG PERUT IN LITERATURE

With the above description as background, I now turn to some other works on the same subject. The details vary but no one writing on the subject questions that the basic *lenggang perut* is pre-Islamic and very old.

It is therefore curious that Skeat, an English turn-of-the-century writer, never mentioned it although he devoted 674 pages to *Malay*

Magic[19] and wrote about hundreds of minor rites as well as major ceremonies. He detailed a ritual of engaging a *'Bidan (sage femme)'*,[20] the Malay and the French both generally being translated into English as 'midwife', during the seventh month of pregnancy and wrote at some length about brief rituals immediately prior to and following the birth of a child. The *Lenggang perut* was omitted. There are several plausible explanations for the omission. The most obvious: Skeat did not know about the *lenggang perut* - although it is not a secret ceremony. Perhaps he had little opportunity to talk with female informants because of Islamic propriety regulations and his male informants failed to mention the ceremony. Or he simply overlooked the *lenggang perut* because it was a women's ceremony. Or he was constrained from discussing pregnancy with anyone because of modesty norms in his own society or his own personal hang-ups.

The last supposition is supported by the fact that on the subject of pregnancy taboos (*pantang*) Skeat gives no original data but quotes Clifford[21] at length, devoting three times more space to an expectant father's observations than to those of those of the pregnant woman. Some of the same or similar taboos are still important and a few must be observed by both the woman and her husband. For example, neither should nail or lash anything closed or the womb might not open fully for the birth, another instance of sympathetic association. But it is the woman who must observe the greater number of taboos in thought, word, and deed.[22]

Wilkinson's 'Papers on Malay Customs and Beliefs: The Incidents of Malay Life' from birth to death appeared a few years later in 1908. When his article was reprinted in the *Journal of the Malay Branch of the Royal Asiatic Society* in 1957, a section on 'Ante-Natal Ceremonies' appeared as an appendix written by Raja Haji Yahya. I have not seen the original but I assume this appendix was part of it because of the way contents are shown in the *JMBRAS* edition following the statement, 'first published in 1908'. It seems odd that the appendix is in Malay, with no translation provided (especially in the 1957 *JMBRAS* monograph), when the articles are in English and intended for an audience that probably included many who could not read formal Malay. At least Wilkinson left a record of the ceremony.

Winstedt[23] gives a brief description of a seventh month ceremony that shares much with the one by Raja Haji Yahya.[24] Winstedt may have drawn from it for his lists Wilkinson's 1908 work among his sources for the relevant chapter. Both Winstedt and the Raja discuss Islamic prayers, lustration of the pregnant woman and her husband on a river bank, use of other symbolic means to avert misfortunes and secure blessings, the couple sitting in state after the procession back to the home, and then the *lenggang perut*. Winstedt's description:

> Shawls are spread on the floor (seven if the patient is a raja), and the expectant mother lies on her back with the shawls under her waist. The midwife seizes the ends of the first shawl and rocks the woman slowly as in a hammock, removes it, seizes the ends of the next shawl and repeats the performance seven times.[25]

The idea that Winstedt used Raja's description as a source for his own is strengthened by his parenthetical note that seven shawls are used for a raja. He makes no comment about the number of shawls appropriate for commoners.

Winstedt begins his description with the word 'everywhere', indicating his belief that involvement of a pregnant woman's husband in parts of the ceremony was universal in Malaya. Yet neither Alwi bin Sheikh Alhady,[26] writing about practices in 'Rhio' (The Riau Archipelago of Indonesia, just south of Singapore) and Johore in the southern part of the Malay peninsula, nor Tunku Pekiram Wira[27] in his discussion of practices in Trengganu mention lustration of the couple, nor, in fact, any ritual involvement of the pregnant woman's husband. Skeat's omission of reference to the *lenggang perut* suggests that if he knew about the ceremony, he did not know about male participation in it. Otherwise, he surely would have described that much.

Assuming that all of the writers who discussed the ceremony are accurate, how is the variation explained? The most obvious answer is time and space.

Unfortunately, several of the cited authors are not very helpful about either. Neither Raja Haji Yahya nor Winstedt designated the area where male participation was found. No male participation in the actual ceremony was noted in Trengganu or Johore. Intra-cultural variation is not surprising and has a very long history. A number of old Malay adages reflect the pattern: *'Lain kampung, lain adat'* (another village, another tradition) is one example.

What about the time element? Encik Alwi states in his introduction that he was born in 1895 and remembers 'the customs and traditions practised by the Malays generally, and by Malay royalty particularly, in Rhio';[28] during 1959 he interviewed 'venerable personages' in Johore and Selangor about customs and traditions 'to refresh, complement, and correct' his own memories. Thus he must be writing about traditions practised during his youth, around the period that Raja Haji Yahya's observations were published in Wilkinson. Was Raja Haji Yahya writing about the contemporary scene of 1908 or from earlier memories? None of the writers cited give any exact dates for the practices they describe.

Is male observational bias problematic? Yes and No. Descriptions of the actual *lenggang perut* ceremony are brief and not very detailed. I assume this is because the male writers did not observe ceremonies but relied on what they were told by women in their families and other informants. Lack of details may indicate a low level of interest. If male participation in any aspect of the ceremony occurred, that would get more space in descriptions by men because they would have the details from their own observations. Such skewing was noted above in my comment about Clifford's treatment of pregnancy taboos (in Skeat).

Are ceremonial differences class based? Only two descriptions can be compared, given the view that differences through time and by region are likely. They are both of *lenggang perut* in Trengganu. Tunku Pekirma Wira states that he writes about 'the Malays of Trengganu'[29] although his title, Tunku, like Haja, denotes royalty. He must be more familiar with practices among royalty that among commoners but his generalisation suggests an attempt to find universals. I find no glaring incongruities between my observations of the ceremony in the villages and what the Tunku describes. My description is far more detailed, but both share several identical features: rolling objects down the woman's abdomen, rocking her with seven cloths, lustration of the woman and the use of *tapong tawar*, opening the *terlepas*, and the use of *nasi semangat*. The comparison suggests the idea that in one region, class differences are more likely to be manifest in the ritual paraphernalia and milieu - elaborate and expensive at one extreme and inexpensive at the other - rather than in the ceremony.

In summary: the variation in the descriptions about male participation in some aspects of the seventh-month-of-pregnancy ceremony does not appear to be due to male bias. Nor do class differences offer an explanation although the Raja and the Tunku are royals and Encik Alwi spent much of his youth at the Rhio court. Even if the authors wrote only about royal or elite practices and made no claims about generalising, the differences among descriptions would remain. Place and time are relevant to an explanation. But where and when the pregnant woman's husband had an impportant role is not established.

That the husband's participation must have been more wide-spread in the past is highly likely: expectant fathers still must observe taboos during a wife's pregnancy. Some people joke about these *pantang* now but observe them anyway with a 'better safe than sorry' approach like that of Americans who 'knock on wood' to avert misfortune.

DISCUSSION

The belief persists, at least as 'superstition', that a man's behaviour can affect the welfare of his wife and unborn child. Hence the elementary questions are: Why was lustration of the couple not universal among Malays? Why was the expectant father not purified and blessed everywhere on the peninsula? Does the answer lie with Islam?

The impact of the religion in a particular form, the degree of orthodoxy and the point of origin of proselytizers, the zeal with which Muslim leaders tried to destroy or just modify pre-Islamic practices via-a-vis the supernatural, and so on, varied according to place, time, the sex of the believer and, very likely, several other factors.

It is easy to imagine Muslim leaders in some locales denouncing male participation in 'pagan' rituals while ignoring women's partici-pation. Men were provided with major ritual roles in Islam; women were given little. Thus women's pre-Islamic ceremonies were not in competition with what was introduced in the name of Islam. Also, proselytizing Indians and Arabs might have considered Malay women's rituals too unimportant or peripheral to their conversion concerns to merit condemnation. The other side of that issue is that Malay women enjoyed a high degree of equality with men, so the sop of their old ceremonies might have kept them from opposing a blatantly patriarchal theology.

Male observations of ante-natal taboos persist because the required behaviours are individual and not usually obvious: they can be ignored as 'superstitions' rather than defined as ritual acts. Participation in a community-wide, public ceremony - the couple escorted to the river bank for lustration - was (is?) an entirely different order of behaviour.

My Trengganu informants believe that the *lenggang perut* in their area has always been for the pregnant woman only and that men were never involved except in what I call the 'prologue', an obvious Islamic tradition. With this in mind, it is notable that the earliest proof of a Muslim community in Malaya is from Trengganu: a stone inscribed with a partly obliterated date that, by the Gregorian calendrical system, might be either 1303 or 1386.[30]

The problem with the argument is this: it fails to account for male participation throughout Malaya in the *bersanding*, a syncretic wedding ceremony when the bride and groom appear together for the first time although they have been officially married in the Muslim *akhad nikah*, an all male ceremony with the bride represented by her guardian. But the *bersanding* is different from the *lenggang perut* in more than just format. It does not have the strong magico-supernatural content of the seventh-month ceremony. It does have an air of playfulness as the groom's kinswomen 'battle' (or buy) his way into the bride's home, and from the suggestive remarks shouted by the groom's male friends outdoors and the responses from some of the older women inside the house. Such aspects give the *bersanding* a secular air. Nevertheless, as of 1979, the *bersanding* was under attack by Muslim fundamentalists. No criticism of the *lenggang perut* was heard at that time. Since then, I do not know.

The extreme fundamentalists have an unlikely ally, an ally they would reject in large part if they could: socio-economic development. Development has brought about enormous changes very rapidly - new forms of health care, increased education and literacy, an emphasis on science as a basic problem-solving technique, expansion of transportation and communication networks, social and spatial mobility, and more. Many of these changes serve to undermine local traditions, including ceremonies like the *lenggang perut*, and lead to the elimination of some traditional roles.

Already *bomoh* (medical-magical pratitioners who use syncretic methods) in this part of Trengganu have become scarce. The old men died and no young ones had learned the art. Landy (1974)[31] refers to an example of role disappearance of Black midwives in the rural south of the United States and gives several reasons, including the failure to recruit women to midwifery from the younger, educated generation. Among Malays, midwifery is not in jeopardy, but the village *bidan kampung* who conducts the *lenggang perut* is being replaced by the formally educated *bidan kerajaan* (government midwife) whose training is medical not ritual. Thus the *lenggang perut* may disappear along with the *bidan kampung* role, with or without the assistance of the extreme Muslim fundamentalists.

REFERENCES

1. Many rural Malay women have shared their understanding and interpretations of the *lenggang perut* as it is practised in parts of Trengganu. And they have permitted me to share their ceremonies. To all of them I express my sincere appreciation. Particular thanks are due to Suri binti Sulaiman who invited me to Asiah's seventh month ceremony, to Asiah and her family for allowing me to attend and to Hajjah Selamah, Hajjah Fatimah, Hajjah Aminah and Hajjah Kulsum.

2. Mohammad Rasjidi, 'Unity and Diversity in Islam', in *Islam, the Straight Path*, edited by Kenneth W. Morgan, New York: Ronald Press, 1958, pp. 403-430.

3. Fouad Ajami, 'Islamic Ideas', *New York Times Book Review*, March 2, 1980, p. 6.

4. See: M.A. Rauf, *A Brief History of Islam with Special to Malaya*, Kuala Lumpur: Oxford University Press, 1964. Also see: C. Geertz, *Islam Observed: Religious Development in Morocco and Idonesia*, New Haven, Conn.: Yale University Press, 1968.

5. Abudl Hamid el-Zein, 'Beyond Ideology and Theology: The Search for the Anthropology of Islam', in *Annual Review of Anthropology*, edited by Bernard Siegal et. al., Palo Alto, CA: Annual Reviews Inc., p. 245.

6. See: C. Geertz, *The Religion of Java*, New York: The Free Press, 1964.

7. Mohammad Marmaduke Pickthall, *The Meaning of the Glorious Koran*, New York: Mentor Books, 1959, p. 83.

8. See: R. Cohen, *The Kanuri of Bornu*, New York: Holt, Rinehart and Winston, 1967.

9. Fatimah Mernissi, *Beyond the Veil: Male Female Dynamics in a Modern Muslim Society*, New York: Schenkman, 1975.

10. Mohammad Rasjidi, op. cit., p. 421.

11. See: Heather Strange, *Rural Malay Women in Tradition and Transition*, New York: Praeger Publishers, 1981.

12. See: Fred Plog et. al., *Anthropology: Decisions, Adaptations and Evolution*, New York: Alfred A. Knopf, 1976, pp. 101-102.

13. E. Fisher, *Woman's Creation: Sexual Evolution and the Shaping of Society*, New York: McGraw Hill, 1980, p. 143.

14. Arnold van Gennep, The Rites of Passage, Chicago: Phoenix Boosk, 1961 (orig. 1908), p. 42.

15. Ibid., p. 41.

16. While it is not part of the ceremony, teasing the pregnant woman beforehand is common. The rationalisation for this treatment is the need for her to accept the situation, everyone's attention and the *bidan's* control. Otherwise, birth will be more difficult. The teasing can have sadistic overtones. I was invited to attend a *melanggang perut* in a village. The young, pregnant woman had been told that a foreign man was going to photograph the ceremony and was nearly hysterical from worry when I arrived. She was relieved when the foreigner turned out to be a female and by assurances that I would not photograph her.

17. Walter William Skeat, *Malay Magic*, New York: Dover

Publications Inc., 1967, (orig. 1900).

18.　George C. Homans, 'Anxiety and Ritual:　The Theories of Malinowski and Radcliffe-Brown', in *Reader in Comparative Religion*, edited by W. Lessa and E. Vogt, Evanston, Ill.　Row, Peterson and Company, 1958, (orig. 1941), p. 116.

19.　W.W. Skeat, op. cit.

20.　Ibid., pp. 332-3.

21.　Ibid., pp. 344-6.

22.　S. Hasnah binti Mohammad Ali has discussed the effects of customary practices, especially food taboos, on a pregnant woman's health.　See her paper 'Islam and Adat-Effect on a Basic Attitude - Health', *Intisari*, (not dated, *circa* 1964), Vol. I, pp. 27-36.　Also see: Christine S. Wilson, 'Food Taboos of Childbirth:　The Malay Example', *Ecology of Food and Nutrition*, Vol. 2, 1973, pp. 267-74.　Carol Laderman, 'Symbolic and Empirical Reality:　A new Approach to the Analysis of Food Avoidances', *American Ethnologist*, Vol. 8, No. 3, 1981, pp. 468-93.

23.　R.O. Winstedt, *The Malay Magician*, London:　Routledge and Kegan Paul, 1961 (orig. 1951).

24.　Raja Haji Yahya, 'Ante-Natal Ceremonies', in R.J. Wilkinson's paper on 'Malay Customs and Beliefs:　The Incidents of Malay Life', monograph of the Malayan Branch of the Royal Asiatic Society, 1957, (orig. 1908), No. 180.

25.　R.O. Winstedt, op. cit., p. 105.

26.　Sheikh Alhady bin Alwi, *Malay Customs and Traditions*, Singapore:　Eastern Universities Press, 1962.

27.　Pekirma Wira, 'Islam and Adat in Trengganu', *Intisari*, not dated (*circa* 1964), Vol. 1, pp. 37-48.

28.　Alwi, op. cit., p. xi.

29.　Wira, op. cit., p. 38.

30.　M.A. Rauf, op. cit., p. 30.

31.　David Landy, 'Role Adaptation:　Traditional Curers under the Impact of Western Medicine', *American Ethnologist*, Vol. I, No. 1, pp. 103-26.

Chapter 7

ISLAM AND THE STATUS OF WOMEN IN TUNISIA

Norma Salem

One of the first actions undertaken by the Tunisian state following independence in 1956 was to promulgate the Code of Personal Status[1] *(Majallat al-Ahwal al-Shakhsiyyah)*[2] effective from 1 January 1957.[3] The Code made marriage and divorce civil matters. It established a minimum age for marriage and gave the spouses a voice in the choice of their mates, previously denied them by society. Prohibitions against Muslim women marrying outside the faith were not mentioned.[4] More surprisingly, the Code forbade polygamy and unilateral repudication by the husband, which are traditionally considered characteristic of Islamic law and society. The Code of Personal Status placed Tunisia in the forefront of all other Arab and Islamic countries (except for Turkey) with respect to the legal rights accorded to women and, in commemoration of its promulgation, the 13th of August was declared a national holiday, 'Woman's Day' (*Yawm al-Mar'ah*).

The question to be asked, therefore, is 'To the extent that the Code of Personal Status reflected the will of the political leaders of Tunisia, was it influenced by Islam or by factors against Islam?'. This study proposes to explore the various dimensions of this question by examining the Code itself within its historical context as well as some of the literature preceding and following its promulgation.[5]

The first part will bear on the most important book concerning the status of women in Tunisia, al-Tahir al-Haddad's *Imra'atuna fi al-Shari'ah wa-al-Mujtama'* ('Our Woman in the Law and in Society'), published in 1930.[6] Al-Haddad's book will be contrasted, on the one hand, with the conservative responses his book provoked and, on the other hand, with the attitude of mainstream leaders of the Tunisian nationalist movement during the 1930s as represented by Habib Bourguiba's (al-Habib Abu Ruqaybah) famous article on the veil.[7]

This will be followed by a discussion of the Code of Personal Status itself and some of the evaluations made about its actual implementation. The third part of the study will consist of an analysis of the essays and speeches made by President Habib Bourguiba, as indicators of the positions taken by the dominant ideology in Tunisia concerning the issue of women.

The Code of Personal Status was not created *ex nihilo* and the impetus towards the advancement of women in Tunisia had its roots deep in the modern history of the country, particularly in that effervescent period following the First World War. The Code of Personal Status was, in fact, the culmination of a long process of intellectual evolution among the political leaders of Tunisia. In the first place, there was a felt need to resolve the contradictions between the servile condition of women, doubly exploited, and their projects of independence from the colonizing power. In the second place, the Code of Personal Status and the following series of related laws translated the will of political leaders to mobilize to the maximum the productive forces of a nation in the struggle for modernity. In both cases, the recognition of women's rights was not the result of a struggle initiated or led by Tunisian women themselves. That it was men who promoted the cause of women's advancement might explain the limitations of this bestowed emancipation.

The most explicit and systematic call for women's emancipation in Tunisia came in the book of al-Haddad, *Our Women in the Law and in Society*, mentioned above. The main argument of the book was that both the law (*shari'ah*) and society had failed to be faithful to the text and the spirit of the Qur'an and the Prophetic *hadiths* (traditions). In order to better understand the book and its main theses, it is important to place it within its historical context.

Invaded by France, Tunisia became a French Protectorate in 1881. But Western influence had penetrated the country as early as Ahmad Bey's reforms (1837-1855),[8] and by 1881 there already existed in Tunisia a nucleus of the elite interested in improving conditions within the country by importing Western techniques, institutions and ideas. From the perspective of this group, the French Protectorate could be viewed as an instrument for the 'modernisation' of the country. The illusion of an 'association' between the French authorities and this Tunisian elite in the pursuit of the goal of 'progress' prevented the articulation of protest against the Protectorate despite inarticulate passive resistance in the towns and sporadic armed resistance in the countryside.

The First World War witnessed the collapse of the Ottoman Empire and the declaration of the Wilsonian doctrine of national self-determination. Thus, the possibility of a wide political unity among Muslims was, for all practical purposes, effectively lost while hopes for independence under the banner of nationalism were raised. Simultaneously, the need for social reform became acute in reaction to the excesses of the unregulated expansion of world capitalism in the late 19th century.

Typically, following the First World War, Tunisia passed through a phase of broad political and social struggle. In 1920, the Free Constitutional Party (*Hizb al-Dustur al-Hurr* - usually referred to as the Destour Party) was established and, in alliance with several splinter factions, demanded some control over the national budget, limitation of land alienation to foreigners and an expansion in the educational system. In 1924, the General Confederation of Tunisian Workers (better known under its French acronym, CGTT, for *Confederation Generale des Travailleurs Tunisiens*) was established but was soon dissolved and its leaders exiled because the Destour did not lend its support. The Destour became radical only in 1934 with the rise of the Neo-Destour which, under the leadership of Habib Bourguiba and in alliance with the heir of the CGTT, the General Union of Tunisian workers (better known under its French acronym, UGTT, for *Union Generale des Travailleurs Tunisiens*) under the leadership of Ferhat Hached (Farhat Hashid) finally succeeded in obtaining the independence of Tunisia in 1956, some 36 years after the creation of the first political party, the Destour, and some 32 years after the establishment of the first Tunisian labour confederation, the CGTT.

Al-Tahir al-Haddad himself had been active first in the Destour Party and later in the CGTT.[9] In fact, he had published a book in 1927, entitled *Al-Ummal al-Tunisiyyun wa-Zuhur al-Harakah al-Niqabiyyah* (Tunisian Workers and the Appearance of the Labour Movement), in which he defended the dissolved CGTT. Although very advanced in his theses, al-Haddad did not suffer any ill consequences upon the publication of this book and it was only with the publication of *Our Woman in the Law and in Society* that his Zaytunah diplomas were stripped from him and he lost his job.[10]

There is no doubt in my mind that al-Haddad's second book, on the Tunisian woman as his first book on the Tunisian workers, flowed from the same source; namely, sympathy with the oppressed and abhorrence for injustice. As a scholar trained in the 'religious' sciences, al-Haddad wrote his book in an attempt to demonstrate that true Islam was not responsible for the sad state of the Tunisian woman. The first part of the book - divided into five chapters: Woman in Islam, Islam against Adultery, Marriage in Islam, Before Divorce, and Divorce in Islam - deals with the status of woman in Islamic law. The second part of the book illustrates al-Haddad's debt to European sociology since he attempts to analyse woman's place in society as it actually was at that point in time. The main thrust of the book is that Islam, properly understood, does not oppress women but that Muslim society in Tunisia had failed to understand or to apply the precepts of Islam.

In the preface to the book, al-Haddad wrote:

> I believe, without the shadow of a doubt, that Islam is innocent of the accusation of arresting reform but that, on the contrary, it is the .... inexhaustible source of reform. The collapse of our (social) structure is but the result of illusions we have believed in, of pernicious and terrible customs we have tied ourselves to. This is what led me to write this book about woman in Islamic Law and society so that we may see what leads to and what misleads away from (the right path).[11]

The methodological premise of the first part of the book is basically that of Muhammad 'Abduh and of most other Muslim reformists; namely, that Islamic law is not immutable and was not revealed all of a piece but developed as the historic Islamic community developed. Al-Haddad goes beyond the temporality of the *shari'ah* - and here is the daring audacity - to claim that the precepts of the Qur'an itself were not eternal but subject to historical

143

contingency.

> It (Islam) wished to be operative in its day and have effect on the people and on the state which it established. Consequently, its verses were revealed following (historic) events; it did not assume these historic events before deciding upon its judgements. For the same reason, the Qur'an did not separate its judgements into chapters depending on the subject, according to theoretical principles governing the recording of principles and of books. Thus, its law (*shari'ah*) was the result of actual (historic) developments and not of articles laid down beforehand in order to make life conform to them.[12]

and, al-Haddad repeats, 'Islam is the religion of reality; it evolves as reality evolves and that is the secret of its eternal glory'.[13]

He continues to clarify this point by distinguishing between the eternal principles in Islam; such as, the creed of unity, ethical requirements, justice and equality, and those precepts dependent upon human contingencies; particularly as they related to conditions in the *Jahiliyyah* (pre-Islamic) period in Arabia.[14] According to al-Haddad, the basic tendency within Islam, actually within the Qur'an itself, is to take a gradualist approach such that its precepts are suited to its historic reality and, thus, effective.[15]

> (Islam) is the religion which holds to the principle of gradualism in legislating its laws according to (limiting) capacity. There is nothing which states or indicates that the stage achieved during the Prophet's lifetime was the hoped-for final (stage) after which there would be no end since gradual (evolution) is linked to the difficulties of those issues for which gradual (steps) are to be taken . . . .[16]

In the first chapter of his book, *Woman in Islam*, al-Haddad gives the usual apologetic reformist position: that Islam improved upon the condition of woman as it existed in pre-Islamic Arabia in that it gave her the right to testify and to sit in judgement;[17] to own and to dispose of her property;[18] to have the custody of minors and to be the executor in cases of inheritance. Al-Haddad also holds that the Qur'an does not impose the veil on women but simply asks for decency.[19]

Al-Haddad believes that the Quranic precepts did not go to the limit of full equality between man and woman in all respects because of the limitations imposed by the actual Arab society of the time such that only a step-by-step approach could be accepted and implemented. Nonetheless, he deduces the general principle of equality of the two sexes from the tendency to balance the respective rights and duties of man and woman within the framework of that Arabian society of the 7th century; while the woman inherits only half the share of her brother, she is to be fully supported by her male kin.[20] Thus, he explains away the two famous Quranic verses:

> . . . . men are a degree above them (women) (2: 228).

Men are in charge of women .... (4: 34).[21]

which, on first impression, could be understood to mean that men are superior to women. According to al-Haddad, all they mean is recognition that, under the economic and social conditions of 7th century Arabia, men had a greater economic responsibility than women.

> In truth, Islam did not give us a decisive judgement, beyond time and the changes time works, on the essence of Woman in her self. There is nothing in its texts that is clear about the issue; what is to be found (in the texts) are expositions of the weakness and backwardness of woman in (7th century Arabia) as factual reports on existing conditions .... [22]

In sum, although these verses might be understood to indicate a Quranic position in support of the superiority of men over women, this is a contingent precept and does not prevent the application of the principle of equality between the two sexes whenever the passage of time creates the necessary conditions in society since 'Islam, in its essence, aims at perfect justice in the spirit of highest Truth'.[23]

The chapter on adultery again attempts to understand the Quranic precepts against adultery and fornication within a historical framework. Applied to the contemporary situation in Tunisia, al-Haddad calls for strong measures against fornication and adultery in order to encourage marriage and procreation since an increase in population would be critical factor in limiting colonization by foreigners.[24]

His third chapter on marriage in Islam by emphasizing the emotional bond between the two partners that is the basis of all solid relationships. He demonstrates that most schools of Islamic law agree that the spouses have the right to choose their future mates, to one degree or the other. Nonetheless, al-Haddad seems to be calling for some restrictions on the Muslim man's right to marry a non-Muslim[25] rather than broadening that principle to give the same right to the Muslim woman to marry a non-Muslim man; he reasons that in Tunisia's situation, non-Muslims are in the dominant position and the children of any mixed marriage will tend to be absorbed by the dominant culture[26] and will be lost to Islam or, more specifically, to Tunisia. Al-Haddad comes out clearly against polygamy.[27]

In his fourth chapter on divorce, al-Haddad quotes the Prophetic tradition which states that: 'Divorce is the most hateful to God of licit acts'.[28] In the first place, al-Haddad argues that divorce was given into the hands of men because of the backward level of women in the early period of Islam.[29] He does not rule out divorce out of hand but admits that 'when agreement becomes impossible', divorce is inevitable.[30] Al-Haddad explains the famous triple divorce, traditionally considered the prerogative of the Muslim man, as an abuse of the clear intention contained in the traditions. According to al-Haddad, the triple repudiation was actually instituted in order to give several chances for the reconciliation of the spouses. Again, al-Haddad goes beyond the usual apologetic reformist position which holds that, in some of the law schools, the woman could obtain the right to divorce if she takes the precaution of including it as an article in her marriage contract. He calls for special divorce courts to have jurisdiction over all cases of divorce and, effectively, withdraws the husband's right to unilaterally repudiate his wife. Moreover, he reminds his readers that marriage in Islam is considered as a contract, and, as such, should also be covered by the principle of indemnity to the wronged partner.

In the summary of this first part, al-Haddad states that the gradualism inherent in Islamic law and dependent on historic conditions tends towards equality between men and women.

> If we examine, in all honesty, the texts of the Shari'ah and their implications, we find that they tend to take woman along with man on the road of equality in all aspects of life.[31]

Al-Haddad concludes this first part by contrasting his presentation with the *response* of six legal authorities, of both the Maliki (covering the majority of Tunisians) and the Hanafi (covering the minority of Tunisians of Ottoman origin) schools of law to 12 questions.[32]

With his critique of the existing legal precepts governing the personal status of women, al-Haddad had also worked in his own vision of what the status of woman should be. Because in essence woman is equal to man, her contingent social situation should be encouraged to tend towards actual equality.

> Islam, despite its gradualist approach, does not leave us in doubt that in its essence it does not call for separating women from men. If it did not demonstrate this clearly in all the precepts connected with personal status, it proved that its higher objective is to consider all of God's worshippers equal. He created them equal ..., defined their final judgement in terms of their actions, commanded them to do good deeds .... without excepting men or women.[33]

He follows the same approach in the second part of his book where, in presenting the sociological condition of Tunisian women, he presents both a critique and a future plan for women in Tunisian society. His main thesis is that education, rather than the suffrage demanded at the time by feminist movements in Western countries, was the key to changing the status of women in Tunisia.[34] This is no surprise in view of the fact that, under the French Protectorate, even Tunisian men lacked suffrage.

Surprisingly, al-Haddad emphasizes general education over and above education for home management or artisanal work in the opening pages but then devotes the greater part of the sociological section to education as a means of improving the woman in her role of wife and mother. He comes out very strongly against the veil and against the seclusion of women; but gives trivial justifications for these positions in order to highlight the inane difficulties brought about by the veil (e.g. the mother cannot supervise her children playing in the alleys and they run wild; she cannot do her own shopping and her husband has to go back and forth to the shops as she takes her time making up her mind). The influence of socialist thought is reflected in the last section of the chapter where al-Haddad traces the causes for the obvious social crisis of Tunisia in the 1930s back to colonialism; as the colonizers enclosed the land the peasants were proletarized and as factory-made cheap goods were introduced, the artisans and the merchants were pauperized. Al-Haddad then argues that, within this situaiton of foreign domination, poor education makes Tunisian women even more vulnerable than Tunisian men to the lures of Western consumerism. The lack of education also makes Tunisian women less attractive than foreign (i.e. non-Muslim) women and encourages Tunisian men to marry non-Tunisian women.

Perhaps in reaction to Bourguiba's article on the veil,[35] published a year before al-Haddad's book, al-Haddad violently attacks the veil which he likens to 'the muzzle used to prevent dogs from biting'. He adds that 'it is the concrete proof of man's basic belief that woman is essentially immoral'.[36] The veil and concomitant seclusion keep the woman in ignorance and prevents her from exercising her legal rights.[37] Again, al-Haddad states that the best way to prevent immoral behaviour is not by imposing the veil on women but by good education of both men and women, inculcating in them the proper ethical principles.

He then moves to a discussion of formal education for women and justifies his encouragement by reference to the various *hadiths* encouraging learning for women as much as for men.[38] Despite this courageous introduction to the topic, al-Haddad quickly reverts to the usual reformist position calling for education for women only to the extent of their roles as wives as mothers; 'By her nature, woman is the mother, the wife and the home-maker'.[39] Here, al-Haddad seems to be consciously putting limits on his project for education for women, probably due to the same concern for pursuing a gradualist policy of 'stages'. Following a paragraph on his general view of education, al-Haddad writes:

> This is the education in the general sense which must be offered to woman and man, equally. It is their natural right limited only by innate talents and human potential. It is out of ignorance, stupidity, cowardice and savage injustice that woman is prevented from obtaining the means to develop her natural talents on the pretext that we have the right to determine her fate as we wish while what we really wish is but lustful and selfish. But let us keep away from (any) talk of equality since we are (actually) far away from that objective in our potentialities or even our thoughts. Let us talk about education for woman according to her functions as a housewife and discuss in general terms the education she needs to accomplish these functions.[40]

Al-Haddad ends his book with the following comments:

We have clarified the rights Islam allots woman and the treasures its texts hold, of tenderness and respect for the woman to the point of equality (with the man). We have also described her actual situation in Tunisian society, her difficulties within the family and her inability to undertake productive work which have prevented us (both men and women) from achieving happiness. The Orient, in its renaissance, has felt the need for that woman hidden within the depths of her house and has built schools and clubs for her. We hear today of the courageous role taken by the woman of the Orient in reviving the patriotic spirit generally. How great is our disgrace among the nations of the world as they seek life and dignity while we stay behind to admire the anachronistic beliefs inherited from our past and erroneously ascribed to Islam. I invite all Tunisians not to take me on my word but to consider our situation and the dangers it holds for the future.

Before concluding, I wish to express my hopes for the progress of women, of the Tunisian people and of the Orient in general. If, today, I see her (woman) far from the sight, I see her close in a union of pain . . . . present in the struggle and sacrifice for knowledge and education. This is the secret of our deliverance from the pains of death and of the dawn of true freedom.[41]

As mentioned previously, *Our Women in the Law and in Society* provoked a strong reaction to the extent that al-Haddad lost his job and died a broken man. Blessed with the official recognition of the Board of Inspectors (*Al-Nizarah al-'Ilmiyyah*) of the Zaytunah Mosque-University, Muhammad al-Salih ibn Murad wrote *al-Hidad 'ala Imra'at al-Haddad aw Radd al-Khata' wa-al-Kufr wa-al-Bid's allati hawaha kitab Imra'atuna fi al-Shari'ah wa-al-Mujtama'* ('Mourning over al-Haddad's Woman or Warding off Error, Apostasy and Innovation included in the Book - Our Woman in the Law and in Society'). Published in 1931, Ibn Murad's book constituted the official response to the 'religious' establishment of Tunisia to al-Haddad.[42]

Surprisingly, Ibn Murad seems to have sidestepped the crucial element in al-Haddad's book, his methodology, by which the Quranic revelations are subjected to history. The main criticism Ibn Murad makes is focussed on the danger al-Haddad's book placed on the traditional family hierarchy based on the power of the father/husband and on the perception that the book was an attempt to synthesize Islamic with positive law.

Another of the flood of books and pamphlets written to refute al-Haddad in the name of Islam, attacked him on the specific issue of the veil; Muhammad al-Madyuni wrote to illustrate the precepts in favour of the veil found in the Qur'an and the hadith collections.[43] Actually, it is not al-Haddad's book as such that al-Madyuni attacks but Shaykh 'Uthman ibn al-Khujah's answer (*fatwa*) to al-Haddad's question: 'What should be covered of the woman's body in order to preserve morality?' Shaykh al-Khujah's answer was that the *man* should not look except at the face and hands of the free woman and that whoever feared temptation had only to avert his gaze.[44] In fact, al-Khujah denies that the veil is inherently Islamic by simply interpreting the relevant Quranic verses according to their literal meaning. In his view, the veil is only a national custom of which Islam is innocent.[45] In contrast, al-Madyuni's refutation is not based on a direct interpretation of the Quranic verses but by subjecting their interpretation to various *hadiths* used to explicate these verses. He arrives at the conclusion that the woman should cover herself completely, including face and hands.[46]

Surprisingly, the same conclusion - based on different grounds - was reached by some of the Tunisian nationalists whose radicalism was beginning to crystallize in the early 1930s. The issue of woman's emancipation had become public when various newspapers published articles covering the special session sponsored by the Socialist Club on 8 January 1929 to discuss the status of the Tunisian woman. Actually, this was the occasion when the future President of Tunisia, Habib Bourguiba, wrote one of his first newspaper articles. Substituting for his brother who had been originally invited to the Club, Bourguiba published an account of the session in an article under the title 'The Veil' in the 11 January 1929 edition of *L'Etendard Tunisien* (The Tunisian Flag).[47]

Bourguiba describes the issue under discussion as the situation of the Tunisian woman, perceived by the majority of the gathering to be 'living under the triple pillories of ignorance, of what-will-the-neighbours-say and .... of the veil'.[48] Under Bourguiba's pen the multiple problems besetting the Tunisian woman of that period are sublimated within the veil; the veil symbolizes not simply woman's prison but the more general characteristic of the Tunisian people. For Bourguiba, the specific situation of Tunisia under the Protectorate meant that the Tunisian personality (or identity) should be defended at all costs; even at the cost of retaining the Tunisian woman behind the veil.

> .... is it in our interests to hasten, without caring for any transitions, the disappearance of our ways, of our customs, bad or good, and of all those little nothings which as a whole - whatever one might say - constitute our personality? My answer, given the very special circumstances in which we live, is categorical: NO! [49]

Nonetheless, Bourguiba is not fundamentally against change. His view of change is that it should be gradualist such that there should remain the possibility of absorbing the change within the national 'personality' and of authenticating it.

> Does this mean that, to maintain our personality, we should resist all progress, appear as prehistoric beings, as antique furniture good only to attract the attention of the tourist? No. Evolution must occur, otherwise it is death. It will be achieved, without break, without rupture in such a way as to maintain unity in the continuous becoming of our personality across time

. . . .[50]

At the meeting, Bourguiba had been preceded to the podium by a Mrs. Menchari who, pleading the cause of Tunisian women, dramatically removed her veil. According to him, this was the second time that the gesture had been made; the first had occurred four years earlier (1924 or 1925)[51] which seems to coincide with the organisation of the Confederation of Tunisian Workers. That the discussion took place at the Socialist Club and that al-Haddad was involved with the CGTT, ostracized by the French socialists, seems to indicate that the issue of woman's emancipation in Tunisia was linked to both the nationalist and the socialist currents flowing through Tunisia at the time.

Only by considering the issue of women's emancipation within the broader framework of the nationalist and socialist tendencies of the time could we then understand the irony of al-Haddad, product of the traditional Zaytunah Mosque-University coming out against the veil compared to Bourguiba, product of the French College Carnot, coming out in favour of the veil. Both al-Haddad and Bourguiba subsumed the precepts of Islam to historic contingency and both proposed a gradualist approach but reached diametrically opposite conclusions. For al-Haddad, the historic situation of Tunisia required that first priority be given to the reform of Tunisian society while, for Bourguiba such reform was impossible as long as Tunisia was subject to foreign domination. Moreover, for al-Haddad, woman makes the nation since 'woman is the one who gives birth to the people and in her arms (the nation) is nurtured and educated'.[52] Implicit in that statement is the deduction that as long as woman is oppressed, the nation - as a whole - will be oppressed.[53] In fact, in the opening paragraph of the sociological section of his book, al-Haddad seems to be aware of Bourguiba's opposite position when he insists on a distinction between the national 'personality' and the weight of customs.

> People are accustomed to educate their children to what they have learned from their ancestors without any intellectual movement or evolution, in a nation which sacralizes its customs as the glory of its ancestors and the symbols of its personality which they imagine would be lost by the loss of these customs and illustion.[54]

Both al-Haddad and Bourguiba are, thus, primarily interested in woman as a social actor and neither deals with the more psychological aspects of relationships between men and women, avoiding any direct consideration of the sexual dimensions.[55]

Where al-Haddad may be compared to Qasim Amin, disciple of Muhammad Abduh, Bourguiba's position may be compared to that of Mustafa Kamil.[56] The reformist tendency heir to Muhammad 'Abduh, gave priority to internal reforms over and above the struggle for independence, perhaps with the 'realistic' view that the Egyptian, or Tunisian, society was too backward to effectively resist foreign encroachment and that only after reform could effective resistance be offered. In contrast, for the new nationalists of the new century, legitimate heirs to the activism of al-Afghani, 'National independence became the demand overriding all other issues';[57] reflecting the implicit assumptions that resistance was in fact possible and that, only with political independence, could effective reforms be carried out. This type of nationalism held that conservatism in the social realm would prevent the disunity of the Tunisian (or Egyptian) identity and, only by maintaining that distinctly non-Western identity could Tunisian (or Egyptian) nationalists promote the independence of their country.[58] The unity of all strata of the society then becomes of utmost importance in the struggle for independence and no possibility of threatening national unity - by exposing the injustices suffered by one half of society at the hands of the other half - is tolerated.

Viewed within its historical framework, the paradox of a Westernised Bourguiba holding the same position as a conservative religious Shaykh becomes easily understandable.[59] The paradox of Bourguiba, defended of the Veil in contrast with Bourguiba, father of the most daring Code of Personal Status in the Arab world[60] also becomes understandable; once independence was achieved, then priority was given to reform.

Consistent with Bourguiba's concern to avoid rupture with the authentic background of Tunisian society, the spirit of the Code of Personal Status remains faithful to Islamic principles, despite its seemingly audacious articles.[61] This corresponds to the general unwillingness to follow the example of Turkey whose reforms in the 1920 represented a total break with its Islamic past. In Tunisia, Islam was made the official religion and Arabic the official language. From this perspective, the Code may be viewed as the realisation of most of al-Haddad's ideas; i.e. as an instrument giving legal weight to what, previously, had been simply moral injunctions buried in the Qur'an.

The Code does not simply cover the status of women as such since it deals with marraige (Book I), divorce (Books II and III), family relationships (Book IV), custody of chilren (Book V), constitution of the family (Books VI, VII and VIII) and inheritance (Books IX and X).[62] As mentioned previously[63] the Code made marriage a civil matter by requiring a formal deed to establish proof of marriage (Article 4). A minimum age for marriage was set, 15 for women and 18 for men (Article 5),[64] the consent of both spouses was required (Article 3) as well as the traditional dowry paid by the man to the woman (Article 12). The most innovative measure included in the Code of Personal Status was the clear-cut prohibition of polygamy (Article 18) making Tunisia the only Arab country, so far, to do this.

The Code also made divorce a civil matter since it required all divorces to take place before the court (Article 30) thus outlawing the husband's unilateral right to repudiate his wife. Here again, the Code takes daring measures by giving equal rights to both man and woman in matters of divorce to the extent that the woman as much as the man is liable to pay an indemntiy. Thus, Article 31 states:

A divorce decree is given:

(1) In pursuance of an application by the husband or the wife for the reasons provided for by this Code.

(2) In pursuance of the mutual consent of both spouses.

(3) In pursuance of the husband's desire to divorce or the request of the wife for same, in which case the judge shall determine the financial indemnity to which the wife may be entitled by way of damages or the indemnity she has to pay to the husband.[65]

Despite the seeming audacity of the Code, opposition was relatively mild compared to the ostracism suffered by al-Haddad upon publication of his book, which might indicate that Bourguiba was closer to the mark than al-Haddad was in assessing the readiness of Tunisian society to accept reform in the status of women but then, the Code was promulgated 26 years after the publication of *Our Woman in the Law and in Society.* Although a group of conservative justices from the religious courts sponsored a petition against the Code,[66] they were unable to mobilize a broad spectrum of opinion and the government kept firm in its resolve to enforce the Code. This is usually explained by the 'historical legitimacy and moral authority'[67] acquired by Bourguiba through the struggle for independence. More fundamentally, the Code does not seem to have gone beyond the actual practices prevalent in Tunisia at the time, at least among the articulate classes of the towns. Moreover, the Code was not as radical as might be assumed.

The conservative facet of the Code is reflected in the image it projects of the marriage relationship between husband and wife. Relationships between men and women are considered only within the framework of the family which is still viewed in hierarchical order with the husband/father as head of the family. Article 23 states:

The husband shall treat his wife with benevolence, live in all those matters envisaged by true maintenance, support her and his children from her in accordance with his circumstances and hers. The wife shall, if she possess any property, contribute to the support of the family. She shall respect her husband in his capacity as head of the family and, within these prerogatives, obey him in whatever he orders her, and perform her marital duties in conformity with usage and custom.[68]

In effect, the traditional equilibrium was preserved such that the responsibility for the financial maintenance of the family was still incumbent upon the man; Article 46 states:

A male descendant (*sic*) to whatever degree removed shall be responsible for the support of his minor descendants and those who are incapable of earning a livelihood to whatever degree removed. Support of the female shall persist until such time as her support becomes the responsibility of the husband. Support of the male shall continue until he has attained the age of sixteen years and is capable of earning a livelihood.

and Article 38 states that 'It is incumbent upon the husband to support a wife with whom he has cohabited . . . .' The traditionally favourable Islamic view that the wife has the right to own and to dispose of property is maintained in Article 24 but the responsibility of the husband to provide for his wife is so strong that she takes precedence over his children; Article 53 states, 'Where there are several persons eligible for support and the person who should provide it is incapable of supporting all those eligible, the wife shall have precedence over the children . . . .' Moreover, if the husband is unable to provide financial support, the wife has the right to seek divorce; Articles 39 states:

> If the husband is in financial straits, maintenance shall not be incumbent upon him. The judge shall, however, after allowing the husband a period of two months and if, after the said period having elapsed, the husband fails to provide his wife with support, grant the wife a divorce from her husband.

In the above articles, the underlying assumption remains the division of labour between man and woman where the man is given the responsibility for the financial maintenance of the family in return for the responsibility of the woman to reproduce the family, i.e. to bear children. On the whole, it would appear that the wife/mother still gets the short end of the stick since she is still obligated to contribute, if she could, to the support of the family without any proviso for a reciprocal decrease in the authority of the husband/father.

The hesitancy of the Code of Personal Status to radically alter its assumptions about woman's economic role and her share in the national wealth are particularly clear in the section dealing with inheritance (Books IX and X).

The basic features of Islamic inheritance laws were preserved, including the famous precept by which the daughter inherited only half the son's share, but whereas, previously, the laws of inheritance tended to distribute wealth among the males of the extended family, the Code tended to favour the nuclear family and, consequently, the share of the female heir within the nuclear family improved but only relative to her share within the extended family.[69] Nonetheless, within the nuclear family she still does not inherit on the same terms as the male; e.g. Article 103 states 'Daughters fall into three categories: (1) A half to one daughter when the only one, (2) Two thirds to two or more; (3) As agnatic heirs with their brothers, in which case the male receives the same as two females'. Outside the framework of the Code, the dissolution of private *habus*[70] (*waqf*, pl. *awqaf* or family trusts), which tended to limit female inheritance, also improved the status of the Tunisian woman in matters of inheritance.[71]

In sum, the Tunisian Code of Personal Status represented the political will of Tunisian leaders to emancipate woman without breaking with the country's Islamic heritage. But this is not the reason why it hesitated to consider woman beyond her roles within the family; the reason relates more to the political leaders' perception of the gradual 'stages' suitable to the actual conditions within Tunisian society. Nonetheless, as an instrument for change, I think that, to the extent the Code does not consider woman as such but only woman in her roles of daughter/wife/mother, it may be judged as relatively conservative and that its 'radicalism' lies simply in its efforts to *improve* upon these traditional roles of woman.

Despite the inability of the opposition to stop the implementation of the Code,[72] we still find resistance to it as late as ten years after its promulgation.[73] In 1964, Muhammad al-Tahir ibn 'Ashur, who is considered among the more progressive elements of the 'religious' establishment and who had supported the Code until then,[74] came out against the prohibition of polygamy in the chapter on 'Woman and Islam' in his book, *Usul al-Nizam al-Ijtima'i fi al-Islam* ('The Bases of the Social Order in Islam').[75] Ibn 'Ashur begins by quoting the Quranic verse 33: 35.

> Lo! men who surrender unto Allah, and women who surrender, and men who believe and women who believe, and men who obey and women who obey, and men who speak the truth and women who speak the truth, and men who persevere (in righteousness) and women who persevere, and men who are humble and women who are humble, and men who give alms and women who give alms, and men who fast and women who fast, and men who guard their modesty, and women who guard (their modesty), and men who remember Allah much and women who remember - Allah hath prepared for them forgiveness and a vast reward.

From this verse the author seems to tend towards deducing the equality of men and women in the eyes of God. Nonetheless, he reasserts the right of a man to take four wives, viewing it as a limitation on the undefined number allowed in pre-Islamic times. Moreover, he insists on the essential division of labour based on the different biological natures of male and female; while woman is prohibited from participating in armed struggle (*jihad*), she is given priority in the custody of children.[76] In this context, he quotes the Quranic verse 4: 32

> And covet not the thing in which Allah hath made some of you excel others; unto men a fortune from that which they have earned, and unto women a fortune from that which they have earned.[77]

He goes even further in arguing that this natural difference results in different actions and even in different motives required by Islamic law of the two categories.[78] He then explicitly rejects the equality of men and women by playing on the philological categories of essence and accident. Both men and women are human beings in essence and the differences between them are accidents. Nonetheless, these accidental differences are permanent preventing women from undertaking the command of armies, or the positions of Caliph or judge or the responsibility for the maintenance of the family.

Another source of resistance came from the civil courts

themselves where the judges tended to give the benefit of the doubt to the man whenever there was ambiguity in the case.[79] This is not borne out by the case-studies of divorce where it is shown that the woman tends to be favoured in terms of the compensation she obtains upon being divorced by her husband.[80]

The Code of Personal Status as promulgated in 1956 was not the final version of legal measures to be applied. On 19 June 1959, Book XI titled 'Testaments and testamentary dispositions' was added for a total of 199 Articles. A number of laws refining and explicating the Code were also legislated.[81] Moreover, on 27 September 1957, religious courts – both Islamic and Jewish – were eliminated or rather amalgamated with the civil courts and the Code became applicable to all Tunisian citizens. Thus, the Code of Personal Status became part of the legal content of the concept of 'Tunisian citizenship',[82] the concrete manifestation of the Tunisian 'personality'.

The Code of Personal Status was promulgated when Habib Bourguiba headed the government of independent Tunisia, as Prime Minister under the Bey. In 1957, the Bey was deposed, a Republic was proclaimed and Bourguiba was elected its Prime Minister.[83] He has been President of Tunisia for almost 25 years and, unquestionably, represents the dominant political ideology in the country. Consequently, his speeches may be considered as the most illustrative sources for understanding the dominant ideology's position vis-a-vis the issue of women in Tunisia.

While the Code of Personal Status was promulgated in 1956, it was only in 1965 and later that Bourguiba *regularly* made an annual speech in celebration of Woman's Day, in remembrance of the promulgation of the Code. Most of the speeches from 1965 on, were made during the annual congress of the National Union of Tunisian Women.[84]

Before embarking upon an analysis of this series of speeches, it is important to consider their political context. Once independence was achieved and the Republic instituted, between 1957 and 1962 the Algerian war and the evacuation of French troops from Tunisian soil occupied most of the energies of the young government and it was only when these problems were solved that the economic situation of Tunisia took first priority. Concerned with the underdevelopment of the various sectors of the Tunisian economy, the government undertook an activist role in the name of socialism. This experimentation with a form of socialism ended with the end of the 1960s and the early 1970s say a reversion to liberalism, both economic and political. The liberal did not last very long and Tunisia entered upon the phase of what may be termed 'planned dependence' in the economic sphere and a *de facto* one-party system in the political sphere. Following social unrest in the late 1970s, a policy of 'pluralism' was declared and only the future will tell what this policy will bring in the 1980s.

The reason for introducing the political context of Bourguiba's speeches is due to the fact that Bourguiba, consistent with his 1929 stand,[85] subordinated the issue of women – and of social reform in general – to his primary concern which was and continues to be 'state-building' or, in other words, the building of a viable structure of political institutions to serve as locomotive of progress and development.

Consequently, in his 3 August 1956 and 10 August 1956 speeches introducing the judicial reforms and Code of Personal Status, Bourguiba insists that improving the lot of women benefits the family, foundation of society,[86] and the justifications of the reforms embodied in the Code of Personal Status are, in the first place, nationalist 'so that Tunisia does not remain an abomination among the civilized nations of the world'.[87] He bases himself on historical legitimacy by demonstrating that the first leaders of the Tunisian nationalist movement, the Young Tunisians,[88] had themselves also called for legal reforms.[89] In the second place, social justice cannot tolerate that half of society should be disadvantaged and, therefore, the issue of the status of women is not simply a private matter but concerns the whole of Tunisian society and the state, representing that society.[90] The third justification is that the rational mind can only accept that, with time, conditions change and adjustments must be made.[91] Finally, he traces the requirements of social justice and of rational effort at adjustment to Islam.[92] In fact, he states that two experts of Islamic law ('ulama'), 'Abd al-'Aziz Ja'it and al-Tahir ibn 'Ashur, were consulted by the legislators and fully supported the Code.[93]

Indirectly, the two 'ulama' represented the contribution of the liberal political elite of Tunis, the capital. When Bourguiba took over power in 1957, this Tunis elite split. While al-Tahir ibn 'Ashur continued to support Bourguiba, at least until the beginnings of the socialist experiment of the 1960s, Ja'it did not.[94]

The next speech formally dedicated to judicial reform and the Code of Personal Status was made on 13 August 1960. During the four intervening years, Bourguiba touched upon the subject only within the framework of more general speeches. Most of these general speeches are not devoted to any one specific topic since Bourguiba views himself as the guide of Tunisia and his speeches as advice to be followed by the Tunisian people;[95] for example, on 19 January 1957, he made a speech in remembrance of his last imprisonment during the national independence struggle and the last part of the speech is devoted to the status of women in which he calls upon women to stop wearing the veil and on men to respect those women not wearing it.[96] He repeats the same theme in his 5 December 1957 speech on dignity.[97] In his 25 November 1958 speech made in the remote southern village of Matmata (Matmatah), he reiterates the social and rational justifications for improving the status of women. He proudly observes that his place in history is assured because of his role in this effort.[98] Interestingly enough, Islam does not enter as a factor justifying the measures taken by the Code of Personal Status but only to justify the non-hereditary principle relating to the head of the newly-declared Republic which he had established.[99]

Despite the generally progressive nature of the ideological climate of Tunisia in the 1960s, the positions taken by Bourguiba himself concerning the issue of the status of women were relatively mild if judged by the standard of equality between men and women. Of course, the same may be said about the political leaders of the

United States of the 1980s who are having such a difficult time accepting the Equal Rights Amendment. It might be relevant also to remember that the essential equality of men and women and its translation into actual social reality is a very recent phenomenon; only in 1965 did women in France obtain the right to hold property and conduct business and, in Switzerland, women obtained their suffrage almost ten years after Tunisian women.[100] It is not surprising, therefore, that in the 1960s and the 1970s Bourguiba proclaimed women 'equal but different'.

> Granting woman her rights does not mean her equality with men in all matters - she is equal in dignity and has equal shares in respect, esteem and deference; men and women have the same degree of consideration but each is capable according to his or her natures; this one for work with things while the other for work with people, that one for sewing and the other for nursing or justice, that one for accounting and the other for physical work. Based on this, there should be tasks specific to man according to his constitution and potential as well as common tasks to be undertaken by both man and woman according to the possibilities and circumstances of each sex.[101]

It is possible that Bourguiba, in the above passage, is reflecting the constraints he perceives as a result of his belief in 'gradual stages' similar to Haddad[102] for a realistic implementation of policies but there is no indication in these texts of such a position. It is also possible that he was simply reflecting the actual situation of public opinion in Tunisia where women themselves seemed to be reluctant to surrender their status in terms of 'respect'[103] in their exclusive roles of wife and mother in return for their 'rights' to compete in a world dominated by men.[104]

The paternalism latent in these speeches becomes explicit in the 13 August 1965 speech when Bourguiba addresses his audience as 'My Beloved Daughters'.[105] This is one of Bourguiba's more structured speeches where he moves from an autobiographic exposition of his own attitude towards women - love and pity for his own mother and sister, the priority he had given to political independence over social and economic reforms, the role of women in the national independence struggle, the promulgation of the Code of Personal Status, the educational reforms for both sexes - to call for improving awareness in order to bring social reality closer to the ideal embodied in the laws. Nonetheless, he strikes a note of warning when he condemns the exaggerated freedom of girls (but not boys) and their refusal to accept parental authority. He calls for freedom without moral corruption and for an equilibrium between rights and duties yet lays the burden of responsibility for probity on the shoulders of the woman rather than equally upon those of the man and of the woman.[106]

The same note, trying to brake the speedy effervescence of the 1960s - the era of the mini-skirt - is found in his 1972 speech,[107] where he explicitly criticizes al-Tahir al-Haddad for being too far ahead of his time.[108] Again, in his 1976 speech,[109] he views the functions of women primarily within the family to the extent that he gives preference to productive activities, such as sewing and weaving which she could undertake in the home; in other words, a state of policy of cottage industries.

Perhaps Bourguiba agrees with the principle of the equality of men and women and simply views Tunisian society not yet ready for it. In fact, Bourguiba is famous for his two tenets of pursuing a policy of stages (*etapisme*) and of 'realism' in his calculations of the possibilities of effectively carrying out the policy.[110] This might explain why Bourguiba, gradualist and realistic that he is, never proclaimed his belief in the principle of perfect equality between men and women simply because he figured that such an ideal could not be effectively translated into social reality in the Tunisia of his time.

> There is no use promulgating legal texts without the benefit of those men who undertake to implement the laws and of the human beings (presumably, women) on whom the implementation is carried out.[111]

It is, therefore very difficult to know whether Bourguiba believes in the essential equality of men and women or whether he holds that there is a limit to women eternal to their nature of reproducers of the human race.

To recapitulate the history of the status of woman in independent Tunisia, we may recall that in the first period of independence, the emphasis lay on reform in the legal and judicial conditions of woman within the family while, when the Neo–Destour embraced socialism in the 1960s, various programs were designed to attract women to the work force.[112] After the failure of the socialist experiment, the interventionalist commitment of the Tunisian political leadership to planned changed in the social sphere seems to have diminished considerably; 'the revolutionary elan that characterised the country earlier dissipated rapidly'.[113] The 1970s represent a period of low levels of planned change when the status of women was left to the hazards of unplanned factors of change.[114] Written in 1977, the following comment is pessimistic indeed.

> .... the situation of women in Tunisia has begun to deteriorate in recent years and the country is resting on its reputation so far as official policies towards women are concerned. The situation of women will have to deteriorate much more before it approaches that of women in conservative Arab countries .... Nevertheless, Tunisia is no longer the radical and daring innovator it once was ....[115]

This was before the bloody demonstrations of 1979, the armed insurrection in Gafsa (Qafsah) in 1980 and the resurgence of Islamic fundamentalist or integralist[116] groups. These developments, directly or indirectly, have led Habib Bourguiba to call for a multi-party political system. In the wake of this call, the Code of Personal Status has been amended and perhaps the 1980s will see the rise of an autonomous women's movement, sorely lacking until now.

In conclusion, it does seem clear that the status of women in Tunisia was historically related both to politics, in its nationalist and socialist forms, and to religion, specifically to Islam. In fact, the two fields of force, politics and religion were separate but not unrelated.[117]

Islam, as religion, played a role in the politics of women's rights in several ways. The spiritual equality between men and women in the eyes of God, as portrayed in the Qur'an, could be interpreted in two ways.[118] Either one kept the spiritual separate from the temporal in order to argue that women was equal to man in her spiritual relationship to God (*'ibadat*) but she was inferior to man in her temporal relationships to him (*mu'amalat*). Or one held that the temporal was subject to the spiritual and deduced that, since woman was equal to man in the eyes of God, she was his equal in the temporal sense as well.[119]

As the study of al-Haddad showed, the two distinctive features of the dominant ideology in Tunisian politics, the ideas of 'gradualism' and 'realism' may be derived from the Qur'an. Interestingly enough, the European ideologies which influenced Tunisian leaders - such as German Social Democracy and French (Reformist) Socialism of the early 20th century - were also characterised by these features.

Thus, following in al-Haddad's tracks, it may be argued that Islam played a role both in enunciating the ideal of full equality between men and women and in defining the approach to be taken to achieve that ideal, 'realistic gradualism'. Finally, Islam played a crucial role in legitimizing the programs and practical steps taken to promote the status of women in Tunisia.

REFERENCES

1. The term 'status' implies two aspects: 'the *rights* given to women and the *respect* given to them'; Nadia H. Youssef, 'The Status and Fertility Patterns of Muslim Women' in *Women in the Muslim World*, edited by Lois Beck and Nikki Keddie (Cambridge: Harvard University Press, 1978), 76. Youssef continues on to note that 'Confusion often ensues because the two distinct factors are erroneously used interchangeably, when in reality they are often inversely correlated'. In this paper, I will be dealing with 'status' in terms of the 'rights' rather than the 'respect' of women.

2. Transliteration from the Arabic follows the Library of Congress system, except that the diacritical marks are dropped and both the ʾ and the ʿ are given by '. When a transliteration into the Latin alphabet is already established, mainly through the prevalent use of French in Tunisia, it is followed by the Library of Congress transliteration given between brackets.

3. A partial English translation of the Code of Personal Status (Books I - X) was made by George N. Sfeir, 'The Tunisian Code of Personal Status' in *The Middle East Journal* 11/3 (Summer 1957), 309-318; while a French translation of the Code as well as of subsequent relevant legislation are given by Maurice Borrmans,

'Documents sur la Famille au Maghreb de 1940 a nos jours; avec les textes legislatifs en matiere de statut personnel musulman' in *Oriente Moderno* LIX/1-5 (January-May 1979), 182-219. The Tunisian Code of 1956 was the second Code of Personal Status promulgated in the Arab world, following upon the Syrian Code of 1953. Despite its relatively early legislative concern with the status of women, Egypt delayed the promulgation of a code as such and instead instituted a whole series of laws in defence of the status of women; see Maurice Borrmans, 'Codes de Statut Personnel et evolution sociale en certains pays musulmans' in *Bulletin d l'Institut des Belles Lettres Arabes* (IBLA) 103 (1963), 205-260.

4. This loop-hole was later covered by the explanatory circulars from the Secretary of State to the Ministry of Interior dated 17 March 1962 and from the Ministry of Justice No. 216 dated 5 December 1973, following the Prime Minister's letter No. 606 dated 19 October 1973. Despite Tunisia's adherence to the New York Conventions of 10 December 1962, a Tunisian Muslim woman cannot marry a non-Muslim foreigner but a Tunisian Muslim man can marry a non-Muslim foreigner; see Naziha Lakehal-Ayat *La Femme tunisienne et sa Place dans le Droit Positif* (Tunis: Editions Dar el-Amel, 1978), 17.

5. As a historian, I am limiting myself more or less to the material offered by written sources. It is up to trained sociologists to deal with the question: 'Was the Code of Personal Status an effective instrument in changing the sociological reality of Tunisian women?' For some insights touching upon this question, see Mark A. Tessler, Janet Rogers and Daniel Schneider, 'Women's Emancipation in Tunisia' in *Women in the Muslim World*, op. cit., 141-158; and L.H. Durrani, 'Employment of Women and Social Change' in *Change in Tunisia*, edited by R. Stone and J. Simmons (Albany: State University of New York Press, 1976); for some views of the general relationships between legislation and society, see Elizabeth H. White, 'Legal Reform as an Indicator of Women's Status in Muslim Nations'; Noel Coulson and Doreen Hinchcliffe, 'Women and Law Reform in Contemporary Islam', both in *Women in the Muslim World*, op. cit., 52-68 and 38-51 respectively; and J.N.D. Anderson, 'Le Droit comme Force Sociale dans l'Histoire et la Culture de l'Islam' in *IBLA* 86 (1959), for a concise picture, see Juliette Bessis, 'Les Femmes et la Politique en Tunisie' in *Les Femmes et la Politique autour de la Mediterranee*, edited by Christiane Souriau (Paris: L'Harmattan, 1980), 219-233. The Center for Economic and Social Studies and Research (Centre d'Etudes et de Recherches Economiques et Sociales, 23 rue d'Espagne, Tunis, Tunisie) has published numerous sociological studies on women in Tunisia. 'Al-Tahir al-Haddad, *Imra atuna fi al-Shari'ah wa-al-mujtama'*, 4th edition (Tunis: Al-Dar al-Tunisiyyah li-al-nashr, 1980). A French summary of the book is given by M. Mutafarrij (pseudonym of Leon Bercher), 'Notre Femme dans le Loi et la Societe' in *Revue d'Etudes Islamiques* 3 (1965), 201-230. This summary was amended and improved by Borrmans, 'Documents', op. cit., 25-69. Mona Mikhail's coverage of the book in her *Images of Arab Women: Fact and Fiction (Washington, D.C.: Three Continents press, 1979), 37-40, is totally*

inadequate; in fact, it shows that she did not read it in full since she completely neglects to mention the second or sociological part of the book. Al-Haddad's book follows in the tradition of the Egyptian Rifa's Rafi' al-Tahtawi, *Al-Murshid al-Amin fi Ta'lim al-Banat wa-al-Banin* (The Good Guide to the Education of Girls and Boys) (1875) and of Qasim Amin who wrote *Fi Tahrir al-Mar'ah al-Jadidah* ('The New Woman') published in 1901. One may trace this genre to John Stuart Mill's *On the Subjection of Women* (1869) and Friedrich Engels' *The Origins of the Family, Private Property and the State* (1884) and it is, indeed, probable that both Amin and al-Haddad were directly or indirectly influenced by this type of European literature belonging to the field of political economy. Nonetheless, writing about women as such was not totally absent from the Arab-Islamic tradition as evidenced by Muhyi al-Din Ibn al-Arabi's special chapter in his *Al-Futuhat al-Makkiyyah*, devoted to the analysis of the common grounds betwen men and women. I thank my colleague, Hoda Lotfi, for the above reference to Ibn al'Arabi's work.

7.   'Le Voile' (The Veil) first published on 11 January 1929 in *L'Etendard Tunisien*;   see Habib Bourguiba, *Articles de Presse, 1929-1934* in the series *Histoire du Mouvement National* (Tunis: Centre de Documentation, 1967), 1-6.

8.   See Leon C. Brown, *The Tunisia of Ahmad Bey, 1837-1855* (Princeton: Princeton University Press, 1974).

9.   Al-Tahir al-Haddad was born around 1899 to a relatively modest family living in Tunis but originally from Gabes (Qabis) in the south of Tunisia.   He enrolled in the famous Zaytunah Mosque-University, Tunisia's al-Azhar, in 1911 and, in 1920, obtained his *tatwi'* diploma, equivalent to Junior College level.   He joined the Destour Party in the same year.   Soon after, he became involved in the movement initiated by Muhammad'Ali al-Hammi (also originally from Gabes) whose ideas, it seems to me, were basically inspired by the contemporary German Social Democrats.   The latter, accepting the principle of stages in social progress, concentrated their efforts in the socio-economic field rather than upon the achievement of political power;   see Eduard Bernstein, *Evolutionary Socialism: A Criticism and Affirmation* (1899) translated from the German by Edith C. Harvey (New York: Schocken Books, 1961), xii-xiv.   Muhammad Ali's first idea was to organise consumer co-operatives upon which would be based financing co-operatives to be followed by production co-operatives.   Unfortunately, he was overtaken by events when the dockers of Tunis and Bizerte (Banzart) struck in 1924.   When the French-dominated General Labour Confederation (CGT - Confeder-ation Generale du Travail) did not help the striking workers, Muhammad Ali decided that a separate Tunisian labour confederation was necessary, and began to organise the General Confederation of Tunisian Workers.   Indirectly, of course, this revived the issue of Tunisian sovereignty within the Protectorate.   Not surprisingly, the French authorities as well as the CGT combated this new organisation and the Destour chose to align itself with this option, allowing the CGTT to be killed in its cradle.   For further information on al-Haddad himself, see Ahmad Khalid, *Al-Tahir al-Haddad wa-al-Bi'ah al-*

Tunisiyyah fi-al-thulth al-awwal min al-qarn al-'ishrin (Tunis: n.p., 1967).

10. Actually, at the celebration held to launch the book, some 60 men attended which shows that al-Haddad did have some support, at least initially among part of the Tunisian elite; see the commemorative photograph in al-Haddad, *Imra'atuna*, p. 13, where not one woman appears, either veiled or unveiled.

11. Ibid., 18.

12. Al-Haddad, *Imra'atuna*, 22.

13. Ibid., 28.

14. Ibid., 22-23.

15. Ibid., 24.

16. Ibid., 43.

17. Ibid., 27-28.

18. Ibid., 30-31.

19. Ibid., 33-38.

20. Ibid., 38-41.

21. These and all other Quranic quotations are given according to the translation by Muhammad M. Pickthall, *The Meaning of the Glorious Koran*.

22. Al-Haddad, *Imra'atuna*, 41.

23. Ibid., 45. The importance of these two verses in the discussions about the status of women in Islamic countries is also illustrated in a study by my colleague, Hanan Awwad, 'Dr. Nazmi Luqa's views on Women in Islam' (unpublished paper).

24. Ibid., 52-54.

25. Ibid., 63-64.

26. Ibid., 65-65.

27. Ibid., 65-68. There is some discrepancy in the various editions of al-Haddad's book concerning the justifications he gives for this position. The 1980 Arabic edition gives the usual reformist argument based on the Quranic verse 4: 3 '. . . . marry of the women, who seem good to you, two or three or four; and if ye fear that ye cannot do justice (to so many) then one (only) . . . .' which is quoted as if it were immediately followed by the verse 4: 129 'Ye will not be able to deal equally between (your) wives however much ye wish (to do so)'. The French summaries, by Bercher and Borrmans, base the argument on the Quranic verse 30: 21 'And of his signs is this: He created for you helpmates from yourselves that ye might find rest in them, and He ordained between you love and mercy'. According to these versions, al-Haddad then argues that this emotional bond of 'love and mercy' is indivisible and, therfore, polygamy is not permitted; see Bercher, op. cit., 209, and Borrmans, 'Documents', op. cit., 31.

28. The term 'divorce' is used here to cover the two meanings of the Arabic term 'talaq'; the unilateral repudiation by the husband and the severing of the marriage bond, in general.

29. Al-Haddad, *Imra'atuna*, 69-70.

30. Ibid., 73.

31. Ibid., 117.

32. Ibid., 88-114. The variety in the answers given by these 6 authorities itself illustrates that the Shari'ah is not immutable or

dogmatic, but offers a wide spectrum of possibilities.

33. Ibid., 118.

34. Most of the commentators on the issue of women in Arab or Islamic countries also emphasized education rather than political rights as the means of improving the status of women: first among whom had been Qasim Amin (see Mikhail, *Images*, 3).

35. See above p.

36. Al-Haddad, *Imraatuna*, 183.

37. That the veil, and seclusion, could be used by women to their own advantage is the thesis presented by Carla Makhlouf (Obermeyer), *Changing Veils: Women and Modernization in North Yemen* (London: Croom Helm, 1979), where she demonstrates that women, using the veil could enter into man's world but that man was absolutely forbidden to enter upon woman's universe without her permission.

38. Al-Haddad, *Imra'atuna*, 203.

39. Ibid., 206.

40. Ibid. In fact, al-Haddad holds that the Qur'an itself was gradualist as mentioned above, p.

41. Ibid., 220.

42. See the summary translated into French by Borrmans, 'Documents', op. cit., 99-119.

43. See the full French translation in ibid., 70-98.

44. Al-Haddad, *Imra'atuna*, 95.

45. Ibid., 99.

46. Ibn 'Ashur in Borrmans, 'Documents', op. cit., 87.

47. See reference 7.

48. Bourguiba, op. cit., 1.

49. Ibid., 3.

50. Ibid., 4-5.

51. Ibid., 1.

52. Ibid., 180.

53. Al-Haddad's fundamental sympathy for woman and his desire for true equality between the sexes is most clearly indicated in his observations about the veil. He holds that responsibility for moral behaviour should not be laid on the shoulders of the woman alone but also on those of the man. He states: 'If we sincerely wish the true purity of woman and we ask for it in an honest and useful fashion, we should combat the licentiousness of man by avoiding scenes of jealousy, ... adultery, sodomy, multiplicity of wives, forced marriages, and giving the reins of divorce into the man's hands without any limitations or supervision'; see ibid., 190.

54. Ibid., 127.

55. For a view of various considerations on the sexual aspects in Islamic societies, see Georges-Henri Bousquet, *L'Ethique sexuelle de l'Islam* (Paris: Maisonneuve-Larose, 1966), revised edition of *La Morale de l'Islam et son Ethique* (Paris: Maisonneuve, 1953) and Abdel-Wahab Bouhdiba, *La Sexualite en Islam* (Paris: Presses Universitaires de France, 1975).

56. For details of the feminist movement in Egypt, see 'The Revolutionary Gentlewomen in Egypt' by Afaf Lutfi al-Sayyid Marsot

and 'Feminism and Nationalist Politics in Egypt' by Thomas Philipp, both of which are found in Beck and Keddie, op. cit., 261-276 and 277-294 respectively.

57.   Philipp, op. cit., 279.

58.   According to ibid., 'Mustafa Kamil's brand of nationalism could perhaps be described by what has been called aptly "counternationalism", that is, a nationalism that is foremost a reaction against foreign domination or the threat thereof rather than a concern with the political and social structure of society itself'.

59.   Shaykh Ahmad Bayram, *Shaykh al-Islam* of Tunisia in 1930, answered al-Haddad's question: 'What should be covered of the woman's body in order to preserve morality?' in the following terms, 'The answer to question 12 is that she should be completely covered including her face and hands during a period when immorality has spread'. (My underline where he is referring to the presence of foreigners in Tunisia); see al-Haddad, *Imra'atuna*, 114.

60.   Lakehal-Ayat, op. cit., 57, calls him 'the most feminist of all leaders in the world'.

61.   Ahmed Mestiri (Ahmad Mistiri) comments in his preface to Es-Snoussi's (Al-Sanusi) *Code annote*, 'Islamic law is based upon principles of indisputable justice, has a universal character, takes into consideration human nature, and can serve as framework at all times in all places, - these virtues were recognised at the International Congress for Comparative Legislation held at the Hague in 1952; (with reference to the Code of Personal Status) the legislator has drawn upon these principles and, inspired by social aims relevant to our period, gave us a corpus of laws accessible to all in a clear and complete text' as quoted by Borrmans, 'Codes', op. cit., 205.

62.   All references and quotations are from the English translation by Sfeir; see Reference 3.

63.   See above p.

64.   This was later amended to 17 years for women and 20 for men; see Lakehal-Ayat, op. cit., 13.

65.   Cf. Lakehal-Ayat, op. cit., 17-23.

66.   Tessler et. al., op. cit., 142.

67.   Slah-Eddine Baly (Salah al-Din Bali) (Minister of Justice in the late 1970s), 'Preface' to Lakehal-Ayat, op. cit., 5.

68.   To the question, 'to what limit this obedience?', Lakehal-Ayat, op. cit., 15, answers, 'The answer is given us by Article 831 of the Code of Contracts and Obligations which stipulates that the married woman may not engage her services as wet nurse or otherwise except with the authorisation of her husband who has the right to break the engagement undertaken without his accord'. But it would seem that this was overruled by Tunisia's ratification of the New York Conventions which provide for 'the equal right of woman as much as man to earn a living by work freely chosen or accepted', ibid., 37.

69.   Youssef, op. cit., 77, correctly focusses on the strength of the family in Islamic countries and on the ability of the family 'to provide economic support for its women at all times' as fundamental factors for the absence of a woman-led feminist movement in most Islamic countries since 'Few women have felt the need to be self-

sufficient through education or employment because of the availability
of economic support (within the male-dominated family)'. Yet she
does not seem to discern the movement away from the extended and
towards the nuclear family and does not distinguish between the
extended family and the nuclear family with respect to the economic
self-sufficiency of the family and the pressures placed on women
within each formation.

70.   Borrmans, 'Codes', op. cit., 255.

71.   The Code of Personal Status was not, in effect, the only
piece of legislation promulgated by the political leaders of independent Tunisia to deal with the situation of women. Following the path
of al-Haddad, the educational reform embodied in law Nos. 58-118 of
4 November 1958 specified the equal access of both girls and boys to
education; see Lakehal-Ayat, op. cit., 35. Also see Marie T. Jones,
'Education of Girls in Tunisia: Policy implications of the Drive for
Universal Enrollment', *Comparative Education Review* 24/2 part 2
(June 1980), S106-S123 which was brought to my attention by my
colleague Mobina Bhinani.

It was only much later, as part of the socialist experiment
of the 1960s and of the general concern for economic development,
that a Labour Code was promulgated on 30 April 1966: Lakehal-Ayat,
op. cit., 40-41. Other legislation covering woman at work were: the
international labour conventions ratified by Tunisia (ibid., 38-40) and a
whole series of laws promulgated during the interventionist 1960s
(ibid., 41-48).

72.   Overall, the most important instrument for actualizing the
implementation of the Code was the Neo-Destour Party, Tunisia's *de
facto* single mass party which became the Destourian Socialist Party
(PSD - Parti Socialiste Destourien) in 1964.   During the following
period of activist government intervention, the Party undertook an
extensive resocialization effort through its more than 1,200 cells
spread throughout the country. To overcome the inability of men to
contact women under seclusion, the National Union of Tunisian Women
(UNFT - Union Nationale des Femmes Tunisiennes) had created in
1957 to explain the rights of women acquired under the Code and to
discuss problems considered specific to women: Tessler et. al.,
op. cit., 143, and personal interview with Fatmah Ya'lawi, UNFT
representative of the Governorate of Jendouba (Jandubah) in August
1980. But it was only under the leadership of Radhia Haddad that it
reached out for political power during the 1960s (Personal interview
with Fatma Haddad, August 1980) and Lucie Pruvost, 'A Propos du IVe
Congress de l'Union Nationale des Femmes en Tunisie', *IBLA* 29 (1966),
439-447.

73.   Thus, it was only in 1964, eight years after the Code of
Personal Status had explicitly prohibited polygamy that the courts
finally declared that a polygamous marriage was actually invalid; see
Coulson and Hinchcliffe, op. cit., 48.

74.   Actually, in a 1956 speech presenting the Code of Personal
Status Bourguiba claimed that Ibn 'Ashur fully supported the Code. It
would seem, to me, that the reservations Ibn 'Ashur made were his way
of expressing his disapproval of the interventionist policies which the

government was beginning to pursue in the 1960s.

75.   A French translation is given by Borrmans, 'Documents', op. cit.

76.   Cf. provisions for custody of children in the Code of Personal Status, Article 57ff.

77.   It would seem that here Ibn 'Ashur was implicitly making a distinction between the sphere of human relations with the Divinity, *'Ibadat*, where men and women are equal in the eyes of God and the sphere of human relations, *mu'amalat*, where men are superior to women.

78.   Borrmans, 'Documents', op. cit., 176-177.

79.   Tessler et. al., op. cit., 142, and Borrmans, 'Codes' op. cit., 212-213 fn. 11.

80.   See Maurice Borrmans, 'Divorce et Abus du Droit en Tunisie', *IBLA* 118-119 (1967), 227-272. Several Tunisian authors also wrote in defence of the Code of Personal Status among whom are M. al-Tayyib al-'Annabi, 'Al-Talaq fi al-Qanun wa-al-Mujtama' (Divorce in Law and Society) in ibid., 346-348; M. al-Bashir Zahrah, 'Al-Tajribah al-Tunisiyyah fi majal al-Ahwal al-Shakhsiyyah' (The Tunisian Experience in Matters of Personal Status), ibid., 349-360, and M. al-Hasan Abu La'abah, 'Al-Talaq al-Hukmi wa-athuruh fi al-Janub' (Court Divorce and its Effect in the South), ibid., 361-381. The last demonstrates, statistically, that the percentages of marriages and divorces had actually declined following the application of the Code and that this may be considered as evidence that, despite its proviso for divorce by mutual consent, the Code had actually encouraged family stability. In any case, it would seem that, compared to other Arab and Islamic countries, Tunisia does very well for the period following the application of the law; where in Egypt divorces were around 30% of the number of marriages contracted in any one year, in Tunisia they were around 5% (see Borrmans, 'Codes', op. cit., 226-227 fn. 5).

81.   Borrmans, 'Documents', op. cit.

82.   Borrmans, 'Codes', op. cit., 211.

83.   It is an open question whether the suffrage given to Tunisian women was a determining factor in the election of Bourguiba as President in 1957. On the legislation covering the political rights of Tunisian women, see Lakehal-Ayat, op. cit., 51-55.

84.   See reference 72 on the UNFT.

85.   See above p.

86.   Habib Bourguiba, *Khutab* ('Speeches') Part II (Tunisia: Ministry of Information, 1974.

87.   Ibid., 260.

88.   See Stuart E. Brown, *The Young Tunisians* (Unpublished Ph.D. dissertation, Institute of Islamic Studies, McGill University, Montreal, 1976).

89.   Bourguiba, *Khutab*, II, 256-257.

90.   Ibid., 273.

91.   Ibid., 261.

92.   Ibid., 262.

93.   Ibid., 264.

94.   Ibid., IX, 38, where Bourguiba violently attacks Ja'it because, according to Bourguiba, Ja'it had not supported the Code. In contradiction, I was informed that the Code – for which Bourguiba is usually given credit – was largely based on a codification of Personal Status laws of the Shari'ah prepared by 'Abd al-Aziz Ja'it, in a personal interview with Ahmed Mestiri, Minister of Justice in 1956 and presently leader of the principle opposition party in June 1981. Also see Ali Dimassi, *Habib Bourguiba, L'Apotre de la Liberte Tunisienne* ('Habib Bourguiba, the Apostle of Tunisian Liberty') (Tunis: Ali Dimassi, 1979), 200. Thus, the Code and the status of women became symbols of political conflict.

95.   Bourguiba, *Khutab*, VII, 242-243 and XX, 261.

96.   Ibid., III, 268-269.

97.   Ibid., V, 271-272.

98.   Ibid., VII, 246.

99.   Ibid., VII, 248.

100. Gamal Moursi Badr, 'Preface' to Mikhail, op. cit., 2.

101. Bourguiba, *Khutab*, XI, 47.

102. See above p. 47.

103. See above, reference 1.

104. Youssef, op. cit., 95.

105. Bourguiba, *Khutab*, XX, 27.

106. Ibid., 25-26.

107. Separate pamphlet dated 14 August 1972 entitled *'Fi al-nuhud bi-al-mar'ah nuhud al-mujtama"* (In the Progress of Woman lies the Progress of Society) (Tunis: Ministry of Inforamtion, 1972).

108. Ibid., 5.

109. Separate pamphlet dated 13 August 1976 and entitled *'Al-Tawfiq bayn Waza'if al-Mar'ah fi al-Mujtama"* (Striking a Balance between the Various Duties of Woman in Society) (Tunisia: Ministry of Information, 1976).

110. See above p.

111. Bourguiba, *Khutab*, XI, 50.

112. Tessler et. al., op. cit., 143. These official measures, taken in both the legal and the practical spheres, were reinforced by unplanned agents of social transformation such as the dramatic urbanisation that occurred in Tunisia after independence (from 15% in 1956 to 45% in 1970), the radio as means for mass communications and education. Within ten years after independence, literacy had climbed from a low of 15% to over 30%, the percentage of children attending primary school grew from 25% to 75% while the proportion of girls attending primary school increased from 31% in 1958 to 39% ibid., 143-144.

113. Ibid., 147.

114. According to a field study made on popular attitudes about women in Tunisia, total support for women's emancipation dropped markedly between 1967 and 1973, declining most among men in smaller towns and least among women in Tunis (ibid., 148-150). The study concludes that 'in general, official efforts are necessary if popular support for changes in the status of women is to be generated' and that 'forces of unplanned change by themselves were not sufficient

to increase support for women's liberation and were in fact associated with a decline in support', ibid., 151.

115.   Ibid., also see the conclusions of Bessis, op. cit., 233.

116.   Personally, I prefer the term 'integralist' since the basic tendency of these new groups is not simply a return to the fundamental tenets of Islam but an attempt to subsume all aspects of life – economic, social and political – to Islam.

117.   Conceptually, I distinguish between 'politics' meaning a set of ideas and institutions dealing with power and 'religion' meaning that set of ideas and institutions premised on the belief in the supernatural. This conceptual differnece is not a characteristic of English or of Western usage alone but is also found in Arabic since the terms 'siyasah' (politics) and 'din' (religion) do exist autonomous of each other. It is usually assumed that the two are inherently unrelated both as theoretical concepts and as historical phenomena in terms of both ideas and institutions in the West. In contrast, the Islamic East is thought, by Westerners, to have misguidedly confused the two fields while Muslim 'integralists' believe that true Islam does not separate between politics and religion. In fact, the Pope is considered by true Catholics to be the Vicar of Christ on earth while the history of Muslims illustrates that the 'integralist' tendency was not, at all times, prevalent as the example of the struggle between the 'khilafah' and the 'saltanah' aptly illustrates.   In sum, the Arab-Islamic heritage distinguishes between 'siyasah' and 'din' on the conceptual and historical levels but not always on the philosophical level.   See the comments along the same lines in my article, 'The Sacred and the Profane: Sadat's Speech to the Knesset', *The Middle East Journal* 34/1 (Winter 1980), 13–14.

118.   Incidentally, the Quranic versions of Genesis and of the Fall do not portray woman as the intermediary between the devil and man.

119.   The first option seems to have been al-Haddad's while the second seems to have been that of his opponents. Of course, the first option also implied that any so-called 'natural' or 'biological' differences are only accidental to the essential equality between the sexes and should be son considered in terms of the legal rights and duties of both men and women.   Nonetheless, a case could be made for the equality of men and women on 'rational' and 'empirical' grounds independent of any religious beliefs.

Chapter 8

FEMALE EDUCATION IN EGYPT: CHANGING ATTITUDES OVER A SPAN OF 100 YEARS*

Hind Abou Seoud Khattab
Syada Greiss El Daeif

HISTORICAL BACKGROUND

Education has always been considered a major factor in shaping a society and in enriching its cultural heritage. Yet the value which is placed upon education and the manner in which a nation educates its citizens are themselves reflective of social, economic, and political forces operative within society. The historical experience, and hence, the tradition of education in Egypt, has further been moulded by centuries of foreign domination. The changes in philosophies, attitudes and practices introduced by those nations which ruled Egypt have heavily influenced the way of life, and in turn, the status of education. Indeed, scholars cite Egypt as an excellent example of a nation whose educational system historically has flourished or deteriorated according to the interests of a dominating foreign power. Thus, in order to obtain a better understanding of the current status of education, and the high esteem in which education is now held in Egyptian society, it is necessary to provide a brief summary of its historical development, emphasizing the contributions of both foreign and Egyptian elements.

The history of education in Egypt dates to the third millennium B.C. The Ancient Egyptians are known to have developed a very sophisticated educational system. Indeed, their contributions to the fields of mathematics, medicine, astronomy, architecture, and art are exemplified by the historical remains of their civilization. The ancient system, however, was geared to the education of the upper and middle classes; and, women of these classes were not denied the privilege of receiving instruction. Ancient records show that, particularly during the period from 1580 to 1085 B.C., women learned to read and write their language correctly, and some became expert scribes.[1]

Since the time of Pharaonic Egypt, the standard of education has traditionally declined during those periods in which an occupying foreign power has allowed the educational system to deteriorate. Thus, during the span of more than 2,000 years in which Egyptians lived under foreign domination, only two brief periods of renaissance occurred. The first was the era following the construction of the

Great Library of Alexandria which served as an intellectual centre during the Hellenistic Age. The second followed the establishment of al-Azhar University, which became the centre of Islamic learning.[2]

Following the foundation of al-Azhar in the tenth century, and until the reign of Muhammad 'Ali (1805-48), the sole type of education available was exclusively religious in nature, and consisted of institutions such as the *kuttab* and *madrasah*. The *kuttab*, a school attached to a mosque, offered elementary instruction in religion, reading and writing, and arithmetic. The *madrasah*, whose more advanced curriculum included Islamic jurisprudence, philosophy, geometry and mathematics, was first introduced into Egypt during the reign of Sultan Salah al-Din al-Ayyubi (1175-93). Like the *kuttab*, the *madrasah* was always affiliated with a mosque and staffed by instructors who were themselves the products of this system of religious education. Hence, al-Azhar and the network of educational institutions over which it presided dominated the cultural life of Egypt for centuries. For it was this system of education which produced the intellectual and religious leadership of the society.

If ambitious young men sought to further their education by attending the *madrasah*, such opportunities were not available to young women in the Mamluk and Ottoman periods. Women were by tradition excluded from attending the *madrasah* and other higher institutions of learning in Egypt. The earliest records mentioning women's education in modern times, which date to the reign of Muhammad 'Ali, reveal that young women of well-to-do families were tutored privately in their homes. Their studies included religious teachings, reading and writing. Girls from less affluent families were sometimes allowed to attend the local *kuttab* in order to learn the fundamentals of religious practice, as well as reading and writing.

The reign of Muhammad 'Ali marked the beginning of a new era in which a utilitarian attitude towards education was adopted. As a part of his program to train large numbers of individuals for assignment to technical or administrative jobs in the government, Muhammad 'Ali established the first government school for girls in 1832. This school was a vocational institution for the training of nurse-midwives to be assigned to the new medical school. This institution remained the only school for women until foreign missionaries established two primary schools for girls in 1846 and 1849 respectively.

These schools were followed by other missionary schools, and later by four private Egyptian schools. In 1875, three of the foreign schools extended their educational system to the secondary level. The Egyptian government opened the first primary school for girls in 1873, and a second in 1875. The number of girls enrolled in primary schools in 1875, as indicated in Table I (see Appendix), totalled 3,723.

Under the British occupation, which began in 1882, few substantial improvements were made in the system of education. Instead of opening additional elementary schools, British policy makers preferred to attempt the transformation of traditional *kuttabs* into elementary schools. Europeanised schools were favoured by British supervision and financial aid as well.

Educational opportunties for young women were further limited by the unavailability of classroom seats. Despite numerous requests to open additional primary schools for girls, by as late as 1900 no new schools had been established. Hence, only those fortunate girls who obtained entrance to a government school, or whose parents could afford the high tuition fees charged by the foreign and missionary schools, received a primary education.

The end of the nineteenth century witnessed a rapid change in attitudes toward the education of women. The movement was pioneered by Muslim religious leaders and social reformers who had had more extensive contact with societies which advocated the emancipation and education of women. Shaykh Muhammad 'Abduh, a Muslim scholar well known for his interpretations of the teachings of Islam, pointed out that Islam accorded women a high status by making them equal to men in communal rights and obligations; and, that it was ignorance rather than Islam that lowered the status of women. This movement was further strengthened by the writings of Qasim Amin who expressed the view that educated women are an asset and a vital element in the reform and development of their society.

Egyptian intellectuals, both male, and those few women who participated in the intellectual community, voiced these opinions in meetings, conferences, and in their own writings. By the turn of the twentieth century, a general public consensus on the need for primary education for girls pressured authorities to open primary schools for girls in almost all of the Governorates of Egypt. The resulting increase in the number of primary schools was accompanied by an increase in the number of waqf schools,[3] urban and rural private schools, private co-educational schools supervised by the government, and railway department schools (Table II: see Appendix).

The growth of nationalism and the struggle for independence from the British made Egyptian leaders aware that they could not succeed in gaining independence as long as the majority of Egyptians remained illiterate. Thus, the period following World War I also witnessed a growing public desire for reform of the existing system of education. *Kuttabs* were converted into four-form elementary schools. Ideas on the universality of education for all boys and girls between the ages of six and twelve were materialised in Article 19 of the Egyptian Constitution of 1923, which called for compulsory education for all Egyptian children. In order to provide for their instruction, existing government schools were used on a two-shift basis to enable more children to attend. Attention was also given to the expansion of training schools for male and female teachers.

From this period until the Revolution, the government made several attempts to reform an educational system which had encouraged the creation of a society characterised by conflicting values, attitudes, and beliefs.[4] Undoubtedly, this state of affairs was to a great extent due to the existence of a heterogeneous educational system. As mentioned earlier, Egypt possessed no unified system of education, rather, a network of *kuttabs*, Egyptian private schools, foreign private schools, and foreign missionary schools.

While the number of schools offering elementary, primary, and secondary instruction gradually increased, higher education continued to be limited to al-Azhar until 1908, when the first Egyptian university was established as a private secular institution. It later became affiliated with the Ministry of Education in 1925. The first nineteen women were admitted to the Egyptian University during the academic year 1909-10.[5]

With the 1952 revolution, Egypt entered a new era of vigorous and extensive reform and development in the political, social, economic, industrial, and educational fields. During the last three decades, the Egyptian educational system has reached a level of development unprecedented in the history of the nation. The most striking phenomena in the development of education has been the extensive expansion in the number of schools, classes, teachers and students; and, in the budget, organisation, administration, activities, and curricula of Egyptian schools.[6]

Two of the most significant developments in the reform of the educational system have been the unification of the system under the supervision of the Ministry of Education, and the tremendous increase in opportunities which are made available without cost to both boys and girls. As an example, the only condition for enrollment in the primary schools is now one of age – no distinction is made between the sexes for purposes of admission.

Consequently, the number and percentage of girls enrolled at all levels increased by two to threefold during the first two decades following the Revolution. At present, Egyptian girls are enjoying educational opportunities equal to those available to boys at all levels and in all fields of specialisation. In fact, it is worth mentioning that the number and ratio of women's enrollment in some faculties have surpassed that of men. Tables III, IV, V, VI, VII, VIII and IX indicate increases in ratio and percentage between 1953-1979 (see Appendix).

The present Egyptian educational system is comprised of four distinct divisions beginning with the primary level and concluding with university and graduate programs. The primary level covers a six year period. Children are enrolled in school at the age of six, and upon completion of the primary examination, they are promoted to the three year preparatory program. Following their examinations, graduates of the preparatory schools may enroll in the various branches of the secondary level, or in vocational training schools. Until 1980, primary educaton was compulsory for all Egyptian children. Since 1981, however, the Ministry of Education has recommended the extension of compulsory education to include the preparatory level as well.

Secondary education, which covers a three year period, is divided into three branches. The first division is Secondary General which prepares students for an academic education in the Egyptian universities. After their first year in this program, students have a choice between concentration in the liberal arts or sciences. Thereafter, those students who have chosen the latter may specialise during their final year in either mathematics or science (biology, physics or chemistry). This three year program is terminated by a national general examination. Graduates of this level then become eligible for enrollment in the various universities and institutes of higher learning. The second division of the secondary level consists of the technical schools. These schools comprise three branches; the industrial, agricultural, and the commercial. Some schools offer a three year program to prepare students to enter the skilled labour force; while others offer a five year program to train qualified technicians. Students who acquire a 75% average upon completion of these programs become eligible to enroll in a university.

The third division of the secondary level is composed of the teachers training schools. These schools offer a five year training program in which students are prepared to become primary school teachers. Students who achieve an average of 75% or above may likewise enroll in a university.

The fourth level of the Egyptian educational system consists of the universities and other higher institutes. Admission to the various faculties of specialisation is based upon a student's score on the general national examination, his area of specialisation in secondary school, and his own career preferences. Through all these stages, it is important to mention that there is no discrimination between the sexes.

Despite the existence of a free and non-discriminatory system of education, the rate of literacy among Egyptian women is still dramatically lower than that of men. At the turn of the twentieth century, the percentage of illiteracy in the country for the total population averaged around 90%. In 1947, the illiteracy rate had decreased to 75%. During that year, the percentage of females categorized as illiterate was 84%, as compared to 65% of the male population. The next census, which was taken in 1960, revealed that although the male illiteracy rate had declined from 65% to 56%, female illiteracy showed a mere one percent decline (from 84% to 83%). The last official census of 1976 showed a more proportionate decrease in illiteracy among females as compared to that of males. The percentage of illiterate males declined from 57% to 43% of the total population, while female illiteracy dropped from 83% to 70%. Hence, while substantial progress has been made in the eradication of illiteracy among Egyptian citizens, the fact remains that seven out of ten women in Egypt can neither read nor write.

RESEARCH PURPOSES AND RATIONALE

This study is based on data collected for longitudinal research focusing on factors involved in the prolongation of female education and its termination at various points in the educational process. The purpose of the study is threefold: (1) to determine the antecedent and contextual factors important in influencing girls' continuation (or non-continuance) to the next educational level at the institutional 'break points' of primary school, preparatory school and secondary school; (2) to describe the contexts of the girls' lives for both the continuers and non-continuers for the purpose of discovering which element might be hypothesized to influence later fertility; and (3) to monitor important events in the girls' lives over a period of three years. The purpose of this monitoring will be to answer a number of questions including: (a) whether continuation in school appreciably delays age at marriage; (b) whether continuation or non-continuation in school has an impact on employment outside the home in significantly different numbers; and (c) types of employment at the different educational levels.

Numerous studies have indicated the serious dangers of Egypt's rapid population growth to the country's social and economic development. The implications of such a high rate of population growth are becoming more evident and more enormous in magnitude as the rate of population growth impedes the rate of economic development.

It was not until 1962, however, that Egyptian policy makers showed serious concern about the relationship between the country's population growth and its social and economic development. At present, Egypt's population and family planning policy seeks to sustain an annual reduction in the birth rate of one-per-thousand over a ten year period. To achieve this goal, the policy specified a set of nine factors to be promoted simultaneously in order to transform the socio-economic and cultural systems into a level conducive to low fertility:

1. Family socio-economic level
2. Education
3. Women's employment
4. Agricultural mechanisation
5. Industrialisation
6. Infant mortality reduction
7. Social security
8. Population and family planning information and communication
9. Family planning services.

It is obvious from this list of factors that education and the employment of women constitute a major concern for Egypt's population and family planning programs.

Interest in this research grew out of the relationship between education and fertility. The persistent patterns associated with education include: (1) low fertility, (2) high female participation in the labour force, (3) emancipation of women, and (4) delayed age at marriage.

The relationship between women's education and fertility has often been studied, and it is usually found to be negative. While the shape, and sometimes the direction of the relationship, differs from one nation to another, it has been found to be definitely inverse in several Muslim countries (Algeria, Lebanon, Egypt, Turkey and Syria). Exactly how education affects fertility is not clearly understood, but some links have been seriously suggested. Education may indirectly affect fertility through its relationship with labour force participation and women's age at marriage.

Female labour force participation has been found to be inversely related to low fertility in such different cultural settings as the United States and Brazil. However, the relationship between women's labour force participation and fertility is also sometimes positive and sometimes non-existent. Various explanations have been suggested for inverse relationships between employment and fertility, such as the incompatability of some types of work and mother roles, and modern attitudes which accompany such new roles for women.

The relationship between female age at marriage and fertility has been somewhat better elucidated. An inverse relationship between age at marriage and fertility has been stated for China, Tunisia, and Morocco. This relationship might be expected to be particularly marked in countries where effective contraception is not widely practised, and where women are exposed to pregnancy mainly within marriage. The relationship between education and age at marriage has frequently been found to be positive: the more the education, the later the age at marriage.

It is important to note at this point that the relationship of early marriage and employment of women to other aspects of Egyptian culture is far more complex than might be inferred from the above statements. Specialists believe that reductions in Egypt's rate of population increase are not likely to be achieved without substantial changes through formal and informal education.

The more direct effects of female education on fertility may, to a great extent, be through attitudinal changes resulting from (1) the use of literacy and increased access to written materials; (2) alternative role models to wife and mother, and exemplified by teachers, and as read about in books, magazines, and newspapers; and (3) exposures to peers from different backgrounds, persons other than neighbours and relatives.

This ongoing research project is currently exploring, and will later elucidate the ramifications of prolonged female education, a complex of behaviour that is in turn believed to be related to fertility.

RESEARCH METHODOLOGY

Site Selection

Cairo was selected as the research site because it represents the most important urban centre in the Arab region. Cairo is also known for its superior educational facilities, particularly those available to girls. Hence, a city like Cairo is an especially appropriate site for the study of girls' educational experience and all the factors concomitant with it, as well as the development of female education in the region.

The southern and western educational zones in Cairo were selected for the research on the basis that these zones have many public schools for girls, and that the majority of the inhabitants of these zones are from the lower-middle and lower socio-economic classes. These two zones cover the districts of Sayida Zeinab, Abdeen, Old Cairo, Manial, Garden City, El Mounira, and Dar El-Salam.

Sample Selection

For the purpose of the study, three cohorts of school girls were selected from the three levels at the institutional 'break points' of primary school, preparatory school, and secondary school. Cohort I consists of girls who were graduating from primary school after completing six grades in the month of June, 1980 preceding the initiation of field research. Since girls begin school at the age of six, the average age of girls in this cohort is around twelve. Cohort II consists of girls who were graduating from preparatory school after completing three additional years by June, 1980 (i.e. seventh to ninth grade). Their ages average about fifteen years. Cohort III consists of girls graduating from school after completing three or five years additional years by June, 1980. These girls average between eighteen and twenty years of age, according to the type of secondary school attended.

Our sample of students was drawn from eighteen schools[7] located in the two educational zones mentioned earlier. The number of classes in preparatory and secondary levels was secured from school records, after which thirty-five classes were selected at random. A larger number of primary schools and classes were included to meet the required quota in the sample, since primary schools are co-educational.

The proposed number for each cohort was a minimum of two hundred girls. However, to allow for refusals, difficulty in locating addresses, etc., a larger sample was secured. The initial screening included 310 primary students, 314 preparatory students, 332 secondary, and 153 secondary technical (commerce and teachers training school) students. The last schools offer intermediate education wherein students are trained and prepared for employment rather than university studies.

Data Collection and Field Work

Field methods used for data collection consist of structured as well as open-ended interviews and participant observation. Since this research is longitudinal, covering a period of three years, the work was divided into three phases. During the first year of research (Phase I), two interview schedules and an informal interview were administered to the girls in our sample, and either of their parents. During these interviews information was ascertained on the educational status of students, their perceptions of and aspirations toward continuing education, their attitudes toward the employment of women, ideal age at marriage, and compatability of roles for married, employed women. Moreover, data was collected on the family's socio-economic background, the parents' educational and occupational status, and their aspirations and attitudes toward their daughter's education and employment.

The second and third phases are planned to provide information on variables antecedent to continuance or non-continuance in school, and to current context effects of continuance or non-continuance in school. Upon completion of the third year, longitudinal information will be available on those factors which were involved in the prolongation of education for some and the termination of education for others in our sample. Such information would indicate the impact of prolongation or non-continuance of education for girls, on age at marriage, employment, and later fertility behaviour. This paper is primarily based on data collected during Phase I.

PRELIMINARY FINDINGS

The information obtained from the respondents interviewed revealed the following characteristics which will be presented here as background information.

Socio-economic Status of Families under Study

Social mobility within socio-economic levels in urban Cairo is becoming more flexible due to several factors of which the most important are: (1) the availability of free education for all, and (2) the substantial increase in the income of skilled and unskilled Egyptian labourers who migrated to work in neighbouring countries and of those labourers employed in Egypt. During the past decade, Egypt has experienced some rapid upward movement within the various socio-economic levels as well as changes in the criteria characterising the different levels.

For the purpose of our study, the following criteria was used to classify our sample. Variables used were: education of both parents, occupation of both parents, neighbourhood of residence, living conditions, density per room, and ownership of material goods.[8] If we were to use the classic classification of upper, middle and lower classes, our sample would fall within the lowest socio-economic level. The focus of the study on girls attending public schools automatically eliminated the upper, and the great majority of the middle classes in urban Cairo, since these groups would enrol their children in foreign or Egyptian private schools.

Further classification of our sample indicated that 63% fall into the middle-lower class, 27% fall into the lower class, 9% in the upper-lower class, and only 1% in the lower-middle class.

Characteristics of Parents

It is quite clear that illiteracy among mothers is much higher than among fathers. While 41% of the mothers are illiterate, only 14% of the fathers are classified in this category. Similarly, the percentage of fathers who can barely read and write[9] is again higher than that of the mothers (28% for fathers as compared to 22% for mothers).

Comparisons between the education of fathers and mothers in the remaining categories, namely those who achieved primary, preparatory, secondary and university levels of education reveal significantly marked differences in one category. The number of fathers who are university graduates is almost four times greater than that of mothers (19% for fathers and 5% for mothers). The relatively high percentage of fathers with a university education may be attributed to the fact that a free university education has been available to all since the early fifties.

The above findings are representative of the overall level of the

177

educational status of women in Egypt, indicating that women's education lags behind that of men. Moreover, the figures for those with preparatory education suggest that the rate of school drop-outs decreases with this level, since graduates equipped with only a preparatory education are less likely to find appropriate employment. Hence, once a preparatory education is attained, the probability of pursuing one's education to the secondary and university levels greatly increases.

Occupation of Fathers and Mothers

The occupations[10] of the fathers range between those holding professinal positions to those engaged in skilled labour. Fifty percent are government employees, while 13% are employed in private business. Twenty-three percent manage their own small businesses. The majority of the mothers are housewives (82%). Around eighteen percent are presently working, and the majority of these (81%) are employed by the government in professional and semi-professional jobs. The remaining nineteen percent are employed in the private sector (as servants, etc.), or manage their own small businesses (as seamstresses, candy and cigarette vendors, etc.).

The number of women who are actively employed in our sample is much higher than the 1976 census figures for active participation of women in the labour force. This is due primarily to the fact that the definition of active employment for women used in the census excludes those women who work in private domestic service or assist in a family business, and women who help the family in agriculture or in the marketing of agricultural products. Hence the contributions of these women to their family income are not recognised.

Household composition

Household composition was examined in terms of the number of people residing in the household, as well as their relationship to the student. The number of people residing in each household ranged from three or less (2.5%) to eleven or more persons (3%). The majority (65%), however, had five to seven members (21%, 24% and 20% respectively). The average number of persons per household is 6.5. This figure closely corresponds to the 1976 census figure for the same family-type.

The great majority of the students live in nuclear families.[11] In twelve percent of the families, the students are living with one parent because either the father (10%) or the mother (2%) is deceased. One percent of the students live with grandparents or uncles because both parents are deceased. The remaining three percent fall into three categories: the parents are divorced, and the student lives with relatives[12] (1%); the student lives with a stepmother (1%); the student lives with a stepfather subsequent to the divorce or death of her natural mother (1%).

An analysis of the family background of the students reveals that most of the girls' parents were born in Cairo or other urban areas. The majority of the fathers were born in Cairo (49%); thirty percent were born in other cities, and 21% were born in rural areas. As compared with fathers' places of birth, a slightly higher percentage of mothers were born in Cairo (55%). Twenty six percent of the mothers were born in other cities, and 15% were born in rural areas.

Characteristics of Students

The age distribution of the respondents at the three institutional 'break point' levels is shown in Table X (see Appendix). The majority of the students in the primary level (75%) were twelve years old, representing the appropriate age level for that group. Seven and a half percent were younger, while 17.5% were older. Similarly, the majority of the girls in the preparatory level (55%) were fifteen years old, again representing the appropriate age for that category. The ages of the students in the secondary levels were more widely distributed between 17 and 23. As was mentioned earlier, by the terminal level of secondary teachers school, which is a five year program, students usually have reached the age of twenty.

By the second interview, which took place a few months later, those respondents who had succeeded in passing the national examinations in all of the various levels (92%) had been promoted to the next level. All of the students who failed (8%) expressed their determination to repeat the year; none of the respondents stated that they would drop out of school or marry. Students who had completed a terminal level, i.e. in secondary commercial (31 students), and in secondary teachers (48 students), were prepared for a change of status regarding employment or marriage.

Almost half of the graduates of commercial schools found employment immediately. Six students went on for higher education, and nine were awaiting employment. None of the girls reported engagement or marriage. On the other hand, eighty-one percent of the graduates of teachers training schools found immediate employment. The higher employment percentages among graduates of secondary teachers schools reflect the current need for teachers in Egypt and the neighbouring countries. Fifteen percent left the country with their husband or family; hence, there is no information on their employment status. Four percent of the students are pursuing a university education. Of the graduates of the teachers training schools, nine have married; four of them are among the employed group, and five are among those who left the country.

Parents' Aspirations and Attitudes towards Education & Employment

Since the 1952 Revolution, and the expansion and popularisation of education throughout the country, there has been a shift in the priority order of values related to status symbols. Prior to agrarian reform, the size of one's land holdings provided the desired socio-economic security which was associated with higher status. Hence, land acquisition for many Egyptian families, regardless of the size of land ownership, took precedence over investment in their children's education, particularly university education. Many parents believed that the future socio-economic security of their children could best be achieved through land acquisition. The introduction in the early 50s of agrarian reform, which restricted land owernship, initiated a basic shift in the priority order of values associated with parents' aspirations for their children. The popularisation of education and the establishment of new schools in rural and urban areas, which started at the same time, satisfied the need which was felt for an alternative means of achieving high social and economic status. Hence, educating one's children became more popular among the various socio-economic classes in society. Undboubtedly, the policy of free education for all facilitated and enhanced this shift in values. The shift could further be attributed to the high esteem placed on higher education by Egyptian policy makers. The 1962 National Charter declared that 'The Universities are progressive leaders who point the way of life out to the people'.[13] Moreover, admission to a university, which is based solely on academic merit, augmented levels of aspiration. For example, those students graduating from high school with the highest averages are automatically enrolled in the faculties of medicine and engineering which prepare them for the most highly regarded and lucrative professions. Our findings indicated that parents' aspirations for their daughters have to a large extent been influenced by this trend.

The values related to the importance of education for girls are best exemplified by the parents' responses, as well as by their investment in their children's education in the form of private tutoring. The overwhelming majority of the parents (94.5%) intend to allow their daughters to pursue their education; and of those, 84% aspire for their daughters to receive a university education. When asked why they wanted them to pursue their education to that particular level, parents stated several reasons. Many want to see their daughters appointed to prestigious positions which cannot be acquired without a university education. For others, the education of their daughters was seen as compensation for their own lack of education. And, in many families, the tradition of education in the family was a deciding factor.

Education is seen as a means of raising one's status both socially and financially. Examples of some of the parent's responses further indicate why an education is today regarded as an important asset:

People today look up to those with a univeristy education.
Life's present circumstances require the pursuit of education up to the university level.
I want my daughter to have a career; she will help make up for our poverty, and she is our hope in this world.
This is the era of certificates, these are the means of achieving happiness at present.

In the last decade, private tutoring has become a widespread phenomena in Egypt. Around 72% of the students in our sample admitted to having had private tutoring in various subjects prior to sitting for the national exam. Despite the fact that the majority of respondents (82%) feel that the cost of private tutoring is a burden on the family budget, they also feel such assistance is necessary in order to prepare adequately for the national exams. Because a student's further educational options are determined from the earlier education- al levels by examination scores, the national examinations are highly competitive. Hence, many parents, as our figures indicate, were willing to make financial sacrifices in order to further assure their daughter's chances of high scholastic achievement.

For those few who said that they did not intend to allow their daughter to pursue a higher education, the lack of financial means and the poverty of the family were given as the main reasons. The majority of these parents wanted to have their daughters work after the termination of secondary technical education to help support their families. It is interesting to note that of the forty-six cases in this group, early marriage was reported for only six cases, whereas financial need was stated in twenty-six cases.

Aspirations of the Students towards their own Education

The students' own aspirations again demonstrate the high esteem given to education. Ninety-four percent of the girls intend to pursue their education; and of those, 89% are planning to pursue their studies up to the university or post-graduate level. University education is closely associated with finding an appealing position in medicine, law, engineering, diplomacy, or commerce, as indicated by the majority of these respondents. The girls see education as the means by which they can achieve independence and a secure future.

It is worthy of note that the majority of girls in the primary level of our sample aspire to become doctors and engineers, reflecting the cultural values prevailing today. The following are examples cited by primary students:

> I want to become a doctor, I love medicine - especially pediatrics because I want to cure sick children.
> Engineering school is my choice. I am curious to discover how machines function.
> I want to be a gynaecologist because I believe women should be examined by a woman doctor who will be kinder and more understanding.

Older girls, however, are more realistic, stating that their scholastic achievement and grade point average greatly determine their future careers. Below are some examples given by students:

> If I acquire a high score, I would like to go to the University to be well educated.
> I would like to attend the Faculty of Commerce or even Pharmacology; I have come to realise that medicine is beyond my academic capacity.
> I would like to study fine arts. I don't like mathematics

because it's difficult - I know I can do better in the theoretical schools.

None of the students in our sample expressed a desire to drop out of school. None in the primary, preparatory, and secondary general (academic education) intend to stop after completion of their secondary education. They all aspire to get a university education. Even the majority (76%) of the students enrolled in secondary technical or teachers schools hope to improve their scholastic performance to the level approved for admission to a university.

An attempt to relate the student's level of aspiration to the father's education or occupation indicated that all the students whose fathers have a university education foresee nothing less for themselves than a comparable education. Similar relationships were also noticed between a student's level of aspiration and her mother having completed a university education. On the other hand, more of the girls whose mothers are illiterate foresee a secondary education as their ultimate goal. The great majority of daughters whose mothers can read and write, or completed primary, preparatory, or secondary education intend to seek a university education.

Further analysis of students' aspirations in relation to fathers' occupations shows a high correlation between a student's level of aspiration for university or post-graduate studies and her father's employment in a professional field. One hundred percent of the daughters of fathers who work in professional jobs aim for a university or post-graduate education. Similarly, ninety-six percent of the daughters of fathers working in semi-professional jobs expressed the same desire. The percentage of students aiming at only a secondary education is higher among girls whose fathers work in occupations which are classified as: small business entrepreneurs (10%); religious functionaries, guards, policemen (12%); skilled labourers (20%); unskilled labourers (23%).

The mother's employment status also showed a relationship to her daughter's aspirations for higher education. The great majority (98%) of the daughters of working mothers expressed a desire to pursue a university education; while only two percent were satisfied with a secondary education as their goal. A higher percentage (12%) of the daughters of non-working mothers did not intend to go beyond secondary school.

Students' Attitudes towards the Employment of Women

In answer to the question concerning opinions on the employment of women outside the home, around 79% of the respondents stated that women's employment is an unconditional necessity in our generation; however, their rationale varied for this response. Of these students, the majority (58%) stated that women must work because they should share with men the responsibility of establishing and maintaining a home. Another group (15%) said that the circumstances of life nowadays force women to work in order to supplement the family income. Yet another group of respondents (12%) perceive of female employment as a means of achieving economic independence. The remaining students (15%) believe that employment enriches a woman's life experience, enhances her relationships with others, and keeps her in contact with the world outside her immediate family surroundings.

Another ten percent of the total sample said that women should work, provided they work in a field of specialisation, or when circumstances are suitable. Alluding to the humiliating situations women are subjected to while using public transportation, the majority of these girls added that the employment of women outside the home should be conditional upon improved public transportation. The remaining eleven percent of the total sample stated that women should stay home to raise their children. They too mentioned the problems of public transportation.

When education was related to employment, the girls' responses were more positive in favour of the employment of educated women. This reveals changing concepts related to confining women to the home. The overwhelming majority (93%) believe that once a young woman completes her education, she must work. They further assert that the ultimate goal of education for women is their future employment. The remaining seven percent indicated that a woman should stay at home regardless of her education; three percent said that a girl's future is in marriage and the care of her family; and four percent stated that they are against women working outside the home because of the humiliating situations they encounter while using overcrowded public transportation, in addition to the burden of their home responsibilities. Both of these, they felt, reflected on the health of the woman. Some girls also mentioned that the meagre salaries earned would barely cover personal expenses or transportation costs.

Contrary to our expectations, our respondents' opinions concerning the most suitable jobs for women still reflect the traditional belief in the classification of occupations in terms of their masculinity or feminity. The majority of the respondents (41%) believe that teaching and social work are the most appropriate jobs for a woman because they are less strenuous and are more likely to be compatible with the natural capacities of her sex. Although twenty-seven percent of the students perceive of medicine as an appropriate career for a woman, they restrict her fields of specialisation to paediatrics and gynae-cology, where, they claimed, she can look after and cure sick children, or attend to other women in childbirth. These two roles have traditionally been played by women as mothers, grandmothers, or midwives in Middle Eastern culture. Hence, it is quite obvious that the change perceived by the girls was not actually in the roles played by women as much as in the academic preparation related to these roles.

The remaining responses (24%) again visualise women in the subordinate roles of a secretary, airline hostess, or fashion designer. Only two percent accredited women with more creative jobs such as writing, journalism, law, or jobs related to the mass media; and another two percent said that women are capable of holding any job. That women should be restricted to their familial roles was said by only two percent of the students. The following responses illustrate these cultural images which have become internalised and made a part of the girls' own personalities and beliefs:

Medicine is a job which is suitable to the nature of women which is characterised by love and affection.
Teaching is an appropriate job because working hours and holidays are convenient.
Secretarial or administrative work is not tiring or strenuous job.
Women were born to be housewives and mothers.

Within the last three decades efforts to revolutionise the education of women in Egypt have been quite successful in opening up all fields of specialisation, i.e. medicine, engineering, political science, law, agriculture, economics, etc. Women's enrollment in the above mentioned faculties has more than doubled or tripled. Moreover, labour force statistics also indicate the increased participation of women in these same fields. However, the traditional image of appropriate jobs for women still seems to prevail among the younger generation. Advancement in perceptions of educational achievement has not necessarily been accompanied by changing concepts related to alternative roles for women.

When the girls were questioned concerning continuing employment for married women with pre-school children, their responses confirmed their commitment to the idea that employment is subordinate to a woman's role as a mother and homemaker. The majority of the students (66%) stated that a woman with children should discontinue work until the children grow up. Twenty-three percent replied that once a woman has children, she should stay home to care for them. Eleven percent thought that a mother should continue working.

For the majority, employment is a real economic necessity. Because Egyptian custom demands that a newlywed couple begin their married life in a fully-furnished home, many girls choose to work prior to their marriage in order to contribute to the establishment of their household.[14] Hence, employment is the means by which a young woman helps defray some of the considerable expense involved in the purchase of the suites of furniture and household equipment which are traditionally given by the bride's family.

Further probing was attempted concerning the question of the compatability of the roles of worker and homemaker. Students with working mothers were asked whether their own mother succeeded in combining both roles. The overwhelming majority (90%) indicated that their mother was successful. Of these, however, thirty percent said that this success came at the expense of their mother's physical and emotional health. Only ten percent said that their mothers had failed at combining the two roles.

Similar responses were obtained from the mothers who claimed that the two roles were compatible (91%). Of these women, twenty-eight percent reported that success was not haphazard, but occurred as a result of conscious added efforts, both physical and emotional.

Only nine percent of the mothers admitted to having failed to combine the two roles.

Contrasting opinions and attitudes were expressed by the girls when asked, 'What is your opinion of your mother's status as an employed woman or a housewife?' The majority of the girls with non-working mothers (85%) preferred their mother's status as a housewife. They affirmed that mothers who are housewives devote their attention wholly to raising their children.

> Having my mother at home whenever I came back from school gave me a sense of security.
> She loved us so much that she was always doing things for us; we never helped at home except during vacations.

On the other hand, twelve percent of this group wished that their mothers were working. Some of the reasons they gave were:

> If my mother had been employed, she would have had greater awareness of the problems of having too many children and would have planned her family.
> She would have better comprehended the relationship between income and number of children.

The remaining three percent of respondents did not comment.

Approximately ninety percent of those students with working mothers approve of their mother's employment outside the home, appreciate her contributions to the family income, and assert that she is more understanding toward them. Some even said that 'Working mothers not only secure a steady monthly income which provides for her own needs and those of her children, but employment provides her and her children with social and economic security in cases of marital disagreement'.

Only five percent said that they did not totally approve of their mother working. They maintained that she is often good to them, but sometimes problems at work are reflected in the way she treats them. The remaining five percent stated that their mother's employment should be conditional, i.e. 'If we had had a better income my mother need not have worked'. Further probing indicated that those who were dissatisfied with the employment of their mother were girls whose mothers were working as domestic servants or nurses.[15]

SUMMARY CONCLUSIONS

This study on the life cycle of girls in Cairo has attempted to explore the factors involved in the prolongation of female education, the factors affecting its termination at various levels, and their impact on age at marriage or later fertility behaviour. Although the research is still in its early stages, the preliminary findings have shed light on the interacting factors behind the prolongation of girls' education. The study is also confirming some of the underlying assumptions proposed by the research. Moreover, the initial findings are revealing the major trends arising as a result of continued female education.

During the past three decades, girls' education has undoubtedly assumed primary importance among Egyptian families. This interest grew out of the national movements that forced policy makers to popularise female education. After the 1952 Revolution, more esteem was placed upon educational achievement; and, education became the main channel of upward socio-economic mobility. Consequently, parent aspirations for their children of either sex culminated in a university education.

Concomitant to increased education for women was the movement for her emancipation from her traditional status to a more active role in public, both in the economic and political spheres. The increase in educational opportunities for women has been accompanied by an increased awareness of the importance of employment for women. This was clearly exemplified in the responses of our students and their mothers who visualised education as analogous to a 'weapon'. This in reality means that education is the means by which women can seek employment, hence, socio-economic independence and greater security.

One of the most significant trends revealed in this study is the actual persistence of students in pursuing an education. Of the 827 students in the study, there have been only six drop-outs from the three educational levels. Five of these students dropped out after failing their national exams for two consecutive years. Another consequent trend is the increased employment of educated women. The majority of our respondents saw employment as their ultimate goal. This was confirmed by the actual behaviour of our girls who completed terminal levels that prepared them for employment. The great majority are presently working or awaiting employment through the Department of Manpower in the Ministry of Labour.

Undoubtedly, both prolonged education and the employment of women are having some bearing upon the age at marriage.[16] Only nine out of 827 cases were married during the research period. These, moreover, were girls who had completed five years in teachers training schools, and hence, were twenty years of age or older. The fact that none of our students dropped out of school to marry, or were married before the age of twenty, in itself is indicative of the impact of prolonged education on delayed age at marriage.

The impact of education and employment on fertility behaviour has yet to be tested. Some of the assumptions will be verified during the course of the research; however, more time is required to identify and fully assess the main variables affecting fertility behaviour.

NOTES

*   This research on Life Courses of Egyptian Female Youth grew out of the interest of the late Margaret Gulick (1923-1979) and Dr. John Gulick of the University of North Carolina, who wrote the original proposal. The study was made possible by an N.I.H. grant to the Carolina Population Center in 1978. Collaboration between Dr. John Gulick of C.P.C. and Dr. Hind Khattab of

A.U.C. to conduct this research began in 1980.

REFERENCES

1. Wallis Budge, The Dwellers on the Nile. New York: Dover Publications Inc., 1977, p. 21.
2. Elmer H. Wagner, The United Arab Republic: A Study of the Educational System. Washington: World Education Series - A.A.C.R.A.O., 1970, pp. 12-13.
3. These are schools funded by benevolent endowments (Waqf, pl. awqaf) and under the supervision of the Ministry of Waqfs.
4. I. Hafez, Education in the U.A.R. Cairo: Ministry of Education Publication, 1964, p. 10.
5. Ibid., p. 8.
6. Amir Boktor, The Development and Expansion of Education in the United Arab Republic. Cairo: American University in Cairo Press, 1963, p. 1.
7. These were: 11 primary, 3 preparatory, 2 secondary general, 2 secondary technical.
8. Information on living conditions and ownership of material goods in addition to occupation are used whenever information on income could not be obtained.
9. From our experience, being able to read and write is usually limited to signing one's name or writing a few words.
10. The classification is that used by the Egyptian Statistical Bureau in census surveys.
11. The nuclear family consists typically of a married couple and their offspring.
12. According to Egyptian law the maternal grandmother is given custody of the children should their mother remarry following her divorce. If the maternal grandmother is deceased, custody will then be given to the paternal grandmother.
13. Hekmat Abou-Zeid, et.al., The Education of Women in the U.A.R. during the 19th and 20th centuries. Cairo: Cairo University Press, 1970, p. 37.
14. The financial contribution of a young woman towards the purchase of her household equipment is a recent phenomenon.
15. These two professions are looked down upon socially.
16. The minimum legal age for marriage in Egypt is sixteen for girls.

APPENDIX

TABLE I

The number of girls enrolled in Primary Schools in 1875

2 Primary Schools (Government)		4 Egyptian Private Primary Schools		26 Primary Foreign Missionary Primary Schools	
No. of girls	No. of teachers	No. of girls	No. of teachers	No. of girls	No. of teachers
445	22	445	21	2,833	130

Source: Hekmat Abou-Zeid, et. al., The Education of Women in the U.A.R. during the 19th and 20th centuries. Cairo: Cairo University Press, 1970, p. 4.

TABLE II

Number of schools, their affiliations, and their enrollment during the 1913-1914 school year

Government Girls Schools:	17
Girls: 2,736	
Awqaf Girls Schools:	14
Girls: 932	
Private Urban Girls Schools:	50
Girls: 1,570	
Governorate Girls Schools:	29
Girls: 2,598	
Governorate Co-education Schools:	?
Girls: 3,724	
Rural Private Girls Schools:	7
Girls: 835	
Private Co-education Government Supervised Schools:	?
Girls: 15,859	
Railway Department Co-education Schools:	36
Girls: 84	

Source: Hekmat Abou-Zeid, et. al., The Education of Women in the U.A.R. during the 19th and 20th centuries. Cairo: Cairo University Press, 1970, p. 12.

TABLE III

**Growth in Number of Schools and Students
in Elementary Schools for Girls
1917–1924**

School Year	No. of Schools	No. of Girls	No. of Girls who paid fees	No. of Girls with free tuitiion	No. of percentage of free tuition
1917–1918	2	133	88	45	34%
1922–1923	6	783	682	39	19%
1923–1924	7	899	–	–	–

Source: Hekmat Abou Zeid, et. al., The Education of Women in the U.S.R. during the 19th and 20th centuries. Cairo: Cairo University Press, 1970, p. 14.

TABLE IV

Number of Elementary Schools and General Maktabs in the Country and the Number of Girls in 1944–1945

	Status of the Schools	1944		1945
		No. of Schools	No. of Boys	No. of Girls
1.	Ministry-run elementary schools	476	57,308	49,717
2.	Schools run by other Organisation, e.g. Waqfs, Benevolent Societies, etc.	24	2,427	872
3.	Schools run by the Governorates	736	80,290	62,416
4.	Private Schools supported by the Ministry of Education	385	48,761	23,023
5.	Private School supported by the Governorate	267	24,844	6,115
	Total of Elementary Schools	1,897	213,630	142,143
1.	General Maktabs run by the Ministry	3	442	399
2.	General Maktabs run by the Governorates	2,696	332,879	305,671
3.	General Maktabs supported by the Ministry	1	62	63
4.	General Maktabs supported by the Governorates	51	3,431	1,727
	Total of Maktabs	2,751	336,814	307,869
	Total number of Elementary Schools and General Maktabs	4,648	550,444	450,003

Source: Abou Zeid, et. al., The Education of Women in the U.A.R. during the 19th and 20th centuries. Cairo: Cairo University Press, 1970, p. 20.

TABLE V

**The Increase in Number of Girls Enrolled
in Primary Schools during Scholastic Year
1953/54 to 1978/79**

Scholastic Year	Number of Students			Percentage of Girls
	Boys	Girls	Total	
1953/54	866,631	526,110	1,392,741	37.7%
1963/64	1,918,239	1,211,453	3,129,692	38.7%
1973/74	2,421,853	1,496,543	3,918,396	38.2%
1978/79	2,590,615	169,709	4,288,124	39.6%
Ratio of Increase between 53/54 & 78/79	199%	223%	207%	

Source: Women and Education in Arab Republic of Egypt.   Cairo: Dar al-Alam al-Arabi fil Tiba'ah, 1980, p. 24.

TABLE VI

**The Increase in Number of Girls Enrolled
in Preparatory Schools during Scholastic Year
1953/54 to 1978/79**

Scholastic Year	Number of Students			Percentage of Girls
	Boys	Girls	Total	
1953/54	279,245	72,589	351,834	20.6%
1963/64	322,643	128,419	451,062	28.4%
1973/74	726,720	372,571	1,099,291	33.9%
1978/79	979,626	568,682	1,547,308	36.7%
Ratio of Increase between 53/54 & 78/79	251%	682%	340%	

Source: Women and Education in Arab Republic of Egypt. Cairo: Dar al-Alam al-Arabi fil Taba'ah, 1980, p. 26.

TABLE VII

The Increase in Number of Girls Enrolled in Secondary Schools during Scholastic Year 1953/54 to 1978/79

Scholastic Year	Number of Students			Percentage of Girls
	Boys	Girls	Total	
1953/54	79,159	12,903	92,062	14.0%
1963/64	101,994	29,210	141,204	27.8%
1973/74	217,515	106,088	323,603	32.8%
1978/79	283,140	159,935	443,075	36.1%
Ratio of Increase between 53/54 & 78/79	258%	1140%	381%	

Source: Women and Education in Arab Republic of Egypt.   Cairo: Dar al-Alam al-Arabi fil Taba'ah, 1980, p. 30.

TABLE VIII

**The Increase in Number of Girls Enrolled
in Technical Secondary Schools during Scholastic Year
1953/54 to 1978/79**

Scholastic Year	Number of Students			Percentage of Girls
	Boys	Girls	Total	
1953/54	15,195	3,643	18,838	19.3%
1963/64	68,810	14,563	83,373	17.5%
1973/74	310,815	104,911	415,726	25.2%
1978/79	471,961	181,486	653,447	27.8%
Ratio of Increase between 53/54 & 78/79	3,006%	4,882%	3,369%	

Source: Women and Education in Arab Republic of Egypt.   Cairo: Dar al-Alam al-Arabi fil Taba'ah, 1980, p. 34.

TABLE IX

Number of Students Enrolled in the Various Egyptian Universities and the Ratio between Males and Females

Scholastic Year	Theoretical Faculty (1)			Practical Faculty (2)			Total		
	Boys	Girls	% of Girls	Boys	Girls	% of Girls	Boys	Girls	% of Girls
1951/52	17,574	11,466	8.3%	14,563	938	6.5%	32,137	2,404	7.5%
1970/71	43,067	25,162	58.5%	60,892	16,602	27.25%	103,959	41,764	40.0%
1978/79	172,661	95,805	55.5%	122,873	42,247	34.4%	295,534	138,052	46.7%
Ratio of increase between 50/51 & 78/79	82%	6,435%		744%	4,404%		820%	5,643%	

Source: Women and Education in Arab Republic of Egypt. Cairo: Dar al-Alam al-Arabi fil Taba'ah, 1980, p. 76.

(1) Literature, Law, Commerce, Economics & Political Sciences, Languages, Teachers College, Education, College for Girls.

(2) Medicine, Dental School, Engineering, Sciences, Physiotherapy, Tumor Institute, Veterinary School.

TABLE X

Distribution of Respondents According to Age and Educational Level

Primary	Age in Years	No.	%
	11	18	2
	12	179	23
	13	41	5
	14	1	–
		329	

Preparatory	Age in Years	No.	%
	14	15	4
	15	130	16
	16	45	5
	17	25	3
		235	

Secondary (General, Technical & Teachers)	Age in Years	No.	%
	17	26	3
	18	186	22
	19	40	5
	20	44	5
	21	33	4
	22	14	2
	23	10	1
		323	

197

Chapter 9

THE STRUGGLE OF WOMEN IN THE NATIONAL DEVELOPMENT OF PAKISTAN

Freda Hussain

Although Pakistan was created as an independent, sovereign state in 1947, its social, political and religious development had preceded its creation by many centuries. Different socio-political orders had exercised varied influences on the development of the social structure of its society during that time. A hundred years before its creation, that is, from 1857 onwards, it was directly under British colonial rule as part of the Indian sub-continent. Prior to that, from the 10th century onwards, it had been under Muslim rule. Earlier still, the sub-continent was under the influence of Hinduism and the Hindu political order.

This paper will focus on the educational development of Muslim women and their struggle in the national development of Pakistan. The significance of this role should not be underestimated as women constitute roughly half the population of the country. According to the 1972 Census of Pakistan, the total population of the country was 64.892 million, of which 30.475 million were females. In 1977 the population was estimated to be 73.43 million and of these 20.13 million constituted the urban population. The majority of the male-female population therefore resided in the rural areas.[1] However, most socio-political changes in Pakistan have emanated from its urban sectors. The struggle of urban educated women in Pakistan will form the central theme of the paper.

Since its inception in 1947, these urban educated women have initiated programmes and policies for the improvement of the lot of the women in Pakistan. Over the years, they have made tremendous strides in this area and have helped with national development. In recent years, the social status of such women in Pakistan society has been threatened and undermined by retrogressive Islamic forces. The ideology of these forces and how they have sought to manipulate the political system will form the backdrop for the central theme.

Before examining the above questions in greater detail, a brief survey of the historical background will not only provide a comparative view of the role of women in different political orders, but will also serve to elucidate how some structures of the past have become institutionalized in the present and have come to exert a considerable influence on the lives of women in a post colonial society.

198

In Hindu India, an important feature of societal life was its stratification by the caste system. Within this system the women became victims of their own religion and the Brahmin priestly class who had institutionalized their roles in Hindu society.[2] This was reinforced by law-givers like Manu who had prescribed cruel penalties for women who deviated from Hindu norms. The practice of *Sati*, for example, required the Hindu wife to be burnt to death on the husband's funeral pyre. Millions of Hindu women, young and old, met their death in this way. This practice was finally stamped out by the British. Another practice that prevailed until the earlier part of this century was the use of Hindu women as *deva-dasies* (slaves of the gods). The Brahmin priests could requisition young Hindu women to serve the gods in the temples and hundreds of women were attached to each temple all over India.[3] These women served to fulfil the sexual needs of the Brahmin priests and when they were no longer attractive, they were branded on their thighs and released. Temple service assured them of a respectable status in society.

It was into this oppressive social milieu that Islam was introduced to Hindu India. The early Afghan conquerors destroyed the temples and later ones established a Muslim empire in the 9th century which reached its zenith in the Mughal era (1526-1857). Islam provided salvation for many Hindu women who sought conversion to Islam in order to escape from *Sati* and temple prostitution. However, once the crusading zeal of Islam had subsided, the Muslim rulers became corrupted by their absolute power and immense wealth and started to deviate from the goals of Islam. Like the Brahmin elite, the palaces of the Muslim rulers and noblemen had large harems. Their *Darbars* (courts) were entertained by *natch* (dancing) sessions. The *deva-dasies* of Hindu India were gradually replaced by *natch* girls (dancing girls). The rulers could pick any woman who caught their fancy for their harems. Women were not allowed to participate in matters of state. One very able woman, Sultana Razia, ascended the throne during the Sultanate period but was attacked by nobles and murdered in prison.

As the decadence of the Muslim rulers continued their fun - immorality reached such heights that the only profession which women were allowed to train for was that of *natch* (dance). Some young girls trained for up to sixteen hours a day in the arts of dancing and singing and erotic gratification of males. At the same time, men of the wealthier classes kept their own wives and daughters in strict segregation in the *Zenana Khana* (womens quarters) and there was a marked distinction between them and the *Tawaif* (female entertainers).[4]

Islam and Feudal Politics

The feudal system thrived during the Muslim rule, where dynasties and not the institutions exercised power. Islam was distorted by the *Ulema* to legitimize the dual morality of the ruling elite. Power, wealth and licentiousness had corroded the fabric of the society and weakened the Mughal empire which subsequently crumbled before the

British forces in 1857. Even at that point, it was women like Chand Bibi and an unknown prostitute who proved to be formidable adversaries to the British invaders.

In the British empire, the Islamic religious functionaries who had previously condoned the acts of Muslim rulers, proved to be a retrogressive force for the Muslims of the sub-continent. Their brand of pseudo-Islam, which was derived from and had reinforced the feudal order, could not challenge the colonial rulers. The Muslim community therefore remained backward in the educational and political processes initiated by the British rulers.

Some men like Sir Sayyid Ahmad Khan made a strong plea to the Muslims to educate themselves but he did not press for the emancipation of women from *purdah* (veil). On the contrary, he felt that:

> it was proper for women to follow men in all walks of life . . . . orthodox Muslims branded the advocates of female education as apostates and separate schools for girls began to be established only after the turn of the century, when Christian missionary schools began to have an impact. By the 1920s a few thousand Muslim women in undivided India had received modern education.[5]

Political consciousness developed slowly among Muslims due to a lack of education and it was not until 1906 that the Muslim League was established. The party remained an exclusive elite club until men like Mohammad Ali Jinnah (1876-1948) joined it and realized that the political mobilization of the Muslims had to be done through an Islamic ideology that was different from the retrogressive Islam of the Ulema from Deoband and Lucknow. A Muslim philosopher, Mohammed Iqbal (1873-1938) produced a dynamic interpretation of Islam that was to be an inspiration to many Muslims. According to Iqbal, even:

> A Kafir, before his idol with a wakeful heart,
> Is better than the religious man asleep in the harem.[6]

Both these men advocated the need for educating men and women so that both could play a role in nation-building. In fact Jinnah believed that:

> no nation can make any progress without the co-operation of its women.[7]

Iqbal however was aware of the plight of women and wrote in one of his poems:

> Man's greatness emanates by itself without others aid,
> While woman's quality is always mediated by the other
> I too am very sad over women's helplessness
> But it is not possible to untie the hard knot of her subjugation.[8]

Iqbal's interpretation of Islam and Jinnah's nationalist movement created a strong political consciousness among Muslim men and women. Among educated Muslims there was a growing realization that unless their women folk were dragged out of the mire of ignorance there could be no real progress. But orthodoxy and conservatism had such firm roots in Muslim homes that for a long time no substantial progress was possible. Even in 1907, the number of Muslim girls in public institutions was not more than 77,244 and in private institutions there were about 44,455, thus making a grand total of 121,699 as compared to the non-Muslim total of 5,266,933. Besides there was only one Muslim girl taking a collegiate course, while in secondary schools the number of Muslim girls was less than 150. All the concentration was thus in primary schools where it was easier for girls to abandon their studies as soon as they had reached the age of puberty.[9] In 1932 the Muslim League passed a resolution to safeguard the rights of women. In 1940 Muslim women came out in the streets in support of the Pakistan resolution.[10] One of their important political activities was to canvass for votes among women for the election of candidates because men could not canvass among women.[11] There is no doubt that the Partition of India was a landmark in the lives of Muslim women in terms of raising their national consciousness. Their whole lives were transformed as they threw themselves whole heartedly into the nationalist cause. Women like Fatima Jinnah, a dentist by profession, gave up their careers to join in the movement for the mobilization of women. After the partition of India, women like Raana Liaquat Ali Khan founded the All Pakistan Women's Association and devoted her life to alleviating the problems of women. Scores of other women followed in their footsteps and have been instrumental in contributing to national development. Although their numbers were not large, their impact on the roles and lives of Pakistani women was significant.

Education was the main agent of political activism in women. One female educator stated that:

> The Partition was a great factor in the liberation of women . . . . they learnt that purdah had been useless, they had not got the protection of men, and they lacked the political knowledge to protect themselves. Purdah lost its meaning, the pattern was shattered, there were widows, kidnappings, life in rehabilitation camps . . . . They knew that education would help them.[12]

The interpretation of Islam in Pakistani society was assimilated with the feudal fabric of societal norms and its feudal political culture. Islam had been compromised to suit the needs of feudal elite groups. A comparison of Pakistani Islam with that of its neighbour Iran will help to clarify this point. The interpretation of Islam by leading *Mujtahids* like Ayatollah Khomeini and others from the city of Qom was not assimilated with the culture of Iranian society. It was linked to the Iranian society through Islamic bridges that separated the political culture of Islam from the monarchial political system.

However, although the nationalist movement had raised the

consciousness of women, the politics of Pakistan did not proceed along the same lines. The charismatic leadership of Jinnah ended in 1948 with his death and the feudal structrue which Pakistan had inherited was further consolidated. It could have been challenged by revolutionary Islam but the religious elites tailored Islam to suit the requirements of the feudalistic elites from the military, bureaucracy and landed gentry. The *Mullahs* from the villages were under the control of landlords while many of the well known *pirs* (holy one) from various provinces were themselves landlords. The Islamically oriented political parties were extensions of feudalism and their views on women were similar to those existing in rural areas.

The feudal lords exerted their authority over their lands, peasants and womenfolk. The women were mainly instruments for producing male progeny that would inherit the father's wealth. Family vendettas often led to kidnapping and sexual molestation or raping of women - this being the greatest dishonour one could inflict on the enemy. Feudal thinking mistrusted women's sexuality and this gave rise to the dual standards of morality that are widely prevalent in Pakistani society. Political leaders like General Ayub Khan, General Yahya Khan and Z.A. Bhutto were not above such moral failings or of using the feudal tactics of dishonouring the womenfolk of their opponents. Even General Zia-ul-Haq has used his feudal power to place the daughter of his opponent (Benazir Bhutto) in gaol so that she cannot fulfil her threat of politically opposing Zia's regime.

What then, was the religious ideology of the retrogressive forces who supported the feudal system in Pakistan? It was to institute a male dominated system in which women were guarded strictly, if not in a harem, then within the four walls of the house. It is therefore not surprising to find some religious authorities like Maulana Mawdudi, exalting the harem institution in writing:

> Harem is the last place of refuge where Islam guards its civilization and culture.[13]

Other writers consider that this institution did not exist in the early period of Islam because

> the actual practice in the days of the Prophet, as evidenced by history and tradition, confirm the view that Muslim women came out of their homes frequently for satisfying their economic, intellectual and religious needs, without putting on a veil, but always dressed in full and wearing a loose over-garment (*jilbah*) which completely hid their bodily features and charms.[14]

The system of guarding women behind harem walls was further considered to be the cause of

> 'Muslim degeneration throughout the Middle Ages. The medieval Muslim, of course never questioned its immoral nature, for they were convinced of its Islamic sanction due to the interpretation of the Ulema, who justified polygamy, slavery, servile concubinage

as Islamic institutions', as such 'Maulana Maududi and others now declare this degenerative system of family and social life as essential Islamic institution'.[15]

Feudal societies from medieval times to present, developed a strict system of division of labour in which man was the breadwinner and women the producer of children. This division of labour was given normative sanction by the retrogressive Islamic forces. Taking the feudal cue, this line of thinking considers that there is the division of work which Nature itself has made between the two sexes of mankind. Biology, physiology and all the branches of social science indicate this division. A good civilization is one which accepts this dispensation of Nature as it is. Once it is done, you may give a woman her proper place, give her honour in the society, respect her justifiable cultural and social rights that burden her only with domestic duties, while allot all outdoor responsibilities and the command of the family to man.[16] Man is considered to be 'absolutely free to do whatever he likes in any walk of life' while the 'whole burden (of procreation) has been put upon the women for the performance of which she is prepared from the time when she was a mere foetus in the womb of her mother.[17] Apart from child-bearing women were not considered fit for any work and as such 'to train and prepare women for man's job and work is absolutely against the design and purpose of Nature, and it is neither good for mankind nor for woman herself to do so.[18] But much more than being incapable, women are

> inferior to men. You may try any device, you cannot produce a single woman of the calibre of an Aristotle, an Ibn Sina, a Kant, a Hegel an Umar Khayyam, a Shakespeare, an Alexander, a Napoleon, a Salahuddin, a Nizam ul-Mulk Tusi or a Bismark.[19]

Being inferior they could never be the equal of men and the latter must dominate them for

> if both of them are equal in power or no one has dominance or control over the other, none of them will accept the effect of the other and no action will then take place at all. If the cloth has the same hardness as the needle, no act of sewing will be at all accomplished. If the earth were so hard and impervious as not to accept the effect of the plough or pickaxe, agriculture would not be possible.[20]

As such it logically follows that

> for the purpose of such a regulation of her life, a woman is obliged to obey the man who is responsible for the maintenance of this system - be he her husband, father or brother.[21]

Another *mullah* considers that

> the real field of work is her house not outside. Therefore, her

going out without any genuine purpose, to participate in irrelevant activities, or for outings and excursions for recreation, sight-seeing and picnics or to display her charms and adornments is impermissible .... women's participation cannot be approved even in those areas which can be considered the best of their kind, such as social or religious work or humanitarian service.[22]

This trend of thinking has polarised the thinking on women in Pakistan. One stands for involving them in national development of the country, the other aims to exclude them from it and confine them within the *chardewari* (four walls of the home). This has naturally caused great concern to women for as one observer notes that:

the question probably uppermost in the minds of educated women was wether Islamisation would mean an end to their careers.[23]

Women and Nation Building

Nation-building has been a central problem of many non-western societies. States like Pakistan are beset with problems of economic and political development in a situation where the leadership was in the hands of feudal elite groups who have, on one hand exploited the masses by keeping them illiterate and on the poverty line, and suppressed the women on the other hand. The ruling elites have aligned themselves with retrogressive religious groups with the aim of dominating women and relegating their social status. They have tried to maintain the feudal system in which all decisions pertaining to the lives of women, such as education, choice of marriage partner, number of children etc. were taken by men. Furthermore, male interpretations of Islam have been used to enforce such restrictions.

In the process of nation-building, both sexes contribute equally. Women can contribute in all walks of life at the same time as being mothers and home-makers. In order to achieve this balanced development:

one of the chief means whereby women can be enabled to make a fuller contribution to national development is by education .... It is not a question of girls replacing boys in schools but of the long term aim of a basic primary education becoming the common equipment of all.[24]

Education in Pakistan has been the privilege of a few and least of all of Pakistan women. However, among the middle class educated women, there is a social awareness of the fact that the only safeguard of their sex against male dependency is education and economic security. According to the 1972 Census of Pakistan, the literacy rate of females of age 10 years and over was 30.9 per cent in urban areas and 4.7 per cent in rural areas. This compared with a literacy rate of males of 49.9 per cent in urban areas and 22.6 per cent in rural areas. There has been a gradual improvement in the education of women over the years but the pace is still slow.

At the primary level, the ratio of males to females in schools has risen from 100:16.6 in 1947-48 to 100:42 in 1975-76. At the secondary level, which includes Middle, High and vocational schools, the ratio has increased from roughly 100:13.7 in 1947-48 to 100:30 in 1975-76. The number of Arts and Science Colleges has also been increasing. In 1947-48 there were 35 colleges for males and only 5 for females. In 1978-79 there were 438 colleges for males and 138 for females. Female enrollment in educational institutions has been estimated to have increased by 89.6 per cent during the last decade (1.3 million in 1970-71 and 2.56 million in 1980-81).[25]

Increase in female education has led to more and more females wanting to take up employment in various spheres of national life. Surveys have shown that there has been a change in attitudes towards female employment. A study based on interview responses of ninety-four women between eighteen to twenty-five years of age in Karachi in 1969 concluded that educational obstacles found in patriarchal family systems, such as *purdah*, lack of educational qualifications and the need for help in the home, affected attitude to employment.[26] This was reinforced by another study which carried out an 'examination of the traditional role of women in Pakistan with an attempt to evaluate on-going changes in their status vis-a-vis social relationships, opportunities for education and economic participation .... Purdah was found to be a major constraint to the progress of women.[27] Yet another study showed that religious forces, population explosion patterns of rural-urban living, social stratification, organisation and planning policy were the determining factors in education policies, and attributed the negligence of female education to social reasons.[28] A study of graduate students from four women's colleges in Lahore indicated that there was a preference for employment in government agencies.[29] It reported that with better service conditions and status, as income level rises, the preference for teaching as a profession decreases. However, 75 per cent of the respondents prefered the teaching profession as this met with parental approval and was considered to be respectable and worthwhile.

Some eighty female students residing in a Karachi University hall of residence indicated that vocational attitudes were not influenced by economic factors but by social conditions and attitudes.[30] Teaching was considered to be a dignified and respectful profession, and consequently had prompt approval from parents and husbands. The findings of another study indicated that 90 per cent of the total respondents considered teaching as the best profession for women, 96 per cent were employed with the approval of parents and 90 percent with the approval of their husbands.[31] A 1973 study based on interviews of 125 students from the Faculty of Arts, University of Karachi, also reinforced the high esteem given to the teaching profession but held that this was inversely proportional to income group.[32] Adherence to religion or father's level of education had no influence on these views.

Some 200 career women and 225 domestic women belonging to various occupations and social strata within the Karachi Metropolitan

Area were interviewed in 1974. The findings showed that a high level of education and family income were found to have a salutary effect on the relaxation of 'felt' constraints and showed that as education and income increased, perception of constraints in employment decreased.[33]   Marriage was found to act as a restraint on the participation of women in the labour force.

Another study calculated female participation rate from the 1961 Census and the Pakistan Fertility Survey in 1976.[34] It reported that within the female occupational structure, the most striking finding was a high proportion (33 per cent) of urban women who were classified as working in professional and technical occupations. This was a big gain since only 10 per cent of all women in the non-agricultural labour force were working in professional jobs in 1961. Urban women in general seemed to be better off in terms of their employment status. In addition there were only 14 per cent of women working as unpaid family helpers compared to 56 per cent of the rural women. Participation in employment was in general higher among women aged between 20-49 than those of 50 years of age or more. An interesting educational differential was found between women who were employed and those who were not working, particularly in the urban areas. One third of the employed urban women were literate compared with only 19 per cent of the non-working women. This positive relationship between employment and education combined with a growing proportion of women working in professional occupations indicated that, in the urban areas the chances for employment in occupations with a higher status was greater.

Studies done in the Sahiwal city of Punjab province on 300 males and 300 females indicated that general attitudes favoured female education and also agreed that the education of females improved consciousness, behaviour, economic status and chances of marriage.[35] Preference was given to medicine, teaching and household management as professions for females. Co-education was generally disliked. The results of another study indicated that the highly educated women (graduate and post-graduate) were more resourceful and had a better practical knowledge of child care.[36]

Another study based on 90 female interviews of school teachers and college teachers found that:

1.   The status of women was raised by educational attainment and financial independence.
2.   Increase in age was correlated with less favourable attitudes toward employment.
3.   Higher income of women was correlated with higher status.[37]

The above discussion clearly outlines that most of the studies carried out on Pakistani women indicate a general trend in which education and employment are correlated factors.

Women like Fatima Jinnah and Raana Liaquat Ali mentioned earlier, opened up new frontiers for the women of Pakistan. The former even stood for Presidential election against General Ayub Khan but was defeated because of tampering with ballot boxes. Many other women have joined their ranks and have qualified to join the Central Superior Services as Foreign Service officers, Inland Revenue etc. Others have joined in the professions of medicine, dentistry, Law, University and College lecturing and school teaching. Yet others have gone into nursing, secretarial work, beauticians, social work etc. A few have even been elected to the positions of Chairman of District Councils in various regions of Pakistan.

The increase in female education has been closely examined by Pakistani social scientists who have noted that such female education growth rates establish two points. Among females there has been an overall increase in general rather than vocational education. Furthermore, higher education is generally increasing faster among females than males and that some departments may be labelled as 'female departments' as the number of females exceed males. Such an increase in female education will raise a number of problems in Pakistani society. Firstly, it will increase the proportion of marriages through mutual choice as opposed to those arranged by parents. Secondly, higher education will also increase female involvement in extra domestic activities as their roles will not be restricted to acting as housewives. Thirdly, such a growing disproportion among male and females in higher education will bring about changes in the 'established value system' of the society. This will therefore call for society to make reassessments that would either reinforce the old value system or flexibly absorb new changes. Lastly, it will also bring about role changes between husbands and wives which will again, create problems with regard to male dominance and female independence.[38]

Such concerns correctly project the implications of female education that will emerge in Pakistani society and in other Muslim societies where a similar set of conditions pertain to female education. The main problem confronting the education of females emanates from the feudal structure of Pakistani society. This, as stated earlier, dates back to the Mughal period in history and has used Islam to rationalise male domination and control of women. Women have had to struggle against this to secure some rights for themselves, develop an identity and contribute to national development. Successive governments have failed to secure and recognise the role and rights of women in Pakistani society. Although there are numerous social, cultural, religious and professional women's organisations in Pakistan, the most important one has been the All Pakistan Women's Organisation (APWA) which has worked for the social welfare of women. In recent years, however, it has degenerated into a social club for ladies from the upper classes who do not need economic security. But in the earlier years, it exerted some influence on policy issues relating to women as a political pressure group.

AWPA's efforts succeeded in the setting up of a Commission on Family Laws in 1955. General Ayub Khan passed the Family Law Ordinance in 1961 which dealt with the injustices perpetrated against Muslim women through marriage, divorce, polygamy etc. The retrogressive forces once again retaliated by stating that:

the Family Laws were unacceptable to the people and would never be accepted by the Ulema of the country

and that they

challenged the competency of the Islamic Advisory Council which, he said, was constituted of persons who had no knowledge of Islam, Shariat or Sunnah .... Maulana Ghaus deplored the immodesty and shamelessness of women.[39]

When the women came out on the streets protesting in favour of the Laws, this was condemned by the retrogressive forces who commented that:

Instead of letting the Assembly decide this purely academic and religious issue after a cool consideration of the whole affair in the light of the teachings of the Holy Quran and Sunnah a section of our womenfolk whose entire life is a standing challenge to even the most fundamental teachings of Islam have started a campaign to get this issue decided in their favour by force of demonstration and other such like tactics.[40]

But the protests continued and six women members of the National Assembly voiced their concern by stating that the:

question of Family Laws is not that of women's special interest only, but a question in which the entire nation .... is vitally interested. The entire nation is bound to be affected as a whole if half the population, constituting a most vital section of the nation is deprived of the rightful position in the onward march of the nation.[41]

Since the military government of General Ayub Khan had popular support in its early years – the Family Laws Ordinance withstood its opposition. The misused divorce practices and polygamy were checked and the change was accepted by the people. But the retrogressive forces and the feudal rulers continued their efforts to reinforce their outdated interpretation of Islam.

Further steps were taken to safeguard the rights of women in the constitution of 1973 which made the following provisions:

Article 25:   All citizens are equal before law and are entitled to equal protection of law.

Article 27:   No citizen otherwise qualified for appointment in the service of Pakistan shall be discriminated against in respect of any such appointment on the grounds of race, religion, caste, sex, residence or place.

Article 32:   Steps shall be taken to ensure full participation of women in all spheres of national life.

Article 37:   Make provisions for securing just and human conditions of work, ensuring that children and women are not employed in vocations unsuited to their age or sex and for maternity benefits for women in employment.

These had a limited effect in reducing the discrimination against women by allowing some to enter the most prestigious services in the country but did not make a significant impact on the employment of educated women. In the face of further pressure, Z.A. Bhutto appointed a Pakistan Women's Rights Committee under the chairmanship of the Attorney General of Pakistan. This Committee included women from various walks of life, such as Begum Nasim Jahan (Member National Assembly), Begum Rehana Sarwar (Member Provincial Assembly of Punjab), Begum Samia Fateh (ex-Senator), Begum Rashida Patel (lawyer), Begum Nasima Sultana (advocate), Miss Fazila Alliani (Member Provincial Assembly of Baluchistan), Mrs Mariam Habib (Editor), Mrs Mira Phailbus (College Principal) and Dr Parveen Shaukat Ali (Punjab Education Department). The terms of reference of the committee were:

(i) to consider and formulate proposals for law reforms with a view to improving the social legal and economic condition of the women of Pakistan and providing speedier legal remedies for obtaining relief in matters like maintenance, custody of children etc.

(ii) to make suggestions for improving the social status of Pakistani women;

(iii) to make recommendations for improving their economic condition, and

(iv) any proposal that the committee can make to improve the status and conditions of Pakistani women.[42]

The committee recommended amendments in the following laws:

The Muslim Family Laws Ordinance, 1961;
West Pakistan Family Courts Act, 1964;
Christian Marriages Act, 1872;
Divorce Act, 1869;
Criminal Procedure Code, 1898;
Pakistan Penal Code;
West Pakistan Employees Social Security Ordinance, 1965;
Guardian and Wards Act, 1890;
Political Parties Act, 1962;
West Pakistan Land Revenue Act, 1967;
West Pakistan Maternity Benefits Ordinance, 1958.[43]

Women made the greatest progress during the Bhutto period. Constitutional and legal changes had opened the door for their participation in national development.

The Rise of Feudal Islam

In 1977, Z.A. Bhutto was overthrown in a military coup led by General

Zia-ul-Haq. The new military regime did not have a mandate from the people of Pakistan and therefore needed to seek a means of legitimizing its rule. This it found in the ideologies of Islamic oriented parties in Pakistan. It took the stand that the Muslims of Pakistan were not Islamic enough and therefore the Islamisation of Pakistan was a necessity. How did a colonial institution like the military come to see itself as a vehicle of Islamisation? The military had never been an Islamic institution and no other group or party in Pakistan recognised it to be truly Islamic. The three Islamic parties differed from each other on their interpretations of Islam. The military selected the Jamaat-i-Islami – a party that had established itself in urban areas with Saudi Arabian funding. On entering the political arena for the first time, the Jamaat set about curtailing the progress that women had made between 1955 and 1976.

A National Education Policy that was put forward in October 1978 included some lofty objectives on Islamic education. Such education, it was considered, should foster:

> a deep and abiding loyalty to Islam .... a consciousness of Muslim nationhood .... as a member of the Pakistan nation is also part of the universal Muslim Ummah .... elimination of gaps and contradictions between the professing and practice of Islam .... to provide a minimum acceptable level of junctional literacy and fundamental education to all citizens .... the realization that education is a continuous and lifelong process .... to promote and propagate scientific and technological training and research ....[44]

In theory such a policy was good and its implementation would be the test of its usefulness. However on the subject of university education the report stated that

> For higher education of the females post-graduate classes will be introduced in selected girls colleges of the country. The scope of the post-graduate courses particularly in the field of home economics will be expanded.[45]

It was evident that the objectives of the National Education Policy were not equally applicable to males and females. Only primary education and general education at university was to be available to females. The Zia regime considered co-education to be 'against the Islamic concept of education' and added that 'the present regime was wedded to the Islamic concept of education'. Most professional and technical institutions were co-educational and this meant that the retrogressive forces did not want women to avail of such education.[46] Later the government approved the 'establishment of women's campuses in Lahore and Karachi as a first step towards the establishment of full-fledged Universities for the females' and stated that 'female students already studying in the universities of Punjab and Karachi will be allowed to continue their studies in the co-educational set-up.[47] In 1980-81 the government revealed a new plan in which selected colleges in various provinces would be raised to the status of 'university colleges'. It also called for the establishment of the Institute of Higher Education which would supervise the development of university colleges and

> will impart meaningful education to women which will be intellectual in pursuit, professional in nature, and job-oriented in approach. Thus can women of Pakistan play a creative and constructive role in the national development of the country.[48]

But the APWA and the Woman's Action Forum have both vehemently opposed such educational segregation. The latter

> pointed out that segregated education inevitably perpetuates the discrimination against females in educational development. The basic question raised by opponents has been whether women will be permitted to pursue established programs at the established universities on a co-educational basis in order to achieve their career goals.[49]

Unless the new universities offered a full range of subjects, women stood to be excluded from many professions such as medicine, engineering, architecture, town planning etc.

General Zia asserted that Islam had given equal rights to men and women,[50] and while the Islamic University Ordinance was being formulated he observed that:

> where there were a good number of Ulema among men in Pakistan, he was concerned to know that there was no eminent female Alim.[51]

When the Islamic University was opened in Islamabad its statutes clearly stated that

> The University shall be open to all persons of either sex of whatever religion, race, creed, class or colour who desire to receive higher education with Islamic orientation . . . .[52]

In one of his speeches, Zia made a reference to women wearing the *Chador* (large scarf to cover head and shoulders) and their position within the *Chardewari* (four walls of the house). The women protested at the implication and he clarified his statement by saying that:

> he did not mean restricting women folk to the four walls of their homes. What he meant was that the administration was responsible for protecting the life, honour and the property of citizens of Pakistan.[53]

Such statements by the President did not allay the fears of women. At the APWA Triennial Conference held in Lahore on February 18, 1982, a number of women expressed their concern. One participant articulated that:

> The movement for Islamic laws and the Islamisation process should be concentrating on giving rights to Muslim women and not towards denying her basic human rights by the misinterpretation of the code of Islam. The intrinsic justice of Islam must be rediscovered and applied. In the context of Islamic rights of women we are so often told that Islam has given full rights to women, and we fully agree with this. Our only question is: where are the rights given to women in Islam? In practice we do not find them .... Unfortunately the movement for Islamisation is not restoring to women their true Islamic rights, the movement looks like a misconceived process to push women back. A recent questionnaire circulated by the Islamic ideology council, as reported in the press, questioned whether minorities and women have a right to vote in Islam. This is an affront to the women of Pakistan. Does not a Muslim woman have the responsibilities towards public good?[54]

When General Zia announced his first Cabinet in 1978, the list included one female Minister of State. He had also appointed a woman as a senior Cabinet Secretary and pointed out that these moves were 'a manifestation of the confidence the government has in the ability of women to take part in the affairs of Government'.[55] Within a month, a new cabinet was announced in which members of the retrogressive Islamic group were included and the female Minister had been excluded. However, in a speech to the Federation of Business and Professional Women, Zia asserted that

> Islam had liberated women from the centuries old backwardness and placed them shoulder-to-shoulder with men .... It (had) ended all forms of social and legal discrimination among men and women and made them equal

and he urged his audience 'to step forward and take full part in national reconstruction and progress'.[56] In 1979 Zia allowed Women's Division to be established within the Cabinet Division and entrusted it with the following responsibilities.

> To formulate public policies and laws to meet the special needs of women,
> To undertake and promote research on the conditions and problems of women;
> To ensure that women's interests and needs are adequately represented in public policy formulation by various organs of government;
> To ensure equality of opportunity in education and employment and the fuller participation of women in all spheres of national life.[57]

In April 1980 the Women's Division held a conference on female education which called for representation of women in educational administration and policy-making.[58]   Later in the year another conference was held on Muslim women. It expressed concern that the Family Laws Ordinance should not be scrapped and that discrimination, inequality, subservient status of women, ignorance, illiteracy among women were 'un Islamic customs' and that womens rights should be protected not only in the family but also in education and employment.[59]

The Women's Division has been staffed by women professionals like Dr Sabiha Hafeez, but there are not enough persons like her within the Division nor within the bureaucracy where they could influence high level policy decisions regarding the future of women. In fact the Women's Division operates under instructions from senior policy making male bureaucrats who merely project government policy. The Women's Division therefore does not have the power to make radical suggestions to alter the role of women.

The retrogressive Islamic forces have manipulated the military regime to subjugate women and impose restrictions on them in various areas of national life in which they had previously played an important role. Although the retrogressive forces could not remove women from participating in all spheres of work in the public arena, they did succeed in one area in July 1981 when the Minister of Information and Broadcasting issued instructions to the media that restricted the appearance of female models in advertising. This move was seen as job discrimination by women and Begun Raana Liaquat Ali Khan wrote a letter to the President saying;

> a matter which is disturbing the women of Pakistan as initiating a new discrimination against women. We have been perturbed to read in the news that women are to be limited in advertisements and the female voice on the Radio and T.V. is to be considerably curtailed. We feel that so long as the female figure and voice is not being used as a sex symbol, or the female figure made to appear obscene, there is no reason to curtail the appearance of women in advertisements and on T.V., Radio and Press. Professionally, a large number of women are trained in the communication media, and are dependent for their livelihood on the same. We feel that the media should utilize women in a positive manner to project the image of women not only as mothers, wives, daughters but also as citizens and workers contributing to the national development. We agree that a code of ethics, eliminating any possibility of misuse of the female mode as a sex object, be strictly observed.[60]

At a joint meeting of 18 women's organisations under the chairmanship of Begun Khan, the following resolution was passed:

> .... this move to curtail the participation of women on the media as being a discrimination against women, which is contrary to the Fundamental Rights of women as equal citizens and full human beings.[61]

The Federal Minister assured the President of APWA that the:

> Government of Pakistan desires our ladies to be exalted,
> liberated and prepared with respect and reverence for the role
> which they have to perform in building of their nation and
> discharging their delicate responsibilities. There is no question
> of banning ladies from the media or any other department of the
> Government.[62]

His words were reassuring but no action followed and the regulation
restricting the appearance of women in advertisements, was enforced.

The mass media in Pakistan are reponsible for much damage to
the image of women in society. The media are male dominated and
one estimate indicated that the 'women component in the media is
about 5 per cent, a dismally low participation rate compared to
teaching and medicine.[63] Television, radio, novels, magazines and
films project a low self image of women. One study, that carried out
a content analysis of mass media, found that in 96 per cent of the
cases, marriage and romance were portrayed as being important. 96
per cent of the women in the media behaved on an emotional level, 68
per cent were destroyed by failure in love, 56 per cent accepted being
tortured by their fate etc. The total projection of women was one in
which the women were playthings in the hands of men and showed
deference to them.[64] A seminar on the subject of Women and the
Media observed that there was considerable discrimination against
employing women in the media and that 30 per cent quota should be
reserved for them.

The Pakistan Women's Institute also organised a seminar on the
same subject. It was recommended that efforts should be made by
women:

> to educate the public and to bring about a gradual change in
> social attitudes a deliberate effort should be made by producers,
> script writers, authors, journalists etc. to present a more
> realistic portrayal of women at home and at work. The problems
> and achievements of working women should be discussed and
> analysed .... Women producers and performers should be more
> assertive against exploitation and victimization by boycotting
> programmes which show women in unrealistic roles.[65]

If women could project a different image of themselves, it would be an
achievement in the right direction.

The second major issue that the retrogressive forces raised was
that of Family Planning – they wanted to put a stop to Family
Planning in Pakistan on Islamic grounds. Historically, there is
evidence that preventive methods such as *azl* (coitus interruptus)
rather than abortion, have found justification in Islam.[66]

In a country where the food production has remained constant,
the population explosion presents a serious problem. General Zia did
not, however, accede to the demands of the retrogressive Islamic
group and appointed a very competent woman (Dr Attiya Inayatullah)

as the Presidential Advisor on Population Affairs. A National Population Planning Policy and Population Welfare Plan was drawn up and its aim was to:

1. to raise the level of effective knowledge about population welfare planning services from 33 per cent to 55 per cent by 1984.
2. to achieve a 33 per cent level of motiviation through information and education about responsible parenthood.
3. to raise the level of practice from an estimated 12.5 per cent in 1979-80 to 25 per cent by 1984.
4. to raise the level of current practice from 9.2 per cent in 1979-80 to 19.4 per cent by 1984 and continuous practice from 6.4 per cent to 13.9 per cent.[67]

A third attack on the role of women in Pakistan was launched by a member of the retrogressive forces (Dr Israr Ahmed) in 1982. In a televised lecture on Islam, he stated that women should not engage in any kind of work that takes them outside their homes. No woman should work in hospitals, educational institutions, media services nor venture into the Bazaars where they could be seen by men. He then went on to say that women should not be allowed to vote in national elections.[68] Dr Israr's statements raised much controversy and were perceived by the educated women as a threat to their careers. Women took part in demonstrations in all major cities. Such views showed a complete lack of perception of the economic realities of the country. Most rural women have to work out in the fields to keep their families at subsistence levels. The urban-lower, lower-middle and middle class women too, have to work out of economic necessity. Working women can supplement family income, utilize their education and contribute to national development. Above all, Islam does not forbid education or work for men and women. In fact, Prophet Muhammed's first wife was herself a working woman. The government did not take up this suggestion nor another that women should not be allowed to vote in national elections.

In the face of various threat postures presented by the retrogressive forces in the Zia regime, the women have become aware of the fact that unless they take a stand, they would loose their existing rights. A Womans Action Forum was set up with branches in Karachi, Lahore, Rawalpindi, and Islamabad. At one of its meetings held in Lahore in May 1982, Khawar Sultana spoke of the need for education for the intellectual awakening of women.[70] The WAF group in Karachi held a demonstration outside the Television studios demanding that Dr Israr's programme be banned from television. The Islamabad branch has campaigned actively through regular meetings and articles in newspapers and magazines by members like Shagufta Alizai, Nigar Ahmad, Shahnaz Ahmad, Sarwar Jamil and Jane Hussain.

General Zia has thus been performing a balancing act between the retrogressive forces on one hand and the women's organisations on the other. The latter, however, are not important for the political survival and the Islamic legitimacy of his regime and he could therfore succumb to the wishes of the Islamic forces. His regime, of course, has much to gain from such an alliance. For example, it cannot allow free elections in case Bhutto's Pakistan's Peoples Party returns to power. It therefore needs some way of legitimizing its rule and for this reason it has to give in to the demands of the retrogressive forces. However, the different Islamic groups in Pakistan have no consensus among themselves of what an Islamic state should be. The Jamiat-ul-Ulema-i-Pakistan discredits the Jammat-i-Islami's brand of Islam and considers Zia's Islamization as mere 'cosmetic Islam'.[71]

With such confusion and a lack of unity on the ideas of an Islamic State, it is not surprising to find a similar confusion on the role of Muslim women. This confusion, as mentioned earlier, arises from the situation in which the retrogressive forces do not have a vision of an Islamic society but can only see it as an extension of the feudal socio-political context. Their interpretations have made Islam static and impotent and women as mere objects for the gratification of sexual needs and procreation. The problems of a modern political context are different and both men and women need to play constructive roles in national development. The Quran constantly reminds its readers to think for themselves but the retrogressive forces have stopped thinking. In summing up a case, a Pakistani High Court judge made a significant observation when he stated that:

> If the interpretation of the Holy Quran by the commentators who lived thirteen or twelve hundred years ago is considered as the last word on the subject then the whole Islamic society will be shut up in an iron cage and not allowed to develop in time. It will then cease to be a universal religion and will remain a religion confined to the time and place where and when it was revealed .... Unfortunately since several centuries the doors or interpretation of the Holy Quran in the light of new circumstances have been completely shut out with the result that Muslims have succumbed to religious coma, cultural deteriorations, political paralysis and economic decline .... Muslims have to wake up and march with the time .... In order to apply the general principles of the Holy Quran to the changing needs of the society it has to be interpreted intelligently .... Like all other human beings, Muslims are also endowed with the divine gift of intelligence and it is meant to be used and not grow rusty.[72]

This judgement reflects the conflict between the thinking of retrogressive Islamic forces that want an extension of the feudal 'Islamic' state established by the Mughals in India, and the revolutionary Islamic forces who want to dynamically apply Islam to problems which never confronted the feudal state. Pakistan is still a feudal-colonial state in which the political thinking is feudal and the 'modern' state structures are colonial. It is by no means an Islamic state. Such patchwork reforms will not make Pakistan an Islamic state as radical changes are needed to dismantle the feudal-colonial structures. A real Islamic state will naturally breed Islamic consciousness. Imposition of

Islamization from above is a contradiction in the feudal context. Amidst this confusion and conflict, women will have to fend for themselves and this can only be done through collective measures, strong organisations and the struggle for active political roles in the national development of the country. The future calls for action, as the fact that a young daughter of Z.A. Bhutto is incarcerated in gaol shows how much the regime fears her and the influence she can carry with the masses.

REFERENCES

1. For Population statistics see: Rafique Akhtar, Pakistan Year Book, 1978, Karachi: East and West Publishing Co., 1978.
2. See: J.J. Meyers, *Sexual Life in Ancient India*, London: Routledge and Kegan Paul, 1953. Also see: P. Thomas, *Indian Women Through the Ages*, London: Asia Publishing House, 1964.
3. See: K. Mayo, *Slaves of the Gods*, New York: Harcourt Brace & Co., 1920. Also see: Abbe J.A. Dubois, *Hindu Manners, Customs and Ceremonies*, Oxford: Clarendon Press, 1906.
4. See: R. Misra, *Women in Mughal India*, Delhi: Munshiram Manoharlal, 1967.
5. H. Papanek, Purdah in Pakistan: Seclusion and Modern Occupations for women, *Journal of Marriage and Family*, Vol. 33, No. 3, 1971, p. 523.
6. See: Muhammad Iqbal, The Reconstruction of Religious thought in Islam, London 1934. Quoted in Mushirul Hassan, Some Aspects of the problem of Muslim Social Reforms in Muslims in India (ed) Zafar Iman, New Delhi: Orient Longmans, 1975, p. 224.
7. Speech by Jinnah at Islamia College for Girls in Lahore, November 22, 1942. Quoted in J. Ahmed (ed.), *Speeches and Writings of Mr Jinnah*, Lahore: Shaikh Muhammad Ashraf 1968, p. 476.
8. Quoted in Mazhar-ul-Haq, *Purdah and Polygamy*, Peshawar: Nashiran-e-ilm-o-Taraqiyet, 1972, p. 217.
9. Rafiq Zakaria, *Rise of Muslims in Indian Politics: An Analysis of Development from 1885 to 1906*, Bombay: Somaiya Publications, 1970, p. 208.
10. Sarfaraz H. Mirza, Muslim Women's Role in the Pakistan Movement, Lahore: Research Society of Pakistan, University of the Punjab, 1969, pp. 6-7, 11, 27.
11. See: Mumtaz S. Nawaz, *The Heart Divided*, Lahore: Mumtaz Publications, 1957.
12. Comment by a Muslim woman educationalist, in H. Papanek, op. cit., p. 523.
13. Abul Ala Maududi, Tanquihat: A Commentary on the clash between Islam and Western Civilization and the problems produced by it, p. 149. Quoted in Mazhar-ul-Haq, op. cit., p. 38.
14. Mohammad M. Siddiqi, *Women in Islam*, Lahore: Institute of Islamic Culture, 1966, p. 129.
15. Mazhar-ul-Haq, *Purdah and Polygamy*, op. cit., p. 38, 39.
16. Maududi on Purdah, Ibid., p. 23.
17. Ibid., p. 22.

18.   Ibid., p. 148.
19.   Ibid., p. 199.
20.   Ibid., p. 197.
21.   Ibid., p. 70.
22.   Maulana Amin Islahi, Pakistani Aurat Do-rahe Par, Quoted in, Ibid., p. 77.
23.   Lucy Carrol, Nizam-i-Islam: Processes and Conflicts in Pakistani Programme of Islamisation with Special reference to the position of women, *The Journal of Commonwealth and Comparative Politics*, Vol. xx, No. 1, March 1982, p. 81.
24.   Edith O. Mercer, The Education of Women, in J. Lowe et al., (edited) *Education and Nation Building in the Third World*, Edinburgh: Scottish Academic Press, 1971.
25.   Pakistan Economic Survey. 1980-81. Islamabad: Government of Pakistan, Economic Advisors Wing, n.d. p. 201.
26.   Nazima Anwar, 'A Study of some major Obstacles in the way of Educated women living in Nazimabad in adopting a career', M.A. Research Report, Department of Sociology, University of Karachi, 1969. The surveys referred to in notes 26-38 were listed in a paper by Mr. F. Kazi of the Pakistan Institute of Development Economics, Islamabad.
27.   Lucy Helbock, 'The Changing Status of Women in Islamic Pakistan', Islamabad: USAID, 1975.
28.   Mukhtar Bhatti, 'Sociological Determinants of Education in Pakistan', Doctoral dissertation, Indiana University, Indiana, 1967.
29.   Mussarat Shah, 'A Study of Attitudes of the Students in a Women's College towards adopting Teaching as a Career', M.A. Thesis, Lahore: University of Punjab, 1963.
30.   Nighat Afaq, 'A study of the opinions of girl students about teaching profession', M.A. Research Report, Department of Sociology, Karachi University, 1974.
31.   Bano Musarrat et al., 'Study of career women in Higher Education', M.A. thesis, Dept. of Social Work, University of Punjab, Lahore. 1970.
32.   Khalida Shah, 'Problems of Pakistani Women seeking Employment', *Contemporary Affairs*, Vol. 2, Autumn, 1970, pp. 45-62.
33.   M.S. Baqai, 'Constraints in Employment of Women', Research Report No. 99, Islamabad: P.I.D.E., November, 1976.
34.   Nasira Shah, 'Fertility of working vs. non-working women in Pakistan, 1973', Paper presented at a seminar at Bangladesh Institute of Law and International Affairs, Dacca, 1976.
35.   Imtiaz Ahmad Tahir, 'A study of attitudes of the general population towards formal female education in a small city', M.A. thesis, Institute of Education and Research, University of Punjab, Lahore, 1970.
36.   Nuzhat K. Qureshi, 'Role of female education in development planning of NWFP', Peshawar Board of Economic Enquiry, Publication No. 74, University of Peshawar, May, 1974.
37.   Razia Sultana, 'Role and status of financial independence of women in the family', M.A. thesis, Department of Sociology, University of Punjab, Lahore.

38.   Professor Mohammod A Rauf, Levels of Educational Attainment Amongst Women in Pakistan, Department of Anthropology, Quaid-e-Azam University, n.d. (Mimeo).

39.   Dawn, July 8, 1962.

40.   Dawn, July 7, 1962.

41.   Dawn, July 8, 1962.

42.   For the full text of the Report of the Pakistan Women's Rights Committee See: *The Criterion.* Vol. II.   Nos. 9 & 10, September & October 1976, pp. 77.

43.   Ibid., p. 79.

44.   See: Pakistani Economic Survey. op. cit., p. 198.

45.   Dawn, October 15, 1978.

46.   Dawn, October 15, 1978 & December 31, 1978.

47.   Dawn, April 8, 1979.

48.   Bulletin, University Grants Commission, Islamabad. 1981.

49.   J. Henry Korson, Islamization and Social Policy in Pakistan, *Journal of South Asian and Middle Eastern Studies*, Vol. VI.   No. 2. 1982. p. 77.

50.   Dawn Overseas Weekly, February 26, 1978.

51.   Dawn Overseas Weekly, November 8, 1980.

52.   Ordinance 53 of November 26, 1980.

53.   Dawn Overseas Weekly, April 15, 1978.

54.   Begum Rashida Patel, 'Legal Status of Women in Pakistan', Paper presented at the APWA Triennial Conference, Governing Body meeting held in Lahore on February 18-21, 1982.

55.   Dawn Overseas Weekly, June 10, 1978.

56.   Dawn Overseas Weekly, October 21, 1978.

57.   Quoted in Lucy Carroll, op. cit., p. 82.

58.   Dawn Overseas Weekly, April 19, 1980.

59.   Dawn Overseas Weekly, November 8, 1980.

60.   Mariam Habib, 'Media and the Status of Women', Paper presented at the APWA Triennial Conference held in Lahore in February 1982.

61.   Ibid., p. 1.

62.   Ibid., p. 2.

63.   Ibid., p. 2.

64.   Seema Pervez, 'Content Analysis of Mass Media', Islamabad: National Institute of Psychology, 1982.

65.   Mariam Habib. op. cit., p. 14.

66.   See: B.F. Musallam, *Sex and Society in Islam: Birth Control before the 19th Century*, Cambridge: Cambridge University Press, 1983.

67.   Pakistan Economic Survey, op. cit., pp. 223-24.

68.   For a discussion of his views see: Zena, 'Dr Israr & the Ladies', *MAG*, June 3-9, 1982, p. 17.

69.   Ibid., p. 17.

70.   For various speeches made by different women see: Nigar Zareen Shahid, 'Women's Action Forum', *MAG*, June 3-9, 1982. p. 21.

71.   Dawn Overseas Weekly, December 6, 1978.

72.   Comment of Justice, Muhammad Shafi at the Lahore High Court in a 1960 case concerning custody of a child: Mst, Rashida

The Struggle of Women in Pakistan

Begum v Sahab Din, PLD, 1960, pp. 1153-4.

Chapter 10

LESSONS FROM FIELDWORK IN THE SUDAN*

Carolyn Fluehr-Lobban

After a decade or more of the proliferation of publications, both scholarly and popular, on the subject of Muslim women it is appropriate that the fieldworkers themselves, both Muslim and non-Muslim, take an objective look at what has been produced. My own work with the status of Sudanese women has spanned the decade of the seventies[1] and has included some larger theoretical consideration of the history of women in society.[2] The scholarly literature on Arab and Muslim women during this period can be characterized along the following lines: (1) those which attempt to correct the inherent male bias of earlier ethnographical-historical studies with the inclusion of or exclusive concern with female perspectives;[3] (2) works with a distinctly feminist orientation which often view men and Islamic society as primary sources of the oppression of Muslim women;[4] (3) works with a Marxist and class perspective which takes the political economy of a society as basic to an understanding of gender variables.[5]

I would include my own work within this final category, and in my scholarship on women in the Sudan I have endeavoured to place the status of Muslim women and their struggle for emancipation against a larger background of economic and historical variables. That is to say the 'woman question' has not been treated as a separate issue but in the context of Sudanese social history and political economy. Thus I have viewed the emergence of the struggle for female emancipation in the Arab and African worlds and the origins of feminism itself in these areas as part of the larger historical movement for national independence.[6] I have analysed the origins of the Sudanese women's movement as occurring within the context of the nationalist movement and the growth of the Sudanese Women's Union as tied to its class orientation and involvement with the trade union movement.[7] Its program reached out to peasant women and for the first time in Sudanese history to southern, non-Muslim women. The dual enemies of international imperialism and their local collaboraters have always been clear in the program of the Sudanese Women's Union[8] and neither Muslim men nor Islamic society has been singled out as a source of female subjugation. On this point there is disagreement with the feminist view which tends to reject the prevailing social order because it is controlled by men.

Lessons from the Field 1970-72

In my fieldwork in the Sudan I have experienced similar problems and advantages being a western female in Muslim society as others who have worked in Islamic societies. I will attempt to chronicle here my own development as a fieldworker and make objective statements, in so far as I am able, about my experience over a ten year period.

I began fieldwork as a pre-doctoral student in 1970 and remained in the Sudan until 1972 when I had completed my research in criminal law, making an anthropological study of homicide. Due to the nature of my project, my formal research did not bring me into direct contact with Sudanese women and men except as they appeared as defendants or witnesses in the court records of murder cases. However, my husband, also an anthropologist, was also conducting fieldwork in the major urban centre of Khartoum and through his contacts and our own immersion in Sudanese life we formed bonds with families that have become enriched over the years. As northern Muslim Sudanese society is strictly sex-segregated, except for the most progressive families, I spent most of my time in the company of women and it was with women that I learned colloquial Arabic, and for this I feel indebted to them. This foundation in the language provided the base which has been built upon considerably in the intervening years, however my speech is still skewed in favour of Sudanese women's use of the language.

Although spending time with women was not part of my original research, I endeavoured to make some 'use' of this social time by asking questions of women related to the law. Lively and informal discussion of issues related to women's perception and use of the law resulted. These candid conversations with women forced me to re-evaluate my own western biases regarding the 'passive' and 'subjugated' Muslim women. The consequence was that I was drawn into the powerful story that is the history of Sudanese opposition to foreign domination and women's part in this story as well as the particular history of the Sudanese women's movement. This compelling story had within it a number of lessons for me about Sudanese pride, their history of resistance and more importantly, it gave me a context, historical, political and social, within which to view the status of women and of men from a Sudanese instead of a western perspective. It is a source of personal pride that I was given the name Mihera bint Abboud, a heroine in Sudanese history who fought against the Turkish-Egyptian invaders in the 19th century.

While certain adjustment on my part was required in order to adapt to Sudanese social life, including sexual segregation and a more constrained public life, I did not experience in any of this serious obstacles to the conduct of field research. As a married woman I was not treated as the 'androgynous female' that some women who are alone in the field mention. I was viewed as part of a family, with my husband in 1970-72 and our daughter in 1979-80, and we almost always socialised together, that is we were invited as a family by a family. I therefore did not experience the ambiguity of role that a woman alone might have felt. Through trial and error I did find that having my husband or a male colleague accompany me on first visits to officials or bureaucrats did help in 'being heard' on initial visits and returns. It was a matter of building networks or fitting into existing networks, often exclusively male, that characterised my first fieldwork. The interest in women was initially a side line and I did not systematically pursue the study of women until subsequent trips to the Sudan. However, my dissertation and subsequent publication of its results[9] did include significant sections on women as defendants and as victims of homicide, and the cultural context of the social institution of honour and shame associated with female character was an integral part of my analysis of the social bases of murder.

Lingering Thoughts

Away from the field in the post-dissertation period I began to consider more theoretical questions regarding the status of Sudanese women in particular as well as larger issues regarding the history and position of women in society. During this period, 1973-77, I studied the history of the Sudanese women's movement and wrestled with the question of the involvement of Arab and African women in politics and the issues which draw them into the political arena, perhaps even to deal with the issue of their own emancipation. I looked for common elements in the history of women's political participation in the Arab world and in Africa and found that women with men in modern history have entered the struggle for national self-determination and *then* have organised specifically for progress in women's rights.

In 1975 I returned to the Sudan specifically to conduct interviews with leaders of the women's Union. I also had the opportunity of visiting the People's Democratic Republic of Yemen where I inter-viewed the leadership and members of the Women's Union in Aden. The advanced nature of the ideology and practice of these groups helped to clarify my own thinking on the subject of women in society. I came to understand that no contradiction between men and women exists in society and that real advances in social progress have taken place when women and men are united in a common struggle, such as that for national independence. The separation of the woman issue from larger historical and political forces leads to isolation and failure. This I learned from the examples of the women's movement in Sudan, in Egypt, in Algeria, amomg the Palestinians, in Democratic Yemen and in the nationalist struggles of southern Africa. During this period I wrote and spoke about the lessons which might be learned from the movements for emancipation by women and men outside of the west even though the prevailing ideology of women's liberation ran counter to these ideas. There was talk of female autonomy and matriarchies, of 'Amazons' and the 'natural' superiority of women without much regard to social development or class considerations. After some debate it was finally recognized that the aspirations of working class and of bourgeois women are not the same, however the international dimension of class divisions along economic and not

223

sexual lines is still poorly understood in western scholarship. Into the dialogue regarding the innate superiority of women and natural matriarchies I inserted a critique of the idea of the matriarchate in idealist thought with an updating of its status in Marxist thought.[10] I concluded that the idea of a society where women have ruled or would rule is a western romantic illusion and, contrary to popular belief, the idea has been subjected to serious reconsideration in Marxist scholarship.

meaning

After the initial lesson from the field which broke down the mythology surrounding Muslim women, the second set of lessons were more theoretical involving the status of Arab women in general and the historical position of women in society.

Fieldwork in 1979–80

Although I had returned briefly to the Sudan in 1975, it was not until 1979–80 that I carried out my second major field study in Khartoum. This time, as a more mature field worker with established contacts and credentials, I conducted research into the *Shari'a* law, a field almost entirely dominated by men. Ten years ago, as a pre-doctoral student, I was fearful of approaching one of the sheikhs who taught Islamic law at the University of Khartoum, yet this time I studied the *Shari'a* with the Grand Qadi of the Sudan, Sheikh Mohammed el-Gizouli. The major variables affecting this change I will attempt to describe here.

A major factor in the success of the second fieldwork is simply the act of returning to the field periodically. Relations established during the initial experience are renewed and new social connections and associations are built. The fieldworker and his/her work become known and accepted and a sincere interest in the country and its people are presumed. In my second fieldwork I built upon relations and friendships at the Sudan Judiciary which had been formed ten years earlier. In the first instance these were contacts arranged by men with men, but I found that a woman alone could not penetrate this network very deeply. In the previous fieldwork my husband often would graciously accompany me to office meetings and social gatherings where my status with men as a woman and wife and *then* as a social scientist were legitimized. But this method ultimately proved impractical as my husband was busy with his own fieldwork, although there was some reciprocity in my giving him insights to the world of women to which he had no legitimate access. I continued, instead, to develop relationships with the female employees in the Judiciary, both office personnel and judges. In the first fieldwork I had made the acquaintance of two of the women judges; it was then that I met Syda Najua Kemal Farid, the first woman to be appointed as a *Shari'a* judge, as far as we know, in the contemporary Islamic world. Our mutual interests blossomed into a friendship between us and our families and she became the greatest promoter of my work and my best critic.

At the time of my return to Khartoum in 1979 to carry out a study of the *Shari'a* law and courts a number of new women judges had been appointed in the Civil and *Shari'a* sections of the Judiciary.

Through them and with the increased presence of women workers I had access to almost every office in the Ministry. Through Justice Najua my presence and work were made known to the Grand Qadi who took an interst in my work because of a desire to have the *Shari'a* properly understood outside of the Muslim world. Since he was close to retirement and had some time free he generously took me on as a student and I profitted enormously from his learning and experience with the *Shari'a* in the Sudan. Upon 'graduation' I began the job of collecting cases by attending sessions in the *Shari'a* courts of Khartoum and Omdurman, and in this Justice Najua was an invaluable asset as a companion to each court for the first, introductory visit. With her as a representative from the Judiciary my research was given the stamp of approval and thereafter I had easy access to any court from the lowest court through the Appeals court to the *Shari'a* High Court. I thus collected case material at every level of the court system on subjects related to marriage, divorce, maintenance, child custody, inheritance and other subjects which fall under the personal law jurisdiction of the *Shari'a*. Once my presence was established I was able to interview judges and sit in their courts freely and without restriction. The courts themselves are filled with women litigants whose last resort to a personal problem is seeking some relief in the courts, and I had occasion to interview a number of litigants as they waited for their case to be heard. Lawyers, when they were attached to a case, were also especially helpful in explaining the history and progress of particular cases. Although this is a subjective comment, lawyers and judges working continuously with *Shari'a* cases seem to be very sympathetic with the struggles of women for judicial relief, although they are almost exclusively men. As members of Sudanese culture they understand very well the shame and desperation which brings a woman to court.

Thus it was the utilisation of the network of women in the employ of the Sudan Judiciary and the *Shari'a* court system which opened the way to the study of Islamic law and its observance in action, dominantly a world of men. In the process warm bonds of affection and friendship formed, especially between me and the women involved, but also with a number of Sudanese men as well. In this respect I had much greater mobility than my anthropologist-husband who was unable to establish relations of friendship with women in spite of their closeness to his male friends or my female friends. I could have had wider associations with men, but with a certain risk of loss of good reputation, so I chose a more restricted set of relationships that were fostered in social visiting that involved my husband and, during the second fieldwork, our daughter, Josina.

It might be of interest to the reader to recount some of the experiences of our daughter in the Muslim, northern Sudan.[11] At 2½ years of age she first travelled to the Sudan and was already enough of an American culture bearer that she experienced a degree of culture shock regarding language and social customs. She resented her parents' use of Arabic unless it was used to get something she wanted like a piece of candy or a toy in the *suq*. She invented her own jibberish language as a defence but eventually managed a good comprehension and some limited use of Arabic. With respect to male-female relations she loved to imitate the dress and manner of Sudanese women, but in any home she preferred to play with the more rembunctious boys in the household. She fought against sexual segregation protesting consistently that her father went to the men's salon to visit while her mother went to the women's *hareem*. She had her choice as a small girl to be with either parent and would make liberal use of her special privilege to more back and forth between the men and women, but finally would settle down with her mother and the other children. Once she learned the rules of sexual segregation she became its most rigorous defender and vigorous enforcer refusing to allow men and women to sit together in our living room when we entertained at home. She liked the Sudanese emphasis on feminity with elaborate perfumes and cosmetics for her to try out, but she deplored the lack of mobility outside the home and would frequently escape the *hareem* to run in the compound or in the streets. She resented staying with the women to prepare the food while the men went for a walk in the garden. I might add that I often took my daughter with me when I went without my husband as an advertisement of my status as wife-mother and not a single woman alone in the city. Otherwise I would endeavour to walk with other women, wait with them for taxis or a bus and sit with them at public gatherings. This reinforced a feeling of solidarity among women which I had already developed from spending much time with women in Sudanese homes.

With respect to my own language acquisition, this was accomplished almost entirely in the Sudan, among women, learning by ear with little formal instruction. Language usage varied according to social context with English used in the university and among intellectuals generally. The use of English is heavily skewed toward interaction with males, and many women knowledgeable in the English language will prefer to use Arabic, perhaps from a shyness expected of women and the resulting inexperience. The vast majority of women, of course, know no English and my conversations with them were conducted solely in colloquial Arabic. Obviously, use of Arabic is preferable in fieldwork, and I found that facility in the colloquial language was sufficient to the study of various aspects of the law except for certain specialized topics in the *Shari'a* where classical Arabic is employed.

Certain special ethical considerations arise in research associated with the *Shari'a* and Muslim women. Since *Shari'a* court cases often deal with highly sensitive family matters and since there is a sense of shame attached to settling a case in court (rather than within the family) the reporting of such cases must protect the anonymity of the litigants. Strict concealment of the identity of participants in cases is observed in the law reporting of these cases in the Sudan and I have continued this practice in my own writing by identifying only the court in which the case was heard and the year of the case. To underscore the sense of stigma associated with going to court, let me say that my frequent invitations to female friends to accompany me to court were invariably met with a polite refusal explaining that they did not want to risk the chance of being seen there, the presumption being that they had a case.

The modesty of Muslim women must also be protected by the western researcher. While my friends had no objection to bei͡ng photographed for a personal remembrance, any publication of the photograph of a woman should at first be approved of and consented to by the woman and her family. Out of consideration for the delicacy of relations exposed in the courtroom setting I did not use my camera there although I would have been given permission to do so had I asked. I did photograph some of the judges and lawyers who staged a mock trial for this purpose, but I will still seek their permission should I ever wish to publish these photographs. When I have made public lectures and have shown slides I have been careful to respect the propriety and dignity of the relations with Sudanese as I have experienced this myself.

The lessons I have derived from fieldwork in the Sudan have been taught gently and skillfully to me by the Sudanese. I owe the greatest debt to them for improving my life through my association with the Sudan and its people.

NOTES

* I dedicate this article to Richard Lobban Jr., my husband and partner in fieldwork in the Sudan. His fieldwork was quite separate but he shared the best times and the worst times and was a supporter throughout. Our shared ideology regarding women and men and the progress of social history is the sustenance of a productive and loving relationship.

REFERENCES

1.   See: Carolyn Fluehr-Lobban, An Anthropological Analysis in an Afro-Arab State: the Sudan.   Unpublished Ph.D. dissertation, Northwestern University, 1973.

'Women and Social Liberation: the Sudan Experience', Arab-American University Graduates Information Papers, Number 12; North Dartmouth, 1974, pp. 28-34.

'Agitation for Change in the Sudan', in A. Schlegel (ed.), Sexual Stratification. New York: Columbia University Press, 1977, pp. 127-43.

'The Political Mobilization of Women in the Arab World' in J. Smith (ed.), Women in Contemporary Muslim Socieites. Bucknell University Press, 1980, pp. 235-52.

'Issues in the Islamic Child Custody Law of the Sudan'. Paper presented at the 4th International Conference of the Institute of African and Asian Studies, University of Khartoum, October, 1981.

2.   See: Carolyn Fluehr-Lobban, 'A Marxist Reappraisal of the Matriarchate'. *Current Anthropology*, Vol. 20 No. 2, 1979, pp. 341-59.

3.   See the following works:

Anne Fuller, Buarij: Portrait of a Lebanese Muslim Village. Middle East Monograph Series. Cambridge, Mass.: Harvard Middle

East Monograph Series, 1970.

Lois Beck and N. Keddie, Muslim Women. Cambridge, MA.: Harvard University Press, 1978.

Daisy Hilse Dwyer, Images and Self-Images: Male and Female in Morocco. New York: Columbia University Press, 1978.

Elizabeth Fernea and Basima Bezirgan, Middle Eastern Women Speak for Themselves. Austin, Texas: University of Austin Press, 1977.

J. Smith (ed.), Women in Contemporary Muslim Society. Lewisburg: Bucknell University Press, 1980.

4. See the following works:

Fadela M'Rabet, La Femme Algerienne. Paris, 1964.

Fatima Mernissi, Beyond the Veil: Male-Female Dynamics in a Modern Muslim Society. New York: John Wiley & Sons, 1975.

Nawal El-Saadawi, The Hidden Face of Eve: Women in the Arab World. London: Zed Press, 1980.

5. See the following works:

Karen Sacks, 'Engels Revisited: Women and Organization of Production and Private Poverty' in M. Rosaldo and L. Lamphere (ed.), Women, Culture and Society. Stanford: Stanford University Press, 1974.

Fatima Babiker Mahmoud, The Role of the Sudanese Women's Union in Sudanese Politics. M.A. Thesis, University of Khartoum, 1971.

Sandra Hale, 'Cultural Reproduction: the 'invisible' Domain of Sudanese Nubian Women'. Paper presented to the 81st Annual meeting of the American Anthropological Association, Los Angeles, December, 1981.

6. The Political Mobilization of Women in the Arab World, op. cit.

7. See my 'Women and Social Liberation: The Sudan Experience' and 'Agitation for Change in the Sudan', op. cit.

8. The original Sudanese Women's League was formed in 1946 and later became the Women's Union. Since the 'May Revolution' regime and political repression directed against it after 1971, it has become known as the Democratic Women's Union.

9. See my dissertation, op. cit., and 'An Anthropological Analysis of Homicide in the Afro-Arab Sudan'. *Journal of African Law*, Vol. XX, No. 1, 1976, pp. 20-38.

10. See my 'A Marxist Reappraisal of the Matriarchate', op. cit.

11. A more complete account of our daughter's experience in the Sudan can be found in an anecdotal account published in *Human Organisation*, Vol. 40, 1981, pp. 277-79 entitled 'Josina's Observations of Sudanese Culture'. A more detailed description of fieldwork in the Sudan as a husband-wife pair of anthropologists to be published in 1982 in 'Families, Gender and Methodology' by C. and R. Fluehr-Lobban in A. Whitehead, et. al., (eds.), Gender and Methodology in Anthropology.

THE CONTRIBUTORS

Freda Hussain has a special interest in education and Muslim womens' studies. She is currently a tutor at Sir Jonathan North School in Leicester and is an active worker among migrant Muslim women in the city. She has written and published articles on the problems of migrant Muslim women in U.K. and is presently engaged in work on two studies on the lifestyles and deviancy among Pakistani women.

Kamelia Radwan is currently a post-graduate student in the Department of Religion at Leicester University. She is married to an Egyptian Psychiatrist and her area of special interest is Islamic studies and Muslim women.

Barbara Freyer Stowasser has focussed on the primary sources of Islam: the Qur'an and the Hadith. She has served as a consultant on Islam and Middle East History and Culture to the Foreign Service Institute. Currently she is the Chairperson at the Arabic Department of Georgetown University in Washington, D.C.

Debbie J. Gerner is involved with research on the domestic and systemic effects of First World-Third World political and economic interactions (e.g. arms transfers, foreign aid allocations, petro dollar recycling); she is the author or co-author of several articles in this area. In addition, Gerner is interested in the comparative study of female elites in the Arab world and elsewhere. Gerner is currently Assistant Professor of Political Science at the University of Iowa.

Anne-Marie Nisbet is a Lecturer at the University of New South Wales. Her special interest is in Maghrebian literature and the place of women in these societies. She has published articles and organised several conferences on Francophone and Maghrebian Literatures and Civilisations and edited *Maghrebian Studies* (1980), *Francophone Studies* (1981) and *Francophone Literature and Civilisations* (1982).

Leila Ahmed's interests have focussed on feminist movements in the Muslim world and on Orientalism. Her study entitled: *Edward W. Lane: A study of his life and work* and of *British ideas of the*

Middle East in the 19th century was published by Longmans in the U.K. She is currently a Fellow of the National Humanities Center at North Carolina University (on sabbatical leave from the University of Massachusetts in Amherst).

Heather Strange is an Associate Professor in the Department of Anthropology Rutgers - the State University of New Jersey. She lived in Trengganu, Malaysia for three extended periods beginning in 1965. Dr. Strange served as Senior Fulbright Lecturer in Malay Studies and the Southeast Asia Program at the University of Malaya, Kuala Lumpur, during 1978-79 and she was appointed to a three year term as External Examiner for Sociology/Anthropology in Malay Studies as of 1982. Her diacronic study *Rural Malay Women in Tradition and Transition*, was published by Paeger in 1981.

Norma Salem is affiliated as a Research Fellow at the Center for Developing Area Studies, McGill University and is engaged in research on Tunisia. She is also a Lecturer at the Universite de Montreal at the Department of History.

Hind A. Khattab is currently Director of Social Studies, Delta Business Services International, Cairo. She has been Professor of Sociology and Anthropology at the American University in Cairo and has developed and presented seminars in Women and Development, Family Planning, Resettlement and Community Development. She has had research experience in Egypt, U.S.A., Kuwait and Jordan.

Seyada Greiss El Daief has had research experience in Egypt, U.S.A., Zaire, Japan and Canada. She has taught Sociology at the American College for Girls in Cairo and at the University of Zaire in Kinshasa. Her research has focussed on female delinquency, Palestinian refugees, structure of family and status of women. She is currently the Senior Research Assistant at Delta Business Services International, Cairo.

Carolyn Fluehr-Lobban is an Associate Professor of Anthropology at Rhode Island College in Providence, R.I. and is currently a Mellon Post-Doctoral Fellow in the Humanities at the University of Pennsylvania in Philadelphia. She is a co-founder of the Sudan Studies Association and is currently Secretary of the Association. Her research in the Sudan commenced in 1970 and has continued to the present.

230

INDEX

(handwritten annotation at top: "no ref to Muhammad, et al?")